Application of Essential Oils in Food Systems

Application of Essential Oils in Food Systems

Special Issue Editors

Juana Fernández-López
Manuel Viuda-Martos

MDPI • Basel • Beijing • Wuhan • Barcelona • Belgrade

Special Issue Editors

Juana Fernández-López
Miguel Hernández University
Spain

Manuel Viuda-Martos
Universidad Miguel Hernández
Spain

Editorial Office
MDPI
St. Alban-Anlage 66
Basel, Switzerland

This is a reprint of articles from the Special Issue published online in the open access journal *Foods* (ISSN 2304-8158) from 2017 to 2018 (available at: http://www.mdpi.com/journal/foods/special_issues/Application_Essential_Oils).

For citation purposes, cite each article independently as indicated on the article page online and as indicated below:

LastName, A.A.; LastName, B.B.; LastName, C.C. Article Title. *Journal Name* **Year**, *Article Number*, Page Range.

ISBN 978-3-03897-047-7 (Pbk)
ISBN 978-3-03897-048-4 (PDF)

Articles in this volume are Open Access and distributed under the Creative Commons Attribution (CC BY) license, which allows users to download, copy and build upon published articles even for commercial purposes, as long as the author and publisher are properly credited, which ensures maximum dissemination and a wider impact of our publications. The book taken as a whole is © 2018 MDPI, Basel, Switzerland, distributed under the terms and conditions of the Creative Commons license CC BY-NC-ND (http://creativecommons.org/licenses/by-nc-nd/4.0/).

Contents

About the Special Issue Editors vii

Preface to "Application of Essential Oils in Food Systems" ix

Juana Fernández-López and Manuel Viuda-Martos
Introduction to the Special Issue: Application of Essential Oils in Food Systems
Reprinted from: Foods **2018**, 7, 56, doi: 10.3390/foods7040056 1

Carmen Ballester-Costa, Esther Sendra, Juana Fernández-López, Jose A. Pérez-Álvarez and Manuel Viuda-Martos
Assessment of Antioxidant and Antibacterial Properties on Meat Homogenates of Essential Oils Obtained from Four *Thymus* Species Achieved from Organic Growth
Reprinted from: Foods **2017**, 6, 59, doi: 10.3390/foods6080059 5

Prabodh Satyal, Jonathan D. Craft, Noura S. Dosoky and William N. Setzer
The Chemical Compositions of the Volatile Oils of Garlic (*Allium sativum*) and Wild Garlic (*Allium vineale*)
Reprinted from: Foods **2017**, 6, 63, doi: 10.3390/foods6080063 16

Tamra N. Tolen, Songsirin Ruengvisesh and Thomas M. Taylor
Application of Surfactant Micelle-Entrapped Eugenol for Prevention of Growth of the Shiga Toxin-Producing *Escherichia coli* in Ground Beef
Reprinted from: Foods **2017**, 6, 69, doi: 10.3390/foods6080069 26

Stella W. Nowotarska, Krzysztof Nowotarski, Irene R. Grant, Christopher T. Elliott, Mendel Friedman and Chen Situ
Mechanisms of Antimicrobial Action of Cinnamon and Oregano Oils, Cinnamaldehyde, Carvacrol, 2,5-Dihydroxybenzaldehyde, and 2-Hydroxy-5-Methoxybenzaldehyde against *Mycobacterium avium* subsp. *paratuberculosis* (Map)
Reprinted from: Foods **2017**, 6, 72, doi: 10.3390/foods6090072 36

Farukh Sharopov, Abdujabbor Valiev, Prabodh Satyal, Isomiddin Gulmurodov, Salomudin Yusufi, William N. Setzer and Michael Wink
Cytotoxicity of the Essential Oil of Fennel (*Foeniculum vulgare*) from Tajikistan
Reprinted from: Foods **2017**, 6, 73, doi: 10.3390/foods6090073 52

Karin Santoro, Marco Maghenzani, Valentina Chiabrando, Pietro Bosio, Maria Lodovica Gullino, Davide Spadaro and Giovanna Giacalone
Thyme and Savory Essential Oil Vapor Treatments Control Brown Rot and Improve the Storage Quality of Peaches and Nectarines, but Could Favor Gray Mold
Reprinted from: Foods **2018**, 7, 7, doi: 10.3390/foods7010007 63

Houda Banani, Leone Olivieri, Karin Santoro, Angelo Garibaldi, Maria Lodovica Gullino and Davide Spadaro
Thyme and Savory Essential Oil Efficacy and Induction of Resistance against *Botrytis cinerea* through Priming of Defense Responses in Apple
Reprinted from: Foods **2018**, 7, 11, doi: 10.3390/foods7020011 80

Marika Pellegrini, Antonella Ricci, Annalisa Serio, Clemencia Chaves-López, Giovanni Mazzarrino, Serena D'Amato, Claudio Lo Sterzo and Antonello Paparella
Characterization of Essential Oils Obtained from Abruzzo Autochthonous Plants: Antioxidant and Antimicrobial Activities Assessment for Food Application
Reprinted from: *Foods* **2018**, 7, 19, doi: 10.3390/foods7020019 . . . . **88**

About the Special Issue Editors

Juana Fernández-López, Professor and researcher in the Agro-food Technology Department, Miguel Hernandez University. I have published 150 articles in scientific journals indexed with a relative quality index. All these works are framed within two research lines: (a) use of agro-industrial byproducts for the development of functional foods, and (b) search and application of natural antimicrobials. I have contributed as author or co-author to 40 book chapters in publications by prestigious international and national publishers on topics related to Food Science and Technology, in addition to 75 works accepted in different national and international congresses.

Manuel Viuda-Martos, Assistant Professor and researcher in the Agro-food Technology Department, Miguel Hernandez University. Editorial board member of *Food Research International Journal*. I have published 82 articles in scientific journals indexed with a relative quality index. All these works are framed within two research lines: (a) use of agro-industrial byproducts for the development of functional foods, and (b) search and application of natural antimicrobials. I have contributed as author or co-author to 27 book chapters in publications by prestigious international and national publishers on topics related to Food Science and Technology, in addition to 50 works accepted in different national and international congresses.

Preface to "Application of Essential Oils in Food Systems"

Essential oils have received increasing attention as natural additives for the shelf-life extension of food products due to the risk in using synthetic preservatives. Synthetic additives can reduce food spoilage, but the present generation is very health conscious and believes in natural products rather than synthetic ones due to their potential toxicity and other concerns. Therefore, one of the major emerging technologies is the extraction of essential oils from several plant organs and their application to foods. Essential oils are a good source of several bioactive compounds, which possess antioxidative and antimicrobial properties, so their use can be very useful to extend shelf-life in food products. Although essential oils have been shown to be promising alternative to chemical preservatives, they present special limitations that must be solved before their application in food systems. Low water solubility, high volatility, and strong odor are the main properties that make it difficult for food applications. Recent advances that refer to new forms of application to avoid these problems are currently under study. Their application into packaging materials and coated films but also directly into the food matrix as emulsions, nanoemulsions, and coating are some of their new applications among others.

Juana Fernández-López, Manuel Viuda-Martos
Special Issue Editors

Editorial

Introduction to the Special Issue: Application of Essential Oils in Food Systems

Juana Fernández-López and Manuel Viuda-Martos *

IPOA Research Group (UMH-1 and REVIV-Generalitat Valenciana), Department of AgroFood Technology, Escuela Politécnica Superior de Orihuela, Miguel Hernández University, Ctra. Beniel km. 3,2, E-03312 Orihuela, Alicante, Spain; j.fernandez@umh.es
* Correspondence: mviuda@umh.es; Tel.: +34-9-6674-9661

Received: 23 March 2018; Accepted: 2 April 2018; Published: 5 April 2018

Abstract: Essential oils have received increasing attention as natural additives for the shelf-life extension of food products due to the risk in using synthetic preservatives. Synthetic additives can reduce food spoilage, but the present generation is very health conscious and believes in natural products rather than synthetic ones due to their potential toxicity and other concerns. Therefore, one of the major emerging technologies is the extraction of essential oils from several plant organs and their application to foods. Essential oils are a good source of several bioactive compounds, which possess antioxidative and antimicrobial properties, so their use can be very useful to extend shelf-life in food products. Although essential oils have been shown to be promising alternative to chemical preservatives, they present special limitations that must be solved before their application in food systems. Low water solubility, high volatility, and strong odor are the main properties that make it difficult for food applications. Recent advances that refer to new forms of application to avoid these problems are currently under study. Their application into packaging materials and coated films but also directly into the food matrix as emulsions, nanoemulsions, and coating are some of their new applications among others.

Keywords: essential oil; foods; preservatives

Introduction

The application of essential oils (EOs) in food systems as natural inhibitors or biopreservatives has received increasing attention mainly due to consumer concerns toward chemical preservatives. This increasing interest can be checked by the number of papers published related to EOs application in foods. In a basic search using the Web of Science database, from 1950 to 2017, selecting as search topic "essential oils and foods" and as document type "article" a total of 5559 results were obtained. Although the first article found dates from 1953 [1] and since then a trickle of articles appear in the following years, it is not until 1990 that articles published every year are reported. Figure 1 shows the evolution of the number of papers per year (from 1990 to 2017) published regarding essential oils and foods. As can be seen in this figure, more than 86% of these papers have been published in last decade which reveals the currently of the topic addressed in this special issue.

The application of essential oils for shelf-life extension in foods is mainly due to their antioxidant and antimicrobial properties which also is reflected in the number of papers found when the words "antioxidant" (1920 papers), "antimicrobial" (2473 papers), or both (973 papers) were added as searching criterion. Regarding the type of foods mainly used in these studies, it can be concluded that essential oils have been applied as biopreservatives in all types of foods, although their application in fruits and vegetables has been the highest reported: fruits (657 papers), vegetables (403 papers), fish products (415 papers), meat products (410 papers), milk and dairy products (216 papers), and bread and baked foods (97 papers).

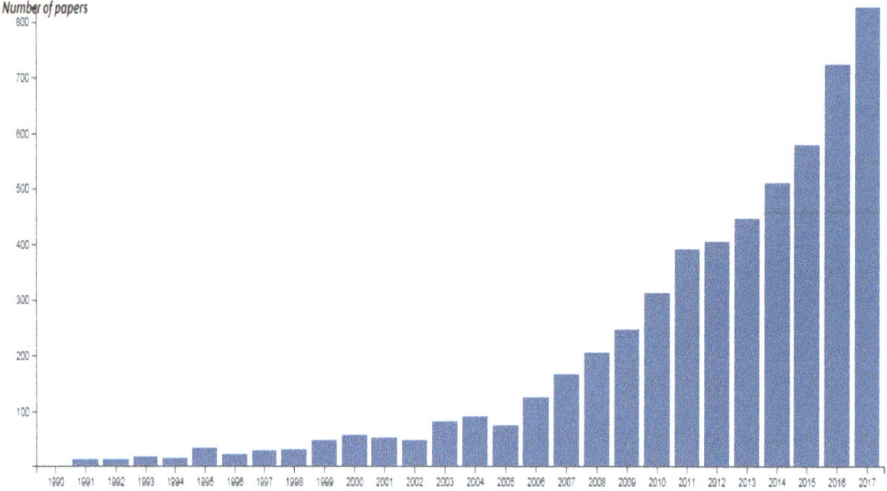

Figure 1. Evolution of the number of papers per year (from 1990 to 2017) published regarding essential oils and foods.

One of the most important aspects that has changed along time is the way in which essential oil has been applied in foods. The first method of application was directly added essential oil to the food matrix, which showed special limitations mainly associated with intrinsic obstacles such as their low water solubility, high volatility, low stability, bioavailability, and strong odor. EOs are unstable volatile compounds which can be degraded easily (by oxidation, volatilization, heating, light, etc.) when they are added to the food matrix. It must be taken into account that most of the food elaboration processes include heat treatment or air and light exposition, all of them factors that increase their degradation. For these reasons, several protection methods to increase their action duration and to provide a controlled release during the shelf-life of food have been proposed. Encapsulation has emerged as a useful alternative to enhance EO stability. The encapsulation of EOs using different materials and methods has been widely studied [2]. EOs have been encapsulated in polymeric particles, liposomes, and solid lipid nanoparticles, which enhanced its stability and efficacy. The recent advances in nanotechnology have made possible the development of novel carrier agents for the delivery and control release of EOs in food system with enhanced chemical, oxidative, and thermal stability [3]. Although nanoencapsulation is a promising tool for effective delivery of EOs into food, the toxicological aspects of most of the nanocarriers and their molecular target site must be further explored.

EOs have also been used as additives in biodegrabable films and coatings for active food packaging [4,5]. EOs can provide the films and coatings with antioxidant and/or antimicrobial properties, depending both on their composition and on the interactions with the polymer matrix. The antioxidant activity depends not only on the specific antioxidant activity of the oil compounds but also on the film's oxygen permeability. The incorporation into edible films can promote the antimicrobial capacity of EOs, and the effectiveness of the edible film against microbial growth will depend on the oil's nature and the type of microorganism. EOs' controlled release from edible films is another aspect that positively affects their effectiveness. In addition, consumers' concern regarding possible negative health effects of applying synthetic preservatives to food products together with the boom of organic culture that promotes the consumption of organic foods (in whose processing synthetic additives are not authorized) have also contribute to boost the interest in organic EOs properties.

In this special issue, the original papers published address all these aspects providing further insights into the application of EOs in foods or assessing specific properties relevant in a specific type of EO.

In the study by Pellegrini et al. [6] the authors focused their interest in EOs from some officinal plants from the Abruzzo territory (Italy), assessing the whole chemical characterization of their volatile fraction and their antimicrobial and antioxidant activities. All these analyses allow establishing which of them could be better candidates for their potential application as biopreservatives depending on the type of food to be incorporated. In addition, the characterization of EOs autochthonous from a specific region will allow their application by local industries contributing to their development.

The study by Sharopov et al. [7] also contributes to increasing the knowledge of local EOs, in this case it is regarding the EO of Fennel from Tajikistan. These authors assessed the chemical composition of this EO by gas chromatographic-mass spectrometric analysis and its antioxidant activity. In addition, these authors also studied the potential cytotoxic activity against several cancer cell lines, which is very important for its potential application in food products.

Consistent with this aspect there is also the paper of Satyal et al. [8] contributing to a deeper knowledge about EOs from a culinary ingredient broadly used around the world (garlic). In this case, EOs from both, garlic (*Allium sativum*) and other type of garlic widely used as its substitute (*Allium vineale*), have been chemically characterized.

Ballester-Costa et al. [9] have focused their study in EOs from four Thymus species from organic growth, contributing to their potential application to organic food processing. Taking into account that thymus is a common specie in the Spain meat industry, the work has assessed its antioxidant and antibacterial properties with the objective of its use for the meat industry. The main novelty of this work is the application, as culture medium for the antibacterial activity evaluation, and of several meat homogenates (minced beef, cooked ham, or dry-cured sausage). This type of study allows that the potential effect of these meat matrices on bacterial survival would be included in the general antibacterial activity that has been evaluated.

In the work carried out by Nowotarska et al. [10] the antimicrobial modes of action of six compounds from cinnamon and oregano EOs against *Mycobacteriun avium* sbsp. *paratuberculosis* were evaluated. It is a pathogenic bacterium that can infect food animals and humans and to be present in milk, cheese, and meat which reveals the interest in studying some compounds to be inhibited and their action mechanisms.

Others two papers are related to the effect of thyme and savory EOs on specific foods: Santoro et al. [11] reported the effect on the control of postharvest diseases and quality of peaches and nectarines, while Banani et al. [12] reported its efficacy on apples. In the first work the authors concluded that both EOs favor a reduction of brown rot incidence (caused by *Monilinia fructicola*) but increased gray mold (caused by *Botrytis cinerea*). Respect to the overall quality of the fruits, both EOs showed a positive effect in reducing weight loos and in maintaining ascorbic acid and carotenoid content. Regarding the second study, apples treated with these EOs showed lower gray mold severity and incidence and the authors reported that the PR-8 gene of apple may play a key role in the mechanism implicated in this inhibition.

The prevention of growth of *Escherichia coli* in ground beef by the application of surfactant micelle-entrapped eugenol was the objective proposed in the paper by Tolen et al. [13]. In this case the authors concluded that this antimicrobial treatment did not significantly decontaminate ground beef and so further studies must be proposed to increase the utility of these EOs for beef safety protection.

Application of essential oils in food systems is an interesting and growing area for researchers whose results could end up having a great use for food industries. It is a wide field of research where different aspects can be addressed. We hope that readers will find this issue interesting and useful and allow them to understand its importance and relevance and so to propose new studies for future papers.

Conflicts of Interest: The authors declare no conflicts of interest.

References

1. Anderson, E.S.; Esselen, W.B.; Handleman, A.R. The effect of essential oils on the inhibition and thermal resistance of microorganisms in acid food product. *J. Food Sci.* **1953**, *18*, 40–47. [CrossRef]
2. Asbahani, A.E.; Miladi, K.; Badri, W.; Sala, M.; Aït Addi, E.H.; Casabianca, H.; Mousadik, A.E.; Hartmann, D.; Jilale, A.; Renaud, F.N.R.; et al. Essential oils: From extraction to encapsulation. *Int. J. Pharm.* **2015**, *483*, 220–243. [CrossRef] [PubMed]
3. Prakash, B.; Kujur, A.; Yadav, A.; Kumar, A.; Singh, P.P.; Dubey, N.K. Nanoencapsulation: An efficient technology to boost the antimicrobial potential of plant essential oils in food system. *Food Control* **2018**, *89*, 1–11. [CrossRef]
4. Atares, L.; Chiralt, A. Essential oils as additives in biodegradable films and coatings for active food packaging. *Trends Food Sci. Technol.* **2016**, *48*, 51–62. [CrossRef]
5. Ribeiro-Santos, R.; Andrade, M.; Ramos de Melo, N.; Sanches-Silva, A. Use of essential oils in active food packaging: Recent advances and future trends. *Trends Food Sci. Technol.* **2017**, *61*, 132–140. [CrossRef]
6. Pellegrini, M.; Ricci, A.; Serio, A.; Chaves-López, C.; Mazzarrino, G.; D'Amato, S.; Lo Sterzo, C.; Paparella, A. Characterization of essential oils obtained from Abruzzo autochthonous plants: Antioxidant and antimicrobial activities assessment for food application. *Foods* **2018**, *7*, 19. [CrossRef] [PubMed]
7. Sharopov, F.; Valiev, A.; Satyal, P.; Gulmurodov, I.; Yusufi, S.; Setzer, W.N.; Wink, M. Cytotoxicity of the Essential Oil of Fennel (*Foeniculum vulgare*) from Tajikistan. *Foods* **2017**, *6*, 73. [CrossRef] [PubMed]
8. Satyal, P.; Craft, J.D.; Dosoky, N.S.; Setzer, W.N. The chemical compositions of the volatile oils of garlic (*Allium sativum*) and wild garlic (*Allium vineale*). *Foods* **2017**, *6*, 63. [CrossRef] [PubMed]
9. Ballester-Costa, C.; Sendra, E.; Fernández-López, J.; Pérez-Álvarez, J.A.; Viuda-Martos, M. Assessment of Antioxidant and antibacterial properties on meat homogenates of essential oils obtained from four thymus species achieved from organic growth. *Foods* **2017**, *6*, 59. [CrossRef] [PubMed]
10. Nowotarska, S.W.; Nowotarski, K.; Grant, I.R.; Elliott, C.T.; Friedman, M.; Situ, C. Mechanisms of antimicrobial action of cinnamon and oregano oils, cinnamaldehyde, carvacrol, 2,5-dihydroxybenzaldehyde, and 2-hydroxy-5-methoxybenzaldehyde against *Mycobacterium avium* subsp. *paratuberculosis* (Map). *Foods* **2017**, *6*, 72. [CrossRef] [PubMed]
11. Santoro, K.; Maghenzani, M.; Chiabrando, V.; Bosio, P.; Gullino, M.L.; Spadaro, D.; Giacalone, G. Thyme and savory essential oil vapor treatments control brown rot and improve the storage quality of peaches and nectarines, but could favor gray mold. *Foods* **2018**, *7*, 7. [CrossRef] [PubMed]
12. Banani, H.; Olivieri, L.; Santoro, K.; Garibaldi, A.; Gullino, M.L.; Spadaro, D. Thyme and savory essential oil efficacy and induction of resistance against botrytis cinerea through priming of defense responses in apple. *Foods* **2018**, *7*, 11. [CrossRef] [PubMed]
13. Tolen, T.N.; Ruengvisesh, S.; Taylor, T.M. Application of surfactant micelle-entrapped eugenol for prevention of growth of the shiga toxin-producing *Escherichia coli* in ground beef. *Foods* **2017**, *6*, 69. [CrossRef] [PubMed]

© 2018 by the authors. Licensee MDPI, Basel, Switzerland. This article is an open access article distributed under the terms and conditions of the Creative Commons Attribution (CC BY) license (http://creativecommons.org/licenses/by/4.0/).

Article

Assessment of Antioxidant and Antibacterial Properties on Meat Homogenates of Essential Oils Obtained from Four *Thymus* Species Achieved from Organic Growth

Carmen Ballester-Costa, Esther Sendra, Juana Fernández-López, Jose A. Pérez-Álvarezand Manuel Viuda-Martos *

IPOA Research Group (UMH-1 and REVIV-Generalitat Valenciana), AgroFood Technology Department, Escuela Politécnica Superior de Orihuela, Miguel Hernández University, Ctra. Beniel km 3.2, E-03312 Orihuela, Spain; carmen.ballester@umh.es (C.B.-C.); esther.sendra@umh.es (E.S.); j.fernandez@umh.es (J.F.-L.); ja.perez@umh.es (J.A.P.-A.)
* Correspondence: mviuda@umh.es; Tel.: +34-966-749-737; Fax: +34-966-749-677

Received: 30 June 2017; Accepted: 22 July 2017; Published: 28 July 2017

Abstract: In the organic food industry, no chemical additives can be used to prevent microbial spoilage. As a consequence, the essential oils (EOs) obtained from organic aromatic herbs and spices are gaining interest for their potential as preservatives. The organic *Thymus zygis*, *Thymus mastichina*, *Thymus capitatus* and *Thymus vulgaris* EOs, which are common in Spain and widely used in the meat industry, could be used as antibacterial agents in food preservation. The aims of this study were to determine (i) the antibacterial activity using, as culture medium, extracts from meat homogenates (minced beef, cooked ham or dry-cured sausage); and (ii) the antioxidant properties of organic EOs obtained from *T. zygis*, *T. mastichina*, *T. capitatus* and *T. vulgaris*. The antioxidant activity was determined using different methodologies, such as Ferrous ion-chelating ability assay, Ferric reducing antioxidant power, ABTS radical cation (ABTS$^{\bullet}$+) scavenging activity assay and 2,2′-diphenyl-1-picrylhydrazyl (DPPH) radical scavenging method; while the antibacterial activity was determined against 10 bacteria using the agar diffusion method in different meat model media. All EOs analyzed, at all concentrations, showed antioxidant activity. *T. capitatus* and *T. zygis* EOs were the most active. The IC$_{50}$ values, for DPPH, ABTS and FIC assays were 0.60, 1.41 and 4.44 mg/mL, respectively, for *T. capitatus* whilst for *T. zygis* were 0.90, 2.07 and 4.95 mg/mL, respectively. Regarding antibacterial activity, *T. zygis* and *T. capitatus* EOs, in all culture media, had the highest inhibition halos against all tested bacteria. In general terms, the antibacterial activity of all EOs assayed was higher in the medium made with minced beef than with the medium elaborated with cooked ham or dry-cured sausage.

Keywords: essential oil; *Thymus*; antibacterial; antioxidant; meat homogenates

1. Introduction

Greater understanding of the relationship between diet, specific food ingredients and health is leading to new insights into the effect of food components on physiological function and health. This awareness has moved consumers to become more health-conscious, driving a trend towards "green", healthy and nutritious foods with additional health-promoting functions. This new approach to improving health status is especially interesting for the meat industry. The study by Grunert [1] on trends in meat consumption identifies the processed meat manufacturing sector as having the most promising future, due, among other reasons, to consumers' demand for products that are easy and quick to prepare. However, to maintain the safety and prolong the shelf-life of meat and meat products, the meat industry uses synthetic preservatives that have been widely used to control the lipid oxidation and to eliminate bacteria or moulds.

The use of these synthetic preservatives enters into controversy with the idea of a healthy and "green" product due to the fact that these compounds could cause health problems for consumers over a long-term period. Thus, aiming at the reduction of the use of chemical additives in the food industry, there has been growing interest recently in the use of natural food additives with antimicrobial and antioxidant properties that do not have any negative effects on human health [2]. In this way, natural antioxidants extracted from plants can be used as alternatives to synthetic preservatives due to their equivalent or greater effect on the inhibition of lipid oxidation and bacterial growth [3].

Essential oils (EOs) obtained from aromatic herbs and spices are aromatic oily liquids formed by aromatic plants as secondary metabolites, which are constituted by a complex mix of compounds, including monoterpens and sesquiterpene hydrocarbons, as well as their corresponding oxidized products (e.g., alcohols, aldehydes, ethers and ketones), several phenylpropane derivatives, phenols and miscellaneous volatile organic compounds (e.g., octanal, dodecanal, 2-undecanone) [4,5]. Although the antioxidant and antimicrobial properties of EOs were acknowledged a long time ago, there are still several investigations that have shown that these compounds exhibit strong antimicrobial and antioxidant properties [6–8], making them interesting ingredients in the meat industry. Additionally, the main advantage of EOs is that they can be used in any food, and are generally recognized as safe (GRAS), as long as their maximum effects are attained with minimal change in the organoleptic properties of the food [9]. Although the antimicrobial properties of EOs reaches in vitro bioactive concentrations at 5% or less, the application of plant EOs for control of food-borne pathogens and food spoilage bacteria requires the evaluation of their efficacy within food products or in model systems that closely simulate food composition [10]. The organic essential oils were obtained from four *Thymus* species: *Thymus zygis*, *Thymus mastichina*, *Thymus capitatus* and *Thymus vulgaris* chemotype linalool, which are common in Spain and are widely used in the meat industry. Additionally, they are widely used as culinary flavoring agents, and their flavor and aroma are familiar to and widely accepted by consumers [11]. Therefore, the aims of this study were to determine (i) their antibacterial activity using, as culture medium, extracts from meat homogenates (minced beef, cooked Ham or dry-cured sausage); and (ii) their antioxidant properties.

2. Material and Methods

2.1. Essential Oils

The essential oils (EOs) of *Thymus zygis* reference (ref.) 11961, *Thymus mastichina* ref. 90001-1284, *Thymus capitatus* ref. 95001-1150, and *Thymus vulgaris* ref. 80001-3577 were used in this work. These EOs were analyzed by Ballester-Costa et al. [11]. These authors reported that in *T. mastichina* EO the major compounds were 1,8-cineole (51.94%), linalool (19.90%) and β-pinene (3.39%). *T. capitatus* EO was characterized by the high monoterpenoid fraction, and especially by the presence of carvacrol (69.83%), and their precursors *p*-cymene (6.12%) and γ-terpinene (6.68%). With regard to *T. vulgaris* EO, the main component was linalool (44.00%) followed by terpineol-4 (11.84%), γ-terpinene (8.91%) and β-myrcene (6.89%). Finally, in *T. zygis* EO, the major components were thymol (48.59%), *p*-cymene (18.79%), γ-terpinene (8.31%) and linalool (4.31%). All EOs analyzed were supplied by Esencias Martinez Lozano (Murcia, Spain). The EOs were certified organic by the Institute for Marketecology (IMO) according to the procedures as outlined in the USDA, AMS 7 CFR Part 205 National Organic Program, Final Rule.

2.2. Antioxidant Activity

2.2.1. 2,2′-diphenyl-1-picrylhydrazyl (DPPH) Radical Scavenging Method

The antioxidant activity of different concentrations (0.23–30 mg/mL) of *Thymus* EOs was measured in terms of hydrogen donating or radical scavenging ability, using the stable radical DPPH [12]. The results were expressed as IC_{50} value: concentration (mg/mL) for a 50% chelating effect.

2.2.2. ABTS Radical Cation ($ABTS^{\bullet+}$) Scavenging Activity Assay

The $ABTS^{\bullet+}$ scavenging activity assay was determined as described by Leite et al. [13] with some modifications. The $ABTS^{\bullet+}$ solution was produced by reacting aqueous ABTS solution (7 mM) with potassium persulfate (2.45 mM). Diluted $ABTS^{\bullet+}$ solution with an absorbance of 0.70 ± 0.02 at 734 nm was employed in the analysis. The reactions were performed by adding 990 μL of $ABTS^{\bullet+}$ solution to 10 μL of each EOs solution (0.23–30 mg/mL). After 6 min of incubation at room temperature, absorbance values were measured on a spectrophotometer at 734 nm. The results were expressed as IC_{50} value: concentration (mg/mL) for a 50% chelating effect.

2.2.3. Ferric Reducing Antioxidant Power

The ferric reducing antioxidant power (FRAP) of different concentrations (0.23–30 mg/mL) of *Thymus* EOs samples was determined by using the potassium ferricyanide-ferric chloride method [14]. The FRAP of the samples was estimated in terms of mg Trolox equivalent (TE) mL of the sample as the mean of three replicates.

2.2.4. Ferrous Ion-Chelating Ability Assay

Ferrous ion (Fe^{2+}) chelating activity (FIC) of different concentrations (0.15–20 mg/mL) of EO samples was measured by inhibiting the formation of Fe^{2+}-ferrozine complex after treatment of test material with Fe^{2+}, following the method of Carter [15]. The results were expressed as IC_{50} value: concentration (mg/mL) for a 50% chelating effect.

2.3. Microbial Strains

The EOs were individually tested against several bacterial strains: *Listeria innocua* CECT 910, *Serratia marcescens* CECT 854, *Pseudomonas fragi* CECT 446, *Pseudomonas fluorescens* CECT 844, *Aeromonas hydrophila* CECT 5734, *Shewanella putrefaciens* CECT 5346, *Achromobacter denitrificans* CECT 449, *Enterobacter amnigenus* CECT 4078, *Enterobacter gergoviae* CECT 587, *Alcaligenes faecalis* CECT 145. These microorganisms were chosen as they are commonly associated with the spoilage of refrigerated foods; as an indicator of pathogenic microorganism or as the spoilage microorganism. All species were supplied by the Spanish Type Culture Collection (CECT) of the University of Valencia (Valencia, Spain).

2.4. Antimicrobial Screening

2.4.1. Preparation of Meat Model Medium

Ten grams of minced beef (MB), cooked ham (CH), or dry-cured sausage (DCS) were added to 90 mL of one-quarter-strength buffered peptone water (pH 7.2) in blender bags and homogenized in a Stomacher until smooth. After that, the samples were filtered through a paper disc Whatman n° 2 to remove solid particles and obtained a clarified extract. Meat model medium was made mixing the extracts obtained from MB, CH or DCS with agar solution (Sharlab, Barcelona, Spain) in order to obtain a final solid medium solution with 1.5% agar. Finally, all prepared meat solutions were autoclaved, separately, at 121 °C for 15 min prior to use, to eliminate contamination from organisms that may already be present in the food.

2.4.2. Disc-Diffusion Method

Screening of EOs for antibacterial activity was determined by the agar diffusion method following the recommendations of Tepe et al. [16]. Petri plates were prepared by pouring 20 mL of previously prepared meat model medium (MB, CH or DCS) at 55 °C and allowed to solidify. Plates were dried for 30 min in a biological safety cabinet with vertical laminar flow. A suspension (0.1 mL of 10^6 CFU/mL) of standardized inoculum suspension was spread on the solid medium plates. The inoculums were allowed to dry for 5 min. Then, a sterile filter paper disk (9 mm in diameter Schlinder & Schuell, Dassel, Germany) was impregnated with 30 µL EO. The plates were left for 15 min at room temperature to allow the diffusion of the EO, and then they were incubated at appropriated temperature for each bacterium for 24 h. At the end of the period, the diameter of the clear zone around the disc was measured with a caliper (Wiha dialMax® ESD-Uhrmessschieber) and expressed in millimeters (disk diameter included) as its antimicrobial activity. According to the width of the inhibition zone diameter expressed in mm, results were appreciated as follows: not active (−) for diameters equal to or below 12.0 mm; moderately active (+) for diameters between 12.0 and 21.0 mm; active (++) for diameters between 21.0 and 30.0 mm and extremely active (+++) for diameters equal to or longer than 30.0 mm [17]. All tests were performed in triplicate.

2.5. Statistical Analysis

Conventional statistical methods were used to calculate means and standard deviations of three simultaneous assays carried out with the different methods. Data collected for antioxidant properties were analyzed by one-way analysis of variance to test the effects of essential oils (levels: *T. zygis*, *T. mastichina*, *T. capitatus* and *T. vulgaris*). Data collected for antibacterial properties were analyzed by two-way analysis of variance to test the effects of two fixed factors: essential oil (levels: *T. zygis*, *T. mastichina*, *T. capitatus* and *T. vulgaris*) and bacterial strains (levels: *L. innocua*, *A. hydrophila*, *S. marcescens*, *A. faecalis*, *A. denitrificans*, *P. fragi*, *P. fluorescens*, *S. putrefaciens*, *E. amnigenus* and *E. gergoviae*). The Tukey's post hoc test was applied for comparisons of means, differences were considered significant at $p < 0.05$. Statistical analysis and comparisons among means were carried out using the statistical package Statgraphics 5.1 for Windows (Statpoint Technologies Inc., Herndon, VA, USA).

3. Results and Discussion

3.1. Antioxidant Activity

The antioxidant activity of EOs obtained from *T. zygis*, *T. mastichina*, *T. capitatus* and *T. vulgaris* was determined using four different methodologies (DPPH and ABTS$^{•+}$ scavenging activity, reducing power and chelating activity), due to the fact that a single method will provide basic information about antioxidant properties, but a combination of methods will describe the antioxidant properties of the sample in more detail [18]. The results are summarized in Table 1. With regard to DPPH assay, the EOs analyzed exhibited varying degrees of scavenging ability. *T. capitatus* EO showed the strongest ($p < 0.05$) radical scavenging effect, with an IC_{50} value of 0.60 mg/mL followed by *T. zygis* EO, which had an IC_{50} value of 0.90 mg/mL. *T. mastichina* and *T. vulgaris* EOs, in that order, showed the lowest scavenging activity ($p < 0.05$). In the case of ABTS$^{•+}$ scavenging activity (Table 1), all EOs analyzed showed this ability. Again *T. capitatus* EO showed the lowest ($p < 0.05$) IC_{50} value, and therefore it had the greatest antioxidant activity. On the other hand, *T. vulgaris* EO had the lowest ($p < 0.05$) IC_{50} value. This strong radical scavenging potential capacity, measured with DPPH and ABTS assays, of the EOs analyzed could explained by the occurrence of hydroxylated compounds such as terpenoids in their composition [19].

Table 1. Antioxidant activity of essential oils obtained from *T. capitatus*, *T. mastichina*, *T. vulgaris* and *T. zygis* determined using four different methods such as DPPH, ABTS, FRAP and FIC.

	DPPH Assay	ABTS Assay	FIC Assay	FRAP Assay
	IC_{50} (mg/mL)	IC_{50} (mg/mL)	IC_{50} (mg/mL)	(mg TE/mL)
T. mastichina	3.11 ± 0.11 [b]	3.73 ± 0.14 [b]	9.61 ± 0.19 [b]	19.26 ± 0.10 [c]
T. zygis	0.90 ± 0.03 [c]	2.07 ± 0.06 [c]	4.95 ± 0.14 [c]	49.56 ± 0.09 [b]
T. vulgaris	4.05 ± 0.09 [a]	6.46 ± 0.11 [a]	13.29 ± 0.18 [a]	12.69 ± 0.03 [d]
T. capitatus	0.60 ± 0.02 [d]	1.41 ± 0.05 [d]	4.44 ± 0.16 [d]	58.12 ± 0.25 [a]

DPPH: 2,2′-diphenyl-1-picrylhydrazyl Radical Scavenging Method; ABTS: Radical Cation (ABTS$^{•+}$) Scavenging Activity Assay; FIC: Ferrous ion (Fe^{2+}) chelating activity; FRAP: The ferric reducing antioxidant power. Values followed by the same lower-case letter within the same column are not significantly different ($p > 0.05$) according to Tukey's Multiple Range Test.

Table 1 shows the ferric reducing antioxidant power obtained using the FRAP assay. *T. capitatus* EO had the highest ($p < 0.05$) ferric reducing capacity in terms of Trolox concentrations. It was followed by *T. zygis* EO. *T. mastichina* and *T. vulgaris* EOs had lower ($p < 0.05$) ferric reducing capacity compared with the other EOs. Ferrous ion, normally present in foods, is recognised as an effective pro-oxidant agent. EOs displayed the ability to chelate pro-oxidant metal ions, such as iron and copper, consequently avoiding free radical formation from these pro-oxidants. The Fe^{+2} chelating capacity of different *Thymus* EOs is shown in Table 1. *T. capitatus* and *T. zygis* EOs, showed the highest values ($p < 0.05$) for chelating Fe^{+2}, with IC_{50} values of 4.44 and 4.95 mg/mL, respectively. Once more, *T. mastichina* and *T. vulgaris* EOs had the lowest capacity ($p < 0.05$) to act as chelating agents.

The antioxidant activities of essential oils obtained from several thyme varieties have been reported by several studies [20–22]. Therefore, Zouari et al. [20] investigated the antioxidant activity of *Thymus algeriensis* Boiss. et Reut EO, which grows wild in Tunisia. They reported that *T. algeriensis* EO was able to reduce the stable free radical DPPH with an IC_{50} of 0.8 mg/mL. Viuda-Martos et al. [4] analyzed the antioxidant activity of *Thymus vulgaris* EO cultivated in Egypt. These authors reported that this EO showed, in a DPPH assay, an IC_{50} of 4.50 mg/mL, while in the FIC assay the EC_{50} was 0.27 mg/mL. Ruiz-Navajas, et al. [6] reported IC_{50} values for *Thymus piperella* EO, in DPPH and FIC assays, of 9.30 and 425 mg/mL, respectively, while for *Thymus moroderi* EO the IC_{50} values were 90 and 6 mg/mL, respectively. In a similar study, Ali et al. [22] analyzed the antioxidant activity of EO obtained from *Thymus algeriensis*. These authors reported that the level of antioxidant activity estimated by the DPPH (IC_{50} = 4.31–9.23 mg/mL) and ABTS (11.69–28.23 µg Trolox Equivalent/mg) tests was moderate. Nikolić et al. [23] reported that *Thymus serpyllum* essential oil showed the highest DPPH radical scavenging activity (IC_{50}: 0.96 µg/mL), followed by the oils of *T. algeriensis* (IC_{50}: 1.64 µg/mL) and *T. vulgaris* (IC_{50}: 4.80 µg/mL).

The difference in the antioxidant capacity measured with four different tests, between the four *Thymus* species analyzed in this work could be explained by the different mechanisms involved in each corresponding assay; each EO had different compounds in its composition with specific capacities to participate in those mechanisms. However, it should be borne in mind that, as mentioned by Viuda-Martos et al. [24], it is very difficult to attribute the antioxidant effect of an EO to one or a few main constituents, due to an EO always containing a mixture of different chemical compounds, meaning that their biological profiles are probably the result of a synergism of all molecules present in the EO. It is even possible that the activity of the main components is modulated by other minor molecules, as mentioned Bakkali et al. [25]. However, it should be borne in mind that the activities of EOs such as antioxidants depend not only on their structural features, but also on many other factors, such as concentration, temperature, light, type of substrate, and physical state of the system, as well as on microcomponents acting as pro-oxidants or synergists [26]. Anyway, the use of EOs or the individual isolated components obtained from them are new approaches for increasing their efficacy, taking advantage of their synergistic and additive effects [27].

3.2. Antibacterial Activity

The antibacterial activity of EOs obtained from *T. zygis*, *T. mastichina*, *T. capitatus* and *T. vulgaris* was determined by the application of disk diffusion against a panel of ten bacteria commonly associated with refrigerated foods, either as indicator of pathogenic microorganism or as spoilage microorganism, using medium extracts obtained from meat homogenates as culture. Table 2 shows the antibacterial activity of *Thymus* EOs using a minced beef extract as culture medium. All EOs studied showed growth inhibitory activity against all strains tested. All EOs tested showed the largest halos of inhibition against *A. faecalis* and *L. innocua* strains. For both bacteria all EOs were extremely active. In the case of *A. faecalis*, the *T. capitatus* EO showed the greatest inhibition halos ($p < 0.05$), followed by the *T. zygis*, *T. vulgaris* and *T. mastichina* Eos; while for *L. innocua*, the EO obtained from *T. zygis* had the greatest inhibition halos ($p < 0.05$), followed by *T. mastichina*, *T. capitatus* and *T. vulgaris* Eos, which showed no differences ($p > 0.05$) between them. For *E. amnigenus*, *E. gergoviae* and *P. fluorescens*, *T. zygis* and *T. capitatus* EOs showed the highest inhibitory activity on these strains, with no statistically significant differences ($p > 0.05$) between them. These EOs were moderately active against *Enterobacter* spp. and active on *P. fluorescens*. For *A. denitrificans*, *A. hydrophila*, *P. fragi*, *S. marcescens* and *S. putrefaciens*, *T. capitatus* EO showed the highest inhibition halos ($p < 0.05$), and their activity against these strains could be classified as active or extremely active. For these bacteria, the next most effective was the *T. zygis* EO, and its activity could be classified as moderately active or active.

Table 2. Antibacterial activity of *T. capitatus*, *T. mastichina*, *T. vulgaris* and *T. zygis* EOs against several bacterial strains using minced beef extract as culture medium.

	Diameter of Inhibition Zone (mm) Including Disc (9 mm)			
	T. capitatus	*T. mastichina*	*T. vulgaris*	*T. zygis*
A. denitrificans	28.37 ± 0.11 aD (++)	11.29 ± 0.00 dE (−)	19.82 ± 0.97 cB (+)	23.92 ± 2.72 bD (++)
A. faecalis	35.12 ± 0.30 aA (+++)	16.91 ± 1.17 dB (+)	32.73 ± 0.33 cA (+++)	33.85 ± 0.36 bB (+++)
A. hydrophila	30.69 ± 1.88 aC (+++)	14.70 ± 0.98 dC (+)	16.04 ± 0.11 cC (+)	19.35 ± 0.07 bE (+)
E. amnigenus	16.80 ± 0.28 aE (+)	10.97 ± 0.01 cF (−)	12.43 ± 0.18 b (+)	17.98 ± 1.67 aE (+)
E. gergoviae	13.78 ± 0.63 aF (+)	10.82 ± 0.06 bF (−)	10.77 ± 1.42 bE (−)	13.92 ± 0.08 aF (+)
L. innocua	34.07 ± 1.68 bA (+++)	34.98 ± 1.67 bA (+++)	33.77 ± 3.35 bA (+++)	45.37 ± 5.98 aA (+++)
P. fluorescens	29.36 ± 2.11 aCD (++)	12.07 ± 1.10 cDE (+)	19.91 ± 2.55 bB (+)	27.72 ± 0.68 aC (++)
P. fragi	29.80 ± 2.16 aCD (++)	11.61 ± 0.01 dE (−)	16.23 ± 2.29 cCD (+)	26.61 ± 1.90 bC (++)
S. marcescens	29.06 ± 1.10 aCD (++)	11.84 ± 0.49 cE (−)	16.84 ± 1.10 bCD (+)	16.96 ± 0.05 bE (+)
S. putrefaciens	32.04 ± 0.01 aB (+++)	13.09 ± 0.40 dD (+)	15.34 ± 0.00 cD (+)	20.85 ± 3.28 bDE (+)

For the same bacteria, values followed by the same lower-case letter within the same row are not significantly different ($p > 0.05$) according to Tukey's Multiple Range Test. For the same essential oil, values followed by the same upper-case letter within the same column are not significantly different ($p > 0.05$) according to Tukey's Multiple Range Test. Essential oils are classified as (−) not active, (+) moderately active, (++) active and (+++) extremely active.

With regard to the antibacterial activity of *Thymus* EOs using a cooked ham extract as culture medium (Table 3); again, all EOs analyzed had antibacterial activity on all bacteria strains tested. Except for *S. putrefaciens*, *T. vulgaris* EO showed the lowest inhibition zones ($p < 0.05$) of all EOs analyzed, and could be classified as not active or active depending of bacteria strain. On the other hand, *T. capitatus* EO showed the greatest ($p < 0.05$) inhibition halos against *A. denitrificans*, *A. faecalis*, *E. amnigenus* and *P. fluorescens*, while *T. zygis* EO had the highest inhibition halos ($p < 0.05$) against *L. innocua*, *A. hydrophila* and *P. fragi*. These EOs, against these strains, could be classified as moderately active or active. For *E. gergoviae* and *S. marcescens*, no statistical differences ($p > 0.05$) were found between *T. capitatus* and *T. zygis* EOs.

Table 3. Antibacterial activity of *T. capitatus*, *T. mastichina*, *T. vulgaris* and *T. zygis* EOs against several bacterial strains using cooked ham extract as culture medium.

	Diameter of Inhibition Zone (mm) Including Disc (9 mm)			
	T. capitatus	*T. mastichina*	*T. vulgaris*	*T. zygis*
A. denitrificans	14.70 ± 0.14 [aE] (+)	13.29 ± 0.61 [bcB] (+)	13.59 ± 0.00 [bE] (+)	13.11 ± 0.13 [cE] (+)
A. faecalis	32.25 ± 0.01 [aA] (+++)	15.34 ± 0.70 [cA] (+)	24.55 ± 1.44 [bA] (++)	25.39 ± 1.96 [bA] (++)
A. hydrophila	14.49 ± 0.39 [bE] (+)	12.13 ± 0.34 [cC] (+)	14.74 ± 0.08 [bD] (+)	18.51 ± 0.24 [aB] (+)
E. amnigenus	16.29 ± 0.50 [aC] (+)	10.69 ± 0.37 [cE] (−)	10.87 ± 0.10 [cF] (−)	15.08 ± 0.90 [bD] (+)
E. gergoviae	16.51 ± 1.73 [aC] (+)	13.81 ± 0.28 [cB] (+)	14.46 ± 0.20 [bDE] (+)	17.32 ± 0.97 [aC] (+)
L. innocua	20.86 ± 0.59 [bB] (++)	15.23 ± 1.22 [cA] (+)	22.35 ± 0.40 [aB] (++)	23.01 ± 0.78 [aA] (++)
P. fluorescens	17.71 ± 0.85 [aC] (+)	12.86 ± 0.56 [dC] (+)	13.93 ± 0.45 [cE] (+)	15.48 ± 0.25 [bD] (+)
P. fragi	15.17 ± 0.15 [bD] (+)	11.78 ± 0.06 [dD] (−)	14.30 ± 0.64 [cDE] (+)	16.68 ± 0.37 [aC] (+)
S. marcescens	16.59 ± 1.09 [aC] (+)	12.69 ± 0.01 [bC] (+)	15.95 ± 0.80 [aC] (+)	15.15 ± 0.00 [aD] (+)
S. putrefaciens	13.75 ± 0.00 [bF] (+)	14.34 ± 0.23 [aA] (+)	9.77 ± 0.04 [dG] (−)	12.98 ± 0.11 [cE] (+)

For the same bacteria, values followed by the same lower-case letter within the same row are not significantly different ($p > 0.05$) according to Tukey's Multiple Range Test. For the same essential oil, values followed by the same upper-case letter within the same column are not significantly different ($p > 0.05$) according to Tukey's Multiple Range Test. Essential oils are classified as (−) not active, (+) moderately active, (++) active and (+++) extremely active.

Table 4 shows the antibacterial activity of *T. capitatus*, *T. mastichina*, *T. vulgaris* and *T. zygis* EOs against several bacteria strains using a dry-cured sausage extract as culture medium. In this case, not all EOs studied showed growth inhibitory activity against all strains tested. Thus, for *E. gergoviae*, only *T. vulgaris* EOs produced inhibition halos while for *A. faecalis* and *E. amnigenus*, only *T. mastichina* and *T. vulgaris* EOs had antibacterial activity, with *T. vulgaris* EOs presenting higher ($p < 0.05$) inhibition halos. For *A. hydrophila*, *A. denitrificans*, *S. marcescens* and *S. putrefaciens* strains, the EOs obtained from *T. capitatus* and *T. zygis* showed the greatest inhibition halos, with no statistically significant differences ($p > 0.05$) between them. These EOs could be classified as moderately active against these bacteria, except on *A. hydrophila*. In this case, their activity is extremely active. In the case of *Pseudomonas* (*P. fragi* and *P. fluorescens*), *T. capitatus* EOs showed the greatest inhibition halos ($p < 0.05$), followed by *T. zygis*, *T. mastichina* and *T. vulgaris* EOs.

Table 4. Antibacterial activity of *T. capitatus*, *T. mastechina*, *T. vulgaris* and *T. zygis* EOs against several bacterial strains using a dry-cured sausage extract as culture medium.

	Diameter of Inhibition Zone (mm) Including Disc (9 mm)			
	T. capitatus	*T. mastechina*	*T. vulgaris*	*T. zygis*
A. denitrificans	20.75 ± 1.57 [aC] (+)	15.87 ± 1.10 [bE] (+)	15.99 ± 1.03 [b] (+)	20.63 ± 0.28 [aC] (+)
A. faecalis	9.00 ± 0.00 [cE] (−)	16.03 ± 0.30 [bE] (+)	21.38 ± 2.08 [a] (++)	9.00 ± 0.00 [cF] (−)
A. hydrophila	38.18 ± 1.48 [aA] (+++)	24.94 ± 0.11 [cA] (++)	29.91 ± 5.12 [b] (++)	40.72 ± 0.85 [aB] (+++)
E. amnigenus	9.00 ± 0.00 [cE] (−)	17.31 ± 0.29 [bC] (+)	19.19 ± 1.08 [a] (+)	9.00 ± 0.00 [cF] (+−)
E. gergoviae	9.00 ± 0.00 [bE] (−)	9.00 ± 0.00 [bH] (−)	12.85 ± 0.44 [a] (+)	9.00 ± 0.00 [bF] (−)
L. innocua	38.59 ± 1.37 [bA] (+++)	19.45 ± 1.03 [dB] (+)	22.82 ± 0.45 [c] (++)	50.97 ± 5.17 [aA] (+++)
P. fluorescens	19.28 ± 0.15 [aC] (+)	16.70 ± 0.33 [cD] (+)	11.49 ± 0.19 [d] (−)	18.99 ± 0.90 [bD] (+)
P. fragi	30.11 ± 0.02 [aB] (+++)	14.19 ± 0.06 [cF] (+)	13.26 ± 0.66 [d] (+)	18.49 ± 0.28 [bD] (+)
S. marcescens	16.60 ± 0.33 [aD] (+)	11.49 ± 0.02 [cG] (−)	14.82 ± 0.76 [b] (+)	16.64 ± 0.10 [aE] (+)
S. putrefaciens	18.96 ± 0.88 [aC] (+)	15.82 ± 0.08 [bE] (+)	13.45 ± 1.66 [c] (+)	18.87 ± 0.51 [aD] (+)

For the same bacteria, values followed by the same lower-case letter within the same row are not significantly different ($p > 0.05$) according to Tukey's Multiple Range Test. For the same essential oil, values followed by the same upper-case letter within the same column are not significantly different ($p > 0.05$) according to Tukey's Multiple Range Test. Essential oils are classified as (−) not active, (+) moderately active, (++) active and (+++) extremely active.

To our knowledge, there are no studies where the antibacterial activity of *Thymus* EOs were determined using extracts from meat homogenates as culture medium. However, the antibacterial activity of EOs obtained from *Thymus* species has been widely determined. Ruiz-Navajas et al. [28] reported that the EOs obtained from two *Thymus* species endemic of eastern of Spain, such as *Thymus moroderi* and *Thymus piperella*, are a source of important bioactive compounds with antibacterial capacities against several Gram-positive and Gram-negative bacteria. The inhibition zones of microbial strains were in the range of 16.0–45.00 mm. Likewise, Fatma et al. [29] investigated the antibacterial activity of *Thymus hirtus* sp. *Algeriensis* EO cultivated in Tunisia against six bacterial strains; namely, *Escherichia coli, Pseudomonas aeruginosa, Salmonella enteritidis, Staphylococcus aureus, Bacillus subtilis* and *Listeria monocytogenes*. These authors found that *T. hirtus* sp. *Algeriensis* EO was capable of inhibiting the growth of bacterial organisms tested with inhibition zones of between 9 and 65 mm. Similarly, Tepe et al. [30] analyzed the antibacterial potential of *Thymus hyemalis* EO against several bacterial strains, and they found that in the presence of this EO, no activity was observed against *Enterobacter aerogenes, Klebsiella pneumonia, P. aeruginosa, L. monocytogenes* and *P. fluorescens*. The most sensitive microorganisms were determined to be *Bacillus cereus* and *B. subtilis*, with an MIC value of 31.25 mg/mL, while *Enterococcus faecalis* and *S. aureus* had MIC values of 62.50 mg/mL. De Martino et al. [31] investigated the antibacterial properties of EOs obtained from *Thymus longicaulis* and *Thymus pulegioides*. These EOs showed important antibacterial activity against *Staphylococcus aureus, Streptococcus faecalis, Bacillus subtilis, Bacillus cereus, Proteus mirabilis, Enterobacter coli, Salmonella typhi Ty2* and *Pseudomonas aeruginosa*.

The antibacterial data obtained in this work showed that certain compounds in the oils were successfully antibacterial, augmenting the oils' significance in inhibiting microbial pathogens [27]. Terpenes have been widely demonstrated as potent antimicrobial compounds, and their considerable contribution to the *Thymus* EOs composition could be responsible for the antibacterial activities achieved in the present study. Thus, some researchers have reported that there is a relationship between the chemical composition of the most abundant components in the EO and the antimicrobial activity [32]. For instance, the main components of the *Thymus* EOs analyzed in this work—thymol, carvacrol, linalool and 1,8-cineol—have been found in previous studies to exhibit strong antibacterial activity [33,34]. Nonetheless, as occurs with the antioxidant activity, the antibacterial properties showed by the *Thymus* EOs analyzed in the present study could result from a synergistic effect of more than one component.

Additionally, it should be borne in mind, that when the EOs are used as antimicrobial agents in food systems, higher concentrations of EOs are needed in order to have comparable antimicrobial effects to those obtained in vitro. Factors present in complex food matrices such as fat content, proteins, water activity, pH, and enzymes can potentially diminish the efficacy of EOs [35]. Thus, high levels of fat and protein in food protect, to a certain extent, the bacteria strains from the action of EOs. Therefore, if the EOs are dissolved in the lipid phase of the food, it will be less available to act on the bacteria strains that are present in the aqueous phase. It is also important to highlight that, depending on the state of the fat fraction of food—either emulsified, degraded by action of the fermentation and curing process, or unaltered—the EOs may exert more or less activity against microbial growth, as is shown in this paper.

Bacteria need water, several sources of nitrogen, and carbon, as well as numerous micronutrients. To have carbon and nitrogen sources such as mono- and disaccharides (as carbon sources) and small amino acids or peptides of molecular weight (as nitrogen sources) favors bacterial growth, and indeed is essential for some bacterial species. The extract of fresh meat has integrity and a low presence of simple sugar proteins or organic acids, and as such is less favorable as a substrate to bacterial growth that extracts cooked product (with dextrose added and caseinates or hydrolyzed soy protein as simple sources of carbon and nitrogen). Extract obtained from dry-cured product is a more favorable substrate for the growth of many bacteria, overcoming the low water activity of additional product due to the extraction, the extract contains dextrose and peptides because of the proteolytic activity of starter cultures. As mentioned above, the higher fat content of the dry-cured product extract can protect some bacteria from the effects of Eos, since they tend to be solubilized by the fat being less available to act on the bacteria. Therefore, EOs in fresh product extracts were more effective inhibitors of bacteria than in cooked and dry-cured extract products.

Although the EOs showed antibacterial properties, the reasons behind this ability are not well documented. For this reason, different mechanisms of action have been suggested. Thus, the available literature data show that the primary site of the toxic action of EOs is generally the plasmic membrane. Therefore, Horvathova et al. [36] mentioned that the effectiveness of EOs against several microorganisms is related to their hydrophobicity, which enables them to integrate into the lipids of the cell membrane and mitochondria, rendering them permeable and leading to leakage of cell contents. Gao et al. [37] reported that membrane function could be disturbed by inhibition of the proton motive force and electron transfer, or disruption of synthesis of critical macromolecules such as nucleic acid and protein. Arques et al. [38] proposed that the EOs affect microbial cells by various antimicrobial mechanisms, including disrupting enzyme systems, compromising the genetic material of bacteria, and forming fatty acid hydroperoxidase caused by oxygenation of unsaturated fatty acids. The essential oils might also inhibit the activity of protective enzymes and sequentially inhibit one or more biochemical pathways, as mentioned by Xing et al. [39]

4. Conclusions

The essential oils obtained from *Thymus vulgaris*, *Thymus mastichina* and mainly from *Thymus zygis* and *Thymus capitatus* may be used, by the food industry in general and the meat industry in particular, as potential natural or "green" additives to replace or reduce the use of chemical ones, since they show significant antioxidant and antibacterial properties. In addition, their efficacy as antibacterial agents have been demonstrated in model systems that closely simulate food composition. However, the use of these essential oils could be restricted by changes to the organoleptic properties of foods to which they are added. So, the most suitable essential oil must be chosen, at the right concentration, for each type of food.

Author Contributions: Carmen Ballester-Costa was responsible for laboratory work and data processing. Esther Sendra was responsible for the statistical analysis. Juana Fernandez-Lopez and Manuel Viud-Martos were responsible for experiment design and writing the manuscript.

Conflicts of Interest: The authors declare no conflict of interest.

References

1. Grunert, K.G. Future trends and consumer lifestyles with regard to meat consumption. *Meat Sci.* **2006**, *74*, 149–160. [CrossRef] [PubMed]
2. Alves-Silva, J.M.; Dias dos Santos, S.M.; Pintado, M.E.; Pérez-Álvarez, J.A.; Fernández-López, J.; Viuda-Martos, M. Chemical composition and in vitro antimicrobial, antifungal and antioxidant properties of essential oils obtained from some herbs widely used in Portugal. *Food Control* **2013**, *32*, 371–378. [CrossRef]
3. Viuda-Martos, M.; Ruiz-Navajas, Y.; Fernández-López, J.; Pérez-Álvarez, J.A. Spices as Functional Foods. *Crit. Rev. Food Sci. Nutr.* **2011**, *51*, 13–28. [CrossRef] [PubMed]
4. Viuda-Martos, M.; El-Gendy, G.S.A.; Sendra, E.; Fernández-López, J.; Razik, K.A.A.; Omer, E.A.; Pérez-Alvarez, J.A. Chemical composition and antioxidant and anti-listeria activities of essential oils obtained from some Egyptian plants. *J. Agric. Food Chem.* **2010**, *58*, 9063–9070. [CrossRef] [PubMed]
5. Carson, C.F.; Hammer, K.A. Chemistry and bioactivity of EOs. In *Lipids and EOs as Antimicrobial Agents*; Thormar, H., Ed.; John Wiley & Sons, Ltd.: West Sussex, UK, 2011; pp. 307–335.
6. Ruiz-Navajas, Y.; Viuda-Martos, M.; Sendra, E.; Perez-Alvarez, J.A.; Fernández-López, J. In vitro antioxidant and antifungal properties of essential oils obtained from aromatic herbs endemic to the southeast of Spain. *Food Prot.* **2013**, *76*, 1218–1225. [CrossRef] [PubMed]
7. Adrar, N.; Oukil, N.; Bedjou, F. Antioxidant and antibacterial activities of *Thymus numidicus* and *Salvia officinalis* essential oils alone or in combination. *Ind. Crops Prod.* **2015**, *88*, 112–119. [CrossRef]

8. Majouli, K.; Besbes Hlila, M.; Hamdi, A.; Flamini, G.; Ben Jannet, H.; Kenani, A. Antioxidant activity and α-glucosidase inhibition by essential oils from *Hertia cheirifolia* (L.). *Ind. Crops Prod.* **2016**, *82*, 23–28. [CrossRef]
9. Viuda-Martos, M.; Ruiz-Navajas, Y.; Fernandez-Lopez, J.; Perez-Alvarez, J.A. Antifungal activity of lemon (*Citrus lemon* L.), mandarin (*Citrus reticulata* L.), grapefruit (*Citrus paradisi* L.) and orange (*Citrus sinensis* L.) essential oils. *Food Control* **2008**, *19*, 1130–1138. [CrossRef]
10. Gutierrez, J.; Barry-Ryan, C.; Bourke, P. Antimicrobial activity of plant essential oils using food model media: Efficacy, synergistic potential and interactions with food components. *Food Microbiol.* **2009**, *26*, 142–150. [CrossRef] [PubMed]
11. Ballester-Costa, C.; Sendra, E.; Fernández-López, J.; Pérez-Álvarez, J.A.; Viuda-Martos, M. Chemical composition and in vitro antibacterial properties of essential oils of four *Thymus* species from organic growth. *Ind. Crops Prod.* **2013**, *50*, 304–311. [CrossRef]
12. Brand-Williams, W.; Cuvelier, M.E.; Berset, C. Use of free radical method to evaluate antioxidant activity. *LWT-Food Sci. Technol.* **1995**, *28*, 25–30. [CrossRef]
13. Leite, A.; Malta, L.G.; Riccio, M.F.; Eberlin, M.N.; Pastore, G.M.; Marostica Junior, M.R. Antioxidant potential of rat plasma by administration of freeze-dried jaboticaba peel (*Myrciaria jaboticaba* Vell Berg). *J. Agric. Food Chem.* **2011**, *59*, 2277–2283. [CrossRef] [PubMed]
14. Oyaizu, M. Studies on products of browning reaction: Antioxidative activity of products of browning reaction prepared from glucosamine. *Jap. J. Nutr.* **1986**, *44*, 307–315. [CrossRef]
15. Carter, P. Spectrophotometric determination of serum iron at the submicrogram level with a new reagent (ferrozine). *Anal. Biochem.* **1971**, *40*, 450–458. [CrossRef]
16. Tepe, B.; Sokmen, M.; Sokmen, A.; Daferera, D.; Polissiou, M. Antimicrobial and antioxidative activity of essential oil and various extracts of *Cyclotrichium origanifolium* (Labill.) Manden. & Scheng. *J. Food Eng.* **2005**, *69*, 335–342.
17. Djabou, N.; Lorenzi, V.; Guinoiseau, E.; Andreani, S.; Giuliani, M.C.; Desjobert, J.M.; Bolla, J.M.; Costa, J.; Berti, L.; Luciani, A.; et al. Phytochemical com-position of Corsican *Teucrium* essential oils and antibacterial activity against foodborne or toxi-infectious pathogens. *Food Control* **2013**, *30*, 354–363. [CrossRef]
18. Číž, M.; Čížová, H.; Denev, P.; Kratchanova, M.; Slavov, A.; Lojek, A. Different methods for control and comparison of the antioxidant properties of vegetables. *Food Control* **2010**, *21*, 518–523. [CrossRef]
19. Kadri, A.; Zarai, Z.; Chobba, I.B.; Gharsallah, N.; Damak, M.; Békir, A. Chemical composition and in vitro antioxidant activities of *Thymelaea hirsuta* L: Essential oil from Tunisia. *Afr. J. Biotechnol.* **2013**, *10*, 2930–2935.
20. Zouari, N.; Fakhfakh, N.; Zouarid, S.; Bougatef, A.; Karraya, A.; Neffati, M.; Ayadie, M.A. Chemical composition, angiotensin I-converting enzyme inhibitory, antioxidant and antimicrobial activities of essential oil of Tunisian *Thymus algeriensis* Boiss. et Reut. (*Lamiaceae*). *Food Bioprod. Process.* **2011**, *89*, 257–265. [CrossRef]
21. Ozen, T.; Demirtas, I.; Aksit, H. Determination of antioxidant activities of various extracts and essential oil compositions of *Thymus praecox* subsp. *skorpilii* var. *skorpilii*. *Food Chem.* **2011**, *124*, 58–64. [CrossRef]
22. Ali, I.B.E.; Chaouachi, M.; Bahri, R.; Chaieb, I.; Boussaïd, M.; Harzallah-Skhiri, F. Chemical composition and antioxidant, antibacterial, allelopathic and insecticidal activities of essential oil of *Thymus algeriensis* Boiss. et Reut. *Ind. Crops Prod.* **2015**, *77*, 631–639.
23. Nikolić, M.J.; Glamočlija, I.C.F.R.; Ferreira, R.C.; Calhelha, Â.; Fernandes, T.; Marković, D.; Marković, A.; Giweli, M.; Soković, M. Chemical composition, antimicrobial, antioxidant and antitumor activity of *Thymus serpyllum* L., *Thymus algeriensis* Boiss. and Reut and *Thymus vulgaris* L. essential oils. *Ind. Crops Prod.* **2014**, *52*, 183–190. [CrossRef]
24. Viuda-Martos, M.; Ruiz-Navajas, Y.; Sanchez-Zapata, E.; Fernández-López, J.; Pérez-Alvarez, J.A. Antioxidant activity of essential oils of five spice plants widely used in a Mediterranean diet. *Flavour Fragr. J.* **2010**, *25*, 13–19. [CrossRef]
25. Bakkali, F.; Averbeck, S.; Averbeck, D.; Idaomar, M. Biological effects of essential oils—A review. *Food Chem. Toxicol.* **2008**, *46*, 446–475. [CrossRef] [PubMed]
26. Yanishlieva, N.V. Inhibiting oxidation. In *Antioxidants in Food: Practical Applications*; Pokorny, J., Yanishlieva, N., Gordon, M., Eds.; Woodhead Publishing Ltd.: Cambridge, UK, 2001; pp. 22–69.
27. Bassolé, I.H.; Rodolfo-Juliani, H.R. Essential oils in combination and their antimicrobial properties. *Molecules* **2012**, *17*, 3989–4006. [CrossRef] [PubMed]

28. Ruiz-Navajas, Y.; Viuda-Martos, M.; Sendra, E.; Perez-Alvarez, J.A.; Fernández-López, J. Chemical characterization and antibacterial activity of *Thymus moroderi* and *Thymus piperella* essential oils, two *Thymus* endemic species from southeast of Spain. *Food Control* **2012**, *27*, 294–299. [CrossRef]
29. Fatma, G.; Mouna, B.F.; Mondher, M.; Ahmed, L. In vitro assessment of antioxidant and antimicrobial activities of methanol extracts and essential oil of *Thymus hirtus* sp. *Algeriensis*. *Lipids Health Dis.* **2014**, *13*, 114–126. [CrossRef] [PubMed]
30. Tepe, B.; Sarikurkcu, C.; Berk, S.; Alim, A.; Akpulat, H.A. Chemical composition, radical scavenging and antimicrobial activity of the essential oils of *Thymus boveii* and *Thymus hyemalis*. *Rec. Nat. Prod.* **2011**, *5*, 208–220.
31. De Martino, L.; Bruno, M.; Formisano, C.; De Feo, V.; Napolitano, F.; Rosselli, S. Chemical composition and antimicrobial activity of the essential oils from two species of *Thymus* growing wild in southern Italy. *Molecules* **2009**, *14*, 4614–4624. [CrossRef] [PubMed]
32. Djenane, D.; Yangüela, J.; Montañés, L.; Djerbal, M.; Roncalés, P. Antimicrobial activity of *Pistacia lentiscus* and *Satureja montana* essential oils against *Listeria monocytogenes* CECT 935 using laboratory media: Efficacy and synergistic potential in minced beef. *Food Control* **2011**, *22*, 1046–1053. [CrossRef]
33. Moon, H.; Rhee, M.S. Synergism between carvacrol or thymol increases the antimicrobial efficacy of soy sauce with no sensory impact. *Int. J. Food Microbiol.* **2016**, *217*, 35–41. [CrossRef] [PubMed]
34. Duarte, A.; Luís, A.; Oleastro, M.; Domingues, F.C. Antioxidant properties of coriander essential oil and linalool and their potential to control *Campylobacter* spp. *Food Control* **2016**, *61*, 115–122. [CrossRef]
35. Burt, S. Essential oils: Their antibacterial properties and potential applications in foods—A review. *Int. J. Food Microbiol.* **2004**, *94*, 223–253. [CrossRef] [PubMed]
36. Horvathova, E.; Navarova, J.; Galova, E.; Sevcovicova, A.; Chodakova, L.; Snahnicanova, Z.; Melusova, M.; Kozics, K.; Slamenova, D. Assessment of antioxidative, chelating, and DNA-protective effects of selected essential oil components (eugenol, carvacrol, thymol, borneol, eucalyptol) of plants and intact *Rosmarinus officinalis* oil. *J. Agric. Food Chem.* **2014**, *62*, 663–6639. [CrossRef] [PubMed]
37. Gao, C.; Tian, C.; Lu, Y.; Xu, J.; Luo, J.; Guo, X. Essential oil composition and antimicrobial activity of *Sphallerocarpus gracilis* seeds against selected food-related bacteria. *Food Control* **2011**, *22*, 517–522. [CrossRef]
38. Arques, J.L.; Rodriguez, E.; Nuñez, M.; Medina, M. Inactivation of gram-negative pathogens in refrigerated milk by reuterin in combination with nisin or the lactoperoxidase system. *Eur. Food Res. Technol.* **2008**, *227*, 77–82. [CrossRef]
39. Xing, Y.; Xu, Q.; Li, X.; Che, Z.; Yun, J. Antifungal activities of clove against *Rhizopus nigricans*, *Aspergillus flavus* and *Penicillium citrinum* in vitro and in wounded fruit test. *J. Food Saf.* **2012**, *32*, 84–93. [CrossRef]

© 2017 by the authors. Licensee MDPI, Basel, Switzerland. This article is an open access article distributed under the terms and conditions of the Creative Commons Attribution (CC BY) license (http://creativecommons.org/licenses/by/4.0/).

Article

The Chemical Compositions of the Volatile Oils of Garlic (*Allium sativum*) and Wild Garlic (*Allium vineale*)

Prabodh Satyal, Jonathan D. Craft, Noura S. Dosoky and William N. Setzer *

Department of Chemistry, University of Alabama in Huntsville, Huntsville, AL 35899, USA; prabodhsatyal@gmail.com (P.S.); craftjd@gmail.com (J.D.C.); nouradosoky@yahoo.com (N.S.D.)
* Correspondence: wsetzer@chemistry.uah.edu; Tel.: +1-256-824-6519

Received: 24 June 2017; Accepted: 28 July 2017; Published: 5 August 2017

Abstract: Garlic, *Allium sativum*, is broadly used around the world for its numerous culinary and medicinal uses. Wild garlic, *Allium vineale*, has been used as a substitute for garlic, both in food as well as in herbal medicine. The present study investigated the chemical compositions of *A. sativum* and *A. vineale* essential oils. The essential oils from the bulbs of *A. sativum*, cultivated in Spain, were obtained by three different methods: laboratory hydrodistillation, industrial hydrodistillation, and industrial steam distillation. The essential oils of wild-growing *A. vineale* from north Alabama were obtained by hydrodistillation. The resulting essential oils were analyzed by gas chromatography-flame ionization detection (GC-FID) and gas chromatography-mass spectrometry (GC-MS). Both *A. sativum* and *A. vineale* oils were dominated by allyl polysulfides. There were minor quantitative differences between the *A. sativum* oils owing to the distillation methods employed, as well as differences from previously reported garlic oils from other geographical locations. *Allium vineale* oil showed a qualitative similarity to *Allium ursinum* essential oil. The compositions of garlic and wild garlic are consistent with their use as flavoring agents in foods as well as their uses as herbal medicines. However, quantitative differences are likely to affect the flavor and bioactivity profiles of these *Allium* species.

Keywords: *Allium sativum*; *Allium vineale*; essential oil composition; allyl polysulfides; cluster analysis

1. Introduction

Garlic (*Allium sativum* L., Amaryllidaceae) likely originated in Central Asia [1]. The plant has been used as a flavoring agent and a traditional medicine since antiquity, and is now cultivated worldwide [1,2]. *Allium vineale* L. (wild garlic, crow garlic) is native to Great Britain, most of Europe, North Africa, and the Middle East. The plant has been introduced to North America, Australia, and New Zealand [3].

Allium sativum has been used as a diaphoretic, diuretic, expectorant, and stimulant [4]. Extracts of *A. sativum* have shown broad-spectrum antibacterial [5] and antifungal [6] activity and the plant has been used to treat tuberculosis, coughs, and colds [7]. Garlic preparations have demonstrated hypotensive activity in moderately hypertensive subjects, and garlic-based phytotherapeutic products are used in France for minor vascular disorders [8]. There is an inverse correlation between regular consumption of garlic and stomach cancer frequency [8], but there seems to be no correlation between garlic consumption and other cancers. Garlic has been used in food preparation not only for its flavor, but also as a digestive aid [4]. *Allium vineale* has been used as a substitute for *A. sativum* in cooking; the bulb is used as a flavoring agent and the leaves as an addition to salad [9,10]. Cherokee Native Americans used both *A. vineale* and *A. sativum* as carminatives, diuretics, and expectorants [11,12].

Although there have been numerous investigations on the phytochemistry of garlic (*A. sativum*) [1,13,14], the chemistry of wild garlic (*A. vineale*) has not been investigated, and because of the history of the uses of *Allium* species as both condiments and phytopharmaceuticals, we have investigated the essential oil compositions of *A. sativum* from Spain, obtained by different isolation methods, and *A. vineale* growing wild in north Alabama, USA.

2. Materials and Methods

2.1. Plant Material

2.1.1. Allium sativum

Bulbs of *Allium sativum* were collected from a field in Las Pedroñeras, Spain (39°26′59″ N, 2°40′23″ W, 745 m elevation), in December 2015. Garlic bulbs were finely chopped, and were subjected to three different distillation methods: laboratory hydrodistillation using a Clevenger apparatus for 3 h, industrial hydrodistillation for 4 h, and industrial steam distillation for 5 h. Pale yellow essential oils were obtained in 0.2%, 0.22% and 0.18% yields, respectively. The obtained essential oils and hydrosol were separated by decantation; remaining water was removed from the essential oils with sodium chloride. The collected essential oil samples were stored under refrigeration ($-4\,°C$) until analysis.

2.1.2. Allium vineale

Four different samples of *Allium vineale* were collected from a field in Huntsville, Alabama (34°38′46″ N, 86°33′27″ W, 191 m elevation) on 10 April 2017, 8 a.m. Each sample was cleaned of debris, the entire plant (leaves and bulbs) chopped, and hydrodistilled using a Likens-Nickerson apparatus for 4 h with continuous extraction with dichloromethane (CH_2Cl_2). Evaporation of the dichloromethane yielded pale yellow essential oils with an extremely pungent odor (Table 1).

Table 1. Essential oil yields of *Allium vineale*.

Sample	#1 [a]	#2	#3	#4
Mass of plant material (g)	94.04	123.29	98.20	72.35
Mass of essential oil (mg)	87.2	258.5	210.5	25.3
Essential oil yield	0.0927%	0.2097%	0.2144%	0.0350%

[a] #1, #2, #3, and #4 are different essential oil samples.

2.2. Gas Chromatography-Mass Spectrometry (GC-MS)

GC-MS characterization of *A. sativum* oils was carried out as previously described using a Shimadzu GCMS-QP2010 Ultra (Shimadzu Scientific Instruments, Columbia, MD, USA) [15,16]. This instrument was operated in the electron impact (EI) mode set at electron energy 70 eV with a scan range of 40–400 amu, a scan rate of 3.0 scans per second, and with GC-MS solution software. A ZB-5 fused silica capillary column (Phenomenex, Torrance, CA, USA), 30 m length × 0.25 mm inner diameter, with a (5% phenyl)-polymethylsiloxane stationary phase and a film thickness of 0.25 µm was used as the GC column. Helium was used as the carrier gas and the pressure was set at 551.6 kPa with a flow rate of 1.37 mL/min on the column head. The temperature of the injector was set at 250 °C and the temperature of the ion source was set at 200 °C. The temperature of the GC oven was programmed to be 50 °C initially and was programmed to increase at a rate of 2 °C/min to a final temperature of 260 °C. The samples were prepared with CH_2Cl_2 in a 5% *w/v* solution. Then, 0.1 µL of the solutions were injected into the instrument with a split ratio of 30:1.

GC-MS analysis of *A. vineale* oils was carried out as previously described [17]: Agilent 6890 GC (Agilent Technologies, Santa Clara, CA, USA), Agilent 5973 mass selective detector (Agilent Technologies), EI mode (70 eV), 40–400 mass scan range, 3.99 scans/s scan rate, and operated through an Agilent ChemStation data system (G1701CA, Agilent Technologies); HP-5ms capillary column

(30 m length × 0.25 mm inner diameter × 0.25 µm film thickness), helium carrier gas, head pressure (92.4 kPa), flow rate (1.5 mL/min); oven temperature program (60 °C initial temperature, which was held for 5 min, temperature increased at a rate of 3 °C/min up to 280 °C), inlet temperature (250 °C), interface temperature (280 °C). *Allium vineale* solutions (1 µL of 1% in CH_2Cl_2) were injected using a splitless mode.

The retention indices were determined by reference to a homologous series of *n*-alkanes. The components of each essential oil sample were identified based on their retention indices and mass spectral fragmentation patterns compared to reference literature [18–22] and our in-house library.

2.3. Semi-Quantitative Gas Chromatography

Semi-quantitative GC was performed with an Agilent 6890 GC with Agilent FID (flame ionization detector) (Agilent Technologies), HP-5ms column (30 m length × 0.25 mm inner diameter × 0.25 µm film thickness), He carrier gas, head pressure (144.1 kPa), flow rate (2.0 mL/min); oven temperature program (as above). The percent compositions of the essential oils were determined from raw peak area percentages without standardization.

2.4. Hierarchical Cluster Analysis

The chemical compositions of *A. sativum* from this current study along with garlic oil compositions from previously published works (hydrodistillations and steam distillations only) [6,23–30] were used as operational taxonomic units (OTUs). The percentages of the major sulfur-containing compounds (diallyl sulfide, allyl methyl disulfide, dimethyl trisulfide, diallyl disulfide, allyl (Z)-1-propenyl disulfide, allyl (E)-1-propenyl disulfide, allyl methyl trisulfide, 2-vinyl-4H-1,3-dithiine, diallyl trisulfide, and diallyl tetrasulfide) were used to evaluate the chemical similarities and differences between the garlic oil samples by agglomerative hierarchical cluster (AHC) analysis using the XLSTAT software, version 2015.4.01 (Addinsoft™, New York, NY, USA). Pearson correlation was used to evaluate similarity and clusters were defined by the unweighted pair-group method with arithmetic averaging (UPGMA).

3. Results and Discussion

3.1. Allium sativum

The garlic (*A. sativum*) essential oils from Spain, obtained using three different distillation methods (Clevenger laboratory hydrodistillation, industrial steam distillation, and industrial hydrodistillation) were characterized by GC-MS (Table 2). The oils were dominated by allyl polysulfides, including diallyl sulfide (1.9–9.5%), diallyl disulfide (20.8–27.9%), diallyl trisulfide (16.8–33.4%), allyl methyl disulfide (4.4–8.3%), and allyl methyl trisulfide (14.5–19.2%). The major components of *A. sativum* essential oil extracted by Clevenger-type laboratory distillation were diallyl trisulfide (allitridin) (33.4%), diallyl disulfide (20.8%), allyl methyl trisulfide (19.2%), allyl (E)-1-propenyl disulfide (5.2%), and allyl methyl disulfide (4.4%) (see Figure 1), whereas the main constituents in the oil extracted by industrial hydrodistillation were diallyl trisulfide (31.2%), diallyl disulfide (25.9%), allyl methyl trisulfide (14.5%), allyl methyl disulfide (5.2%), allyl (E)-1-propenyl disulfide (4.6%) and diallyl sulfide (3.4%). Thus, the two hydrodistillation methods yielded very similar results. Extraction by industrial steam distillation, on the other hand, resulted in the identification of diallyl disulfide (27.9%), allyl methyl trisulfide (17.7%), diallyl trisulfide (16.8%), diallyl sulfide (9.5%), allyl methyl disulfide (8.3%), and allyl (E)-1-propenyl disulfide (3.7%) as the major components. Thus, the steam distillation gave somewhat increased yields of diallyl sulfide and diallyl disulfide with a concomitant decrease in diallyl trisulfide and diallyl tetrasulfide yields. These differences are small, however; the three distillation methods gave comparable results overall.

Table 2. Essential oil compositions of garlic (*Allium sativum*) obtained by different distillation methods.

		Percent Composition		
RI [a]	Compound	Clevenger-Type Hydrodistillation	Industrial Steam Distillation	Industrial Hydrodistillation
739	Dimethyl disulfide	0.4	1.4	- [b]
741	2-Methyl-4-pentenal	tr [c]	0.1	-
743	2-Methylene-4-pentenal	0.4	-	-
787	3-Methylthiophene	-	0.1	-
801	Hexanal	tr	0.1	-
842	1,2-Dithiolane	0.5	0.3	0.4
855	Diallyl sulfide	1.9	9.5	3.4
870	Allyl propyl sulfide	-	0.1	-
886	Allyl (Z)-1-propenyl sulfide	tr	tr	tr
889	Allyl (E)-1-propenyl sulfide	tr	-	-
904	3,4-Dimethylthiophene	tr	0.2	0.1
916	Allyl methyl disulfide	4.4	8.3	5.2
928	Methyl (Z)-1-propenyl disulfide	0.4	0.4	0.4
936	Methyl (E)-1-propenyl disulfide	0.6	0.7	0.6
953	1,2-Dithiolene	0.3	0.1	0.4
968	Dimethyl trisulfide	2.0	2.9	1.3
1080	Diallyl disulfide	20.8	27.9	25.9
1093	Allyl (Z)-1-propenyl disulfide	2.6	2.2	2.6
1100	Allyl (E)-1-propenyl disulfide	5.2	3.7	4.6
1138	Allyl methyl trisulfide	19.2	17.7	14.5
1149	Methyl propyl trisulfide	-	-	tr
1153	4-Methyl-1,2,3-trithiolane	tr	1.2	0.5
1159	Methyl (Z)-1-propenyl trisulfide	0.1	-	0.1
1164	Methyl (E)-1-propenyl trisulfide	0.1	-	0.1
1188	3-Vinyl-4H-1,2-dithiine	0.9	0.8	0.6
1198	1,2,3-Trithia-4-cyclohexene	0.7	0.4	0.6
1208	Allicin	tr	-	tr
1214	2-Vinyl-4H-1,3-dithiine	2.5	1.8	2.0
1292	Methyl (methylsulfinyl)methyl sulfide [d]	0.1	0.1	0.1
1301	Diallyl trisulfide	33.4	16.8	31.2
1313	Allyl propyl trisulfide	0.2	0.3	0.2
1325	Allyl (E)-1-propenyl trisulfide	-	-	0.4
1369	5-Methyl-1,2,3,4-tetrathiane	0.2	0.4	0.6
1379	Unidentified [e]	0.5	0.7	0.7
1411	1,4-Dihydro-2,3-benzoxathiin 3-oxide	0.4	0.2	0.2
1443	[(E)-1-Propenyl] 2-thiopent-3-yl disulfide [d]	-	0.2	-
1540	Diallyl tetrasulfide	1.5	1.0	2.2
1591	Propyl 4-thiohept-2-en-5-yl disulfide [d]	-	0.2	-
1646	4-Methyl-1,2,3,5,6-pentathiepane [c]	-	0.1	0.2
2041	Cyclooctasulfur	0.3	0.1	0.4
	Total Identified	99.2	98.9	99.0
	Sulfur-containing	99.3	99.4	99.5

[a] RI = Retention index determined with respect to a homologous series of *n*-alkanes on an ZB-5 column. [b] - = not detected. [c] tr = trace (<0.05%). [d] Identification based on MS only. [e] MS (m/z): 210 (1%), 184 (3%), 158 (9%), 146 (5%), 120 (32%), 105 (10%), 79 (36%), 64 (60%), 45 (41%), 41 (100%).

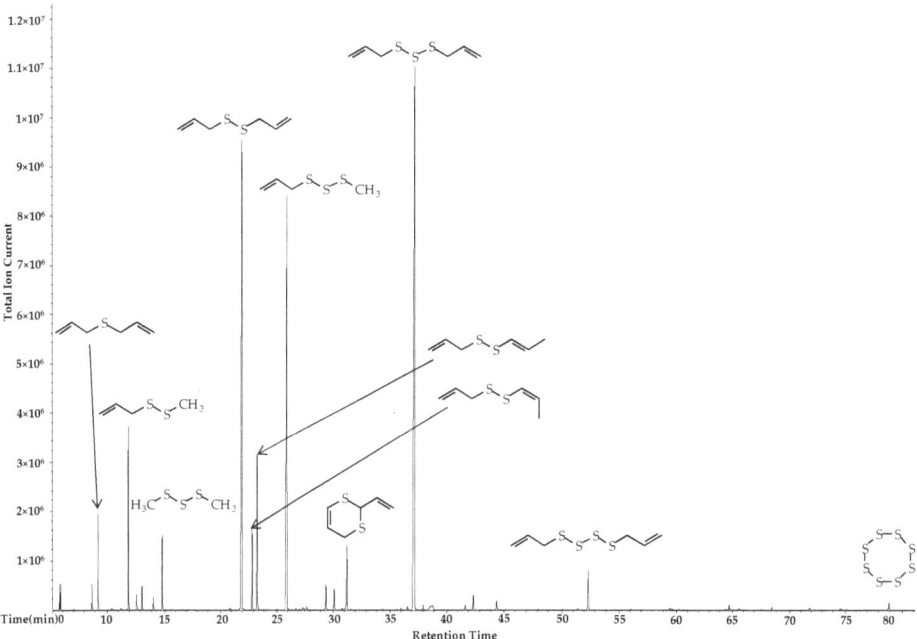

Figure 1. Chromatogram of *Allium sativum* essential oil from Clevenger distillation, including major sulfur-containing compounds.

The oil compositions from this study show quantitative similarities and differences from previously published reports on garlic oil [6,23–30]. Egyptian garlic essential oil extracted by hydrodistillation had diallyl disulfide (25.2%), allyl methyl trisulfide (23.8%) and diallyl trisulfide (21.1%) as the major constituents [29]. The major components of Serbian garlic essential oil obtained by hydrodistillation were diallyl trisulfide (33.6%), diallyl disulfide (28.1%), and allyl methyl trisulfide (17.8%) [26]. Diallyl disulfide (49.1%) and diallyl trisulfide (30.4%) were the main components of Tunisian garlic essential oil obtained by hydrodistillation [31]. The profile identified in this study was also different from French garlic oil presented by Mnayer et al. [27] in which the major components were diallyl disulfide (37.9%), diallyl trisulfide (28.1%), allyl methyl trisulfide (7.3%), diallyl sulfide (6.6%), diallyl tetrasulfide (4.1%) and allyl methyl disulfide (3.7%). Douiri et al. [23] showed that *A. sativum* essential oil obtained by Clevenger hydrodistillation was dominated by diallyl trisulfide (46.5%) followed by diallyl disulfide (16.0%), allyl methyl trisulfide (10.9%) and diallyl disulfide (7.2%). Similarly, Rao and co-workers have analyzed six geographical varieties of essential oils obtained by steam distillation of fresh garlic grown in India. These investigators found diallyl disulfide (27.1–46.8%) and diallyl trisulfide (19.9–34.1%) to be the dominant components, followed by allyl methyl trisulfide (8.3–18.2%), and allyl methyl disulfide (4.4–12.0%) [28]. Commercial Chinese garlic oil has shown abundant diallyl disulfide (45.1–63.2%), diallyl trisulfide (18.5–23.4%), diallyl sulfide (4.5–11.4%), and diallyl tetrasulfide (6.3–10.5%) (unpublished results from our laboratories). Kimbaris and co-workers obtained garlic oil from Greece (Likens-Nickerson hydrodistillation-extraction) and found diallyl disulfide (23.1–28.4%), diallyl trisulfide (18.2–22.1%), allyl methyl trisulfide (16.3–17.5%), and allyl methyl disulfide (8.5–11.2%) [25].

A hierarchical cluster analysis of garlic oils from this work and reported in the literature has been carried out (Figure 2). The cluster analysis revealed greater than 70% similarity between all oils, but five distinct clusters with greater than 90% similarity for each cluster can be defined based on the relative concentrations of sulfur-containing compounds: Cluster #1 (diallyl disulfide > diallyl trisulfide ≈ allyl methyl trisulfide > allyl methyl sulfide), Cluster #2 (diallyl trisulfide ≫ diallyl disulfide ≫ allyl methyl trisulfide ≈ diallyl tetrasulfide), Cluster #3 (diallyl trisulfide > diallyl disulfide > allyl methyl sulfide), Cluster #4 (diallyl disulfide > diallyl trisulfide > allyl methyl trisulfide > allyl methyl disulfide), and Cluster #5 (diallyl disulfide ≫ diallyl trisulfide ≫ diallyl tetrasulfide ≈ diallyl sulfide). Both of the hydrodistilled samples from Spain in this work fall into Cluster #3, while the steam-distilled sample falls into Cluster #1. Five of the Indian garlic varieties [28] (Rajkot, Gondal, Jamnagar, Junagadh, and Gujarat) are in Cluster #4, while the Amreli variety is in Cluster #3. Four different commercial garlic oil samples from China (unpublished data from our laboratories) form Cluster #5.

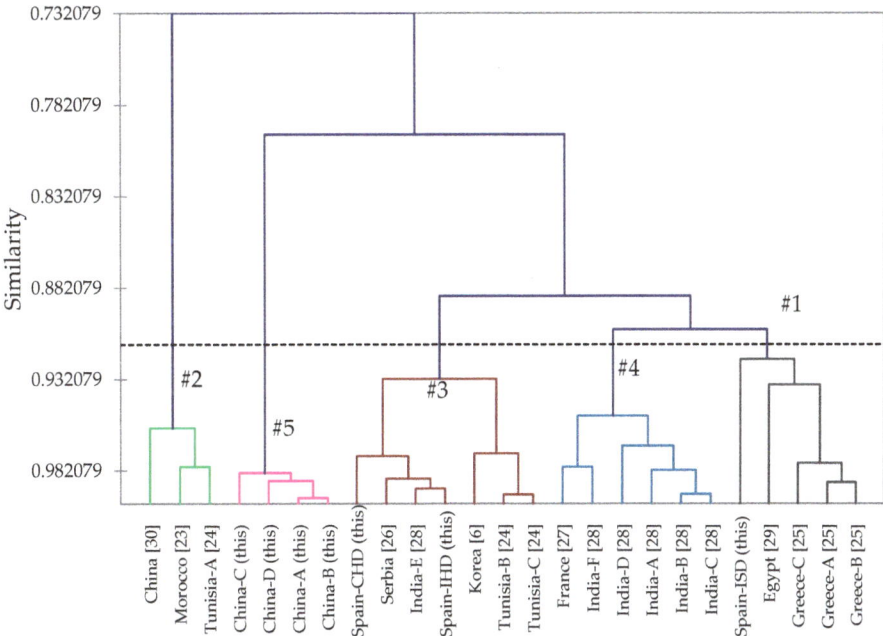

Figure 2. Dendrogram obtained from the agglomerative hierarchical cluster analysis of 25 *Allium sativum* essential oil compositions. Individual clusters are highlighted by different colored lines and numbers (#1–#5). The letters A–F refer to different essential oil samples from the same country of origin. CHD = Clevenger hydrodistillation; IHD = industrial hydrodistillation; ISD = industrial steam distillation.

3.2. Allium vineale

The gas chromatographic analysis of *A. vineale* essential oils is summarized in Table 3. A representative chromatogram (sample #4) is shown in Figure 3. The major components in the essential oils were sulfur-containing compounds allyl methyl trisulfide (7.9–13.2%), allyl (*E*)-1-propenyl disulfide (7.9–12.5%), dimethyl trisulfide (4.3–17.4%), diallyl disulfide (4.4–12.2%), diallyl trisulfide (2.8–10.5%), and methyl (*E*)-1-propenyl disulfide (2.6–12.5%). The high proportion of sulfur-containing components (74.9–91.6%) accounts for the very pungent aroma of the oils.

Table 3. Essential oil compositions of wild garlic (*Allium vineale*) growing wild in north Alabama.

RI [a]	Compound	Percent Composition			
		#1 [b]	#2	#3	#4
837	2-Furaldehyde	2.2	1.0	1.3	1.3
854	(2E)-Hexenal	0.8	2.0	1.9	2.0
856	(3Z)-Hexenol	tr [c]	1.4	tr	tr
902	2,4-Dimethylthiophene	0.8	1.7	2.0	2.2
915	Allyl methyl disulfide	6.1	3.6	2.3	2.3
930	Methyl (Z)-1-propenyl disulfide	3.1	1.1	1.3	1.5
939	Methyl (E)-1-propenyl disulfide	12.5	3.2	2.6	3.0
958	Benzaldehyde	tr	0.6	4.2	16.4
965	Dimethyl trisulfide	17.4	3.8	4.4	4.3
1079	Diallyl disulfide	6.3	12.2	4.4	5.2
1091	Allyl (Z)-1-propenyl disulfide	3.1	4.3	3.4	2.8
1099	Allyl (E)-1-propenyl disulfide	11.6	12.5	7.9	8.2
1115	1-Propenyl propyl disulfide [d,e]	1.4	2.0	1.9	1.7
1123	Methyl methylthiomethyl disulfide	tr	0.5	1.2	0.8
1135	Allyl methyl trisulfide	13.2	9.9	9.9	7.9
1147	4-Methyl-1,2,3-trithiolane [d]	tr	1.8	1.0	1.6
1149	Methyl propyl trisulfide	tr	1.9	2.7	1.8
1158	Methyl (Z)-1-propenyl trisulfide	1.9	0.5	1.4	0.9
1164	Methyl (E)-1-propenyl trisulfide	2.7	1.0	1.7	1.5
1211	Dimethyl tetrasulfide	4.0	0.8	1.2	1.1
1284	Allyl methylthiomethyl disulfide [d]	tr	2.3	2.6	1.9
1291	Diallyl trisulfide	2.8	10.5	7.9	5.3
1302	Allyl (Z)-1-propenyl trisulfide	tr	3.0	2.7	2.3
1309	*p*-Vinylguaiacol	5.3	5.2	6.5	5.4
1320	Allyl propyl trisulfide	tr	1.1	2.4	2.2
1344	5-Methyl-1,2,3,4-tetrathiane [d]	tr	5.5	6.1	4.3
1346	Methyl methylthiomethyl trisulfide	tr	0.7	1.0	1.5
1364	Allyl methyl tetrasulfide	2.4	1.6	2.4	1.8
1483	Allyl methylthiomethyl trisulfide [d]	tr	0.5	1.2	0.9
1599	Unidentified [f]	1.6	1.7	4.6	3.3
1623	4-Methyl-1,2,3,5,6-pentathiepane [d]	tr	0.5	2.0	1.2
1754	Unidentified [g]	0.6	2.0	4.1	3.2
	Total Identified	97.8	96.2	91.4	93.5
	Sulfur-containing	91.6	90.0	86.1	74.9

[a] RI = Retention index determined with respect to a homologous series of *n*-alkanes on an HP-5ms column. [b] #1–#4 are different essential oil samples. [c] tr = trace (<0.05%). [d] Identification based on MS only. [e] (Z)/(E)-Isomer not determined. [f] MS (m/z): 410 (4%), 326 (3%), 221 (21%), 207 (5%), 129 (81%), 69 (100%), 59 (26%), 45 (32%), 41 (31%). [g] MS (m/z): 446 (2%), 405 (2%), 269 (2%), 207 (5%), 129 (71%), 69 (100%), 59 (17%), 45 (27%), 41 (35%).

In contrast to wild garlic (*A. vineale*), garlic (*A. sativum*) essential oils tend to be very rich in allyl polysulfides, especially diallyl disulfide, allyl methyl trisulfide, diallyl trisulfide, and diallyl tetrasulfide (see above) [6,25,27]. The compositions of *A. vineale* are similar to those reported for *Allium ursinum* (broad-leaved garlic, bear's garlic, wild garlic) volatile oils, which showed allyl methyl disulfide (13.0–18.9%), methyl (E)-1-propenyl disulfide (3.4–6.2%), dimethyl trisulfide (3.5–7.5%), diallyl disulfide (16.2–19.9%), allyl (E)-1-propenyl disulfide (7.5–10.2%), and allyl methyl trisulfide (12.6–15.0%) [32]. Both *A. vineale* and *A. ursinum* have qualitative similarities in composition to *A. sativum*, which no doubt accounts for the similar uses of these two "wild garlic" species.

The medicinal properties of garlic have been attributed to the abundance of sulfur-containing compounds. These compounds have also shown antifungal [33,34], antibacterial [27,35,36], acaricidal [37], antiparasitic [38,39], nematicidal [40], antiviral [29], and insecticidal [23,30,41,42] properties. Diallyl disulfide and dipropyl disulfide have hypoglycemic [43] and hypolipidemic actions [44]. Diallyl trisulfide and diallyl disulfide, which are allicin-derivative products, have been shown to activate antioxidant enzymes [45,46] and to possess antimicrobial activity [47,48].

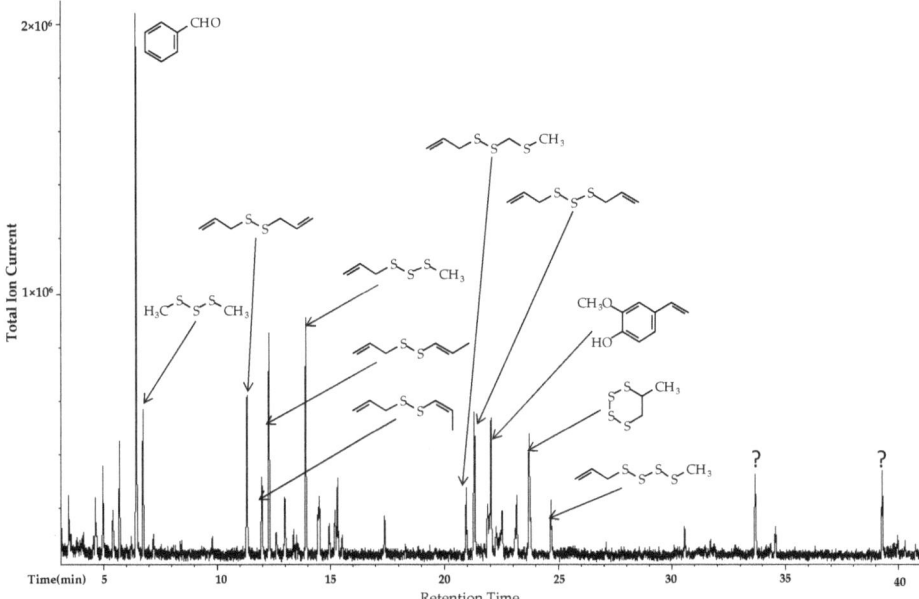

Figure 3. Chromatogram of *Allium vineale* essential oil sample #4 showing major components. ? = unidentified component.

4. Conclusions

The essential oils of garlic and wild garlic are shown to be dominated by sulfur-containing compounds, particularly allyl polysulfides. Garlic oils from various geographical locations have shown qualitative similarities, but quantitative differences in the concentrations of organosulfur compounds, and are likely to affect both the medicinal and the organoleptic properties of the garlic. Wild garlic is qualitatively similar in composition to garlic, but there are some key differences: diallyl disulfide and diallyl trisulfide concentrations are higher in garlic than in wild garlic, while allyl 1-propenyl disulfide and dimethyl trisulfide concentrations are higher in wild garlic than in garlic.

Acknowledgments: The authors are grateful Puri Castillo for providing samples of *Allium sativum* from Spain.

Author Contributions: P.S. and W.N.S. conceived and designed the experiments; P.S., J.D.C., and W.N.S. performed the experiments; P.S., N.S.D. and W.N.S. analyzed the data; P.S. and W.N.S. contributed reagents/materials/analysis tools; P.S., N.S.D., and W.N.S. wrote the paper.

Conflicts of Interest: The authors declare no conflict of interest.

References

1. Block, E. *Garlic and Other Alliums: The Lore and the Science*; Royal Society of Chemistry: Cambridge, UK, 2010.
2. National Center for Complementary and Integrative Health. Garlic. Available online: https://nccih.nih.gov/health/garlic/ataglance.htm (accessed on 5 June 2017).
3. Queensland Government. Allium Vineale. Available online: http://keyserver.lucidcentral.org/weeds/data/media/Html/allium_vineale.htm (accessed on 31 May 2017).
4. Grieve, M. *A Modern Herbal*; Dover Publications: New York, NY, USA, 1971; Volume I.
5. Sharifi-Rad, M.; Mnayer, D.; Tabanelli, G.; Stojanovic-Radic, Z.Z.; Sharifi-Rad, M.; Yousaf, Z.; Vallone, L.; Setzer, W.N.; Iriti, M. Plants of the genus *Allium* as antibacterial agents: From tradition to pharmacy. *Cell. Mol. Biol.* **2016**, *62*, 57–68. [PubMed]

6. Pyun, M.S.; Shin, S. Antifungal effects of the volatile oils from *Allium* plants against *Trichophyton* species and synergism of the oils with ketoconazole. *Phytomedicine* **2006**, *13*, 394–400. [CrossRef] [PubMed]
7. Lewis, W.H.; Elvin-Lewis, M.P.F. *Medical Botany—Plants Affecting Man's Health*; John Wiley & Sons Ltd.: New York, NY, USA, 1977.
8. Bruneton, J. *Pharmacognosy*, 2nd ed.; Intercept Ltd.: London, UK, 1999.
9. Kunkel, G. *Plants for Human Consumption: An Annotated Checklist of the Edible Phanerogams and Ferns*; Koeltz Scientific Books: Königstein, Germany, 1984.
10. Facciola, S. *Cornucopia: A Source Book of Edible Plants*; Kampong Publications: Vista, CA, USA, 1990.
11. Hamel, P.B.; Chiltoskey, M.U. *Cherokee Plants and Their Uses—A 400 Year History*; Herald Publishing Company: Sylva, NC, USA, 1975.
12. Moerman, D.E. *Native American Ethnobotany*; Timber Press, Inc.: Portland, OR, USA, 1998.
13. Block, E. The organosulfur chemistry of the genus *Allium*—Implications for the organic chemistry of sulfur. *Angew. Chem. Int. Ed.* **1992**, *104*, 1158–1203. [CrossRef]
14. Lanzotti, V. The analysis of onion and garlic. *J. Chromatogr. A* **2006**, *1112*, 3–22. [CrossRef] [PubMed]
15. Satyal, P.; Murray, B.L.; McFeeters, R.L.; Setzer, W.N. Essential oil characterization of *Thymus vulgaris* from various geographical locations. *Foods* **2016**, *5*, 70. [CrossRef] [PubMed]
16. Satyal, P.; Jones, T.H.; Lopez, E.M.; McFeeters, R.L.; Ali, N.A.A.; Mansi, I.; Al-Kaf, A.G.; Setzer, W.N. Chemotypic characterization and biological activity of *Rosmarinus officinalis*. *Foods* **2017**, *6*, 20. [CrossRef] [PubMed]
17. Deng, G.; Craft, J.D.; Steinberg, K.M.; Li, P.L.; Pokharel, S.K.; Setzer, W.N. Influence of different isolation methods on chemical composition and bioactivities of the fruit peel oil of *Citrus medica* L. var. *sarcodactylis* (Noot.) Swingle. *Medicines* **2017**, *4*, 1.
18. Adams, R.P. *Identification of Essential Oil Components by Gas Chromatography/Mass Spectrometry*, 4th ed.; Allured Publishing: Carol Stream, IL, USA, 2007.
19. Block, E.; Iyer, R.; Grisoni, S.; Saha, C.; Belman, S.; Lossing, F.P. Lipoxygenase inhibitors from the essential oil of garlic. Markovnikov addition of the allyldithio radical to olefins. *J. Am. Chem. Soc.* **1988**, *110*, 7813–7827. [CrossRef]
20. Yu, T.-H.; Wu, C.-M.; Rosen, R.T.; Hartman, T.G.; Ho, C.-T. Volatile compounds generated from thermal degradation of alliin and deoxyalliin in an aqueous solution. *J. Agric. Food Chem.* **1994**, *42*, 146–153. [CrossRef]
21. Kubec, R.; Velíšek, J.; Doležal, M.; Kubelka, V. Sulfur-containing volatiles arising by thermal degradation of alliin and deoxyalliin. *J. Agric. Food Chem.* **1997**, *45*, 3580–3585. [CrossRef]
22. Iranshahi, M. A review of volatile sulfur-containing compounds from terrestrial plants: Biosynthesis, distribution and analytical methods. *J. Essent. Oil Res.* **2012**, *24*, 393–434. [CrossRef]
23. Douiri, L.; Boughdad, A.; Assobhei, O.; Moumni, M. Chemical composition and biological activity of *Allium sativum* essential oils against *Callosobruchus maculatus*. *IOSR J. Environ. Sci. Toxicol. Food Technol.* **2013**, *3*, 30–36. [CrossRef]
24. Dziri, S.; Casabianca, H.; Hanchi, B.; Hosni, K. Composition of garlic essential oil (*Allium sativum* L.) as influenced by drying method. *J. Essent. Oil Res.* **2014**, *26*, 91–96. [CrossRef]
25. Kimbaris, A.C.; Siatis, N.G.; Daferera, D.J.; Tarantilis, P.A.; Pappas, C.S.; Polissiou, M.G. Comparison of distillation and ultrasound-assisted extraction methods for the isolation of sensitive aroma compounds from garlic (*Allium sativum*). *Ultrason. Sonochem.* **2006**, *13*, 54–60. [CrossRef] [PubMed]
26. Kocić-Tanackov, S.; Dimić, G.; Lević, J.; Tanackov, I.; Tepić, A.; Vujičić, B.; Gvozdanović-Varga, J. Effects of onion (*Allium cepa* L.) and garlic (*Allium sativum* L.) essential oils on the *Aspergillus versicolor* growth and sterigmatocystin production. *J. Food Sci.* **2012**, *77*, 278–284. [CrossRef] [PubMed]
27. Mnayer, D.; Fabiano-Tixier, A.S.; Petitcolas, E.; Hamieh, T.; Nehme, N.; Ferrant, C.; Fernandez, X.; Chemat, F. Chemical composition, antibacterial and antioxidant activities of six essentials oils from the Alliaceae family. *Molecules* **2014**, *19*, 20034–20053. [CrossRef] [PubMed]
28. Rao, P.G.P.; Rao, L.J.; Raghavan, B. Chemical composition of essential oils of garlic (*Allium sativum* L.). *J. Spices Aromat. Crops* **1999**, *8*, 41–47.
29. Romeilah, R.M.; Fayed, S.A.; Mahmoud, G.I. Chemical compositions, antiviral and antioxidant activities of seven essential oils. *J. Appl. Sci. Res.* **2010**, *6*, 50–62.

30. Zhao, N.N.; Zhang, H.; Zhang, X.C.; Luan, X.B.; Zhou, C.; Liu, Q.Z.; Shi, W.P.; Liu, Z.L. Evaluation of acute toxicity of essential oil of garlic (*Allium sativum*) and its selected major constituent compounds against overwintering *Cacopsylla chinensis* (Hemiptera: Psyllidae). *J. Econ. Entomol.* **2013**, *106*, 1349–1354. [CrossRef] [PubMed]
31. Chekki, R.Z.; Snoussi, A.; Hamrouni, I.; Bouzouita, N. Chemical composition, antibacterial and antioxidant activities of Tunisian garlic (*Allium sativum*) essential oil and ethanol extract. *Med. J. Chem.* **2014**, *3*, 947–956.
32. Radulović, N.S.; Miltojević, A.B.; Stojković, M.B.; Blagojević, P.D. New volatile sulfur-containing compounds from wild garlic (*Allium ursinum* L., Liliaceae). *Food Res. Int.* **2015**, *78*, 1–10. [CrossRef] [PubMed]
33. Motsei, M.L.; Lindsey, K.L.; Van Staden, J.; Jäger, A.K. Screening of traditionally used South African plants for antifungal activity against *Candida albicans*. *J. Ethnopharmacol.* **2003**, *86*, 235–241. [CrossRef]
34. Ledezma, E.; Apitz-Castro, R. Ajoene, el principal compuesto activo derivado del ajo (*Allium sativum*), un nuevo agente antifúngico. *Rev. Iberoam. Micol.* **2006**, *23*, 75–80. [CrossRef]
35. Ross, Z.M.; O'Gara, E.A.; Hill, D.J.; Sleightholme, H.V.; Maslin, D.J. Antimicrobial properties of garlic oil against human enteric bacteria: Evaluation of methodologies and comparisons with garlic oil sulfides and garlic powder. *Appl. Environ. Microbiol.* **2001**, *67*, 475–480. [CrossRef] [PubMed]
36. Benkeblia, N. Antimicrobial activity of essential oil extracts of various onions (*Allium cepa*) and garlic (*Allium sativum*). *LWT Food Sci. Technol.* **2004**, *37*, 263–268. [CrossRef]
37. El-Zemity, S.; Rezk, H.; Farok, S.; Zaitoon, A. Acaricidal activities of some essential oils and their monoterpenoidal constituents against house dust mite, *Dermatophagoides pteronyssinus* (Acari: Pyroglyphidae). *J. Zhejiang Univ. Sci. B* **2006**, *7*, 957–962.
38. Zenner, L.; Callait, M.P.; Granier, C.; Chauve, C. In vitro effect of essential oils from *Cinnamomum aromaticum*, *Citrus limon* and *Allium sativum* on two intestinal flagellates of poultry, *Tetratrichomonas gallinarum* and *Histomonas meleagridis*. *Parasite* **2003**, *10*, 153–157. [CrossRef] [PubMed]
39. Ayaz, E.; Turel, I.; Gul, A.; Yilmaz, O. Evaluation of the anthelmentic activity of garlic (*Allium sativum*) in mice naturally infected with *Aspiculuris tetraptera*. *Recent Pat. Antiinfect. Drug Discov.* **2008**, *3*, 149–152. [CrossRef] [PubMed]
40. Abbas, S.; Dawar, S.; Tariq, M.; Zaki, M.J. Nematicidal activity of spices against *Meloidogyne javanica* (Treub) Chitwood. *Pak. J. Bot.* **2009**, *41*, 2625–2632.
41. Park, I.L.K.; Shin, S.C. Fumigant activity of plant essential oils and components from garlic (*Allium sativum*) and clove bud (*Eugenia caryophyllata*) oils against the Japanese termite (*Reticulitermes speratus* Kolbe). *J. Agric. Food Chem.* **2005**, *53*, 4388–4392. [CrossRef] [PubMed]
42. Chaubey, M.K. Insecticidal effect of *Allium sativum* (Alliaceae) essential oil. *J. Biol. Act. Prod. Nat.* **2013**, *3*, 248–258.
43. Jain, R.C.; Vyas, C.R.; Mahatma, O.P. Hypoglycemic action of onion and garlic. *Lancet* **1973**, *2*, 1491. [CrossRef]
44. Bordia, A.; Bansal, H.C.; Arora, S.K.; Singh, S.V. Effect of the essential oils of garlic and onion on alimentary hyperlipemia. *Atherosclerosis* **1975**, *21*, 15–20. [CrossRef]
45. Amagase, H.; Petesch, B.L.; Matsuura, H.; Kasuga, S.; Itakura, Y. Recent advances on the nutritional effects associated with the use of garlic as a supplement. *J. Nutr.* **2001**, *131*, 955S–962S. [PubMed]
46. Tsai, T.H.; Tsai, P.J.; Ho, S.C. Antioxidant and anti-inflammatory activities of several commonly used spices. *J. Food Sci.* **2005**, *70*, C93–C97. [CrossRef]
47. Tsao, S.M.; Yin, M.C. In-vitro antimicrobial activity of four diallyl sulphides occurring naturally in garlic and Chinese leek oils. *J. Med. Microbiol.* **2001**, *50*, 646–649. [CrossRef] [PubMed]
48. Kim, J.W.; Huh, J.E.; Kyung, S.H.; Kyung, K.H. Antimicrobial activity of alk(en)yl sulfides found in essential oils of *Allium sativum* and onion. *Food Sci. Biotechnol.* **2004**, *13*, 235–239.

© 2017 by the authors. Licensee MDPI, Basel, Switzerland. This article is an open access article distributed under the terms and conditions of the Creative Commons Attribution (CC BY) license (http://creativecommons.org/licenses/by/4.0/).

Communication

Application of Surfactant Micelle-Entrapped Eugenol for Prevention of Growth of the Shiga Toxin-Producing *Escherichia coli* in Ground Beef

Tamra N. Tolen [1], Songsirin Ruengvisesh [2] and Thomas M. Taylor [1,*]

[1] Department of Animal Science, Texas A & M University, College Station, TX 77843-2471, USA; ttolen84@tamu.edu
[2] Department of Nutrition and Food Science, Texas A & M University, College Station, TX 77843-2253, USA; songsirin@gmail.com
* Correspondence: matt_taylor@tamu.edu; Tel.: +1-979-862-7678

Received: 20 July 2017; Accepted: 14 August 2017; Published: 16 August 2017

Abstract: Beef safety may be compromised by O157 and non-O157 Shiga toxin-producing *Escherichia coli* (STEC) contamination. The capacity of surfactant micelles loaded with the plant-derived antimicrobial eugenol to reduce STEC on beef trimmings that were later ground and refrigerated for five days at 5 ± 1 °C was tested to determine their utility for beef safety protection. STEC-inoculated trimmings were treated with free eugenol, micelle-encapsulated eugenol, 2% lactic acid (55 °C), sterile distilled water (25 °C), or left untreated (control). Following treatment, trimmings were coarse-ground and stored aerobically at 5 ± 1 °C. Ground beef was then sampled for STEC immediately post-grinding, and again at three and five days of storage. STEC minimum inhibitory concentrations (MICs) in liquid medium for free eugenol and 1% sodium dodecyl sulfate (SDS)-loaded micelles were 0.5% and 0.125%, respectively. STEC numbers on beef trimmings treated by sterile water (6.5 $\log_{10}$ CFU/g), free eugenol (6.5 $\log_{10}$ CFU/g), micelle-loaded eugenol (6.4 $\log_{10}$ CFU/g), and lactic acid (6.4 $\log_{10}$ CFU/g) did not differ compared to untreated controls (6.6 $\log_{10}$ CFU/g) ($p = 0.982$). Conversely, STEC were significantly reduced by refrigerated storage (0.2 and 0.3 $\log_{10}$ CFU/g at three and five days of storage, respectively) ($p = 0.014$). Antimicrobial treatments did not significantly decontaminate ground beef, indicating their low utility for beef safety protection.

Keywords: plant-derived antimicrobial; micelles; non-O157 STEC; *E. coli* O157:H7; ground beef; beef safety; eugenol

1. Introduction

The O157 and non-O157 Shiga toxin-producing *Escherichia coli* (STEC) are known causes of human foodborne disease, inducing both acute and chronic sequelae ranging from mild diarrheal disease to hemolytic uremic syndrome (HUS), renal failure and potentially death [1]. The U.S. Centers for Disease Control and Prevention (CDC) has estimated 265,000 cases of STEC-associated human foodborne disease occur annually in the U.S.; 36% percent of these are reportedly associated with O157 STEC and the balance the result of the non-O157 STEC [2,3]. In addition to *E. coli* O157:H7, six serotypes of the non-O157 STEC have been declared adulterants in fresh non-intact beef products by the U.S. Department of Agriculture-Food Safety and Inspection Service (USDA-FSIS) [4]. Estimates of the annual financial costs of these pathogens in the U.S. with respect to income loss, medical expenses, and other quantifiable costs have ranged from $280 million to $790 million per annum [5,6].

Cattle have been identified as a reservoir for the STEC, potentially facilitating cross-contamination of beef products during handling of meat [7–9]. Fresh beef can be cross-contaminated during the fabrication of beef trimmings destined for use in the production of ground beef [10]. Antimicrobial interventions applied for the decontamination of beef trimmings and/or ground beef have exhibited varying levels of efficacy for STEC reduction. Geornaras et al. [11] reported that the application of antimicrobial interventions on trimmings produced from beef chuck rolls, including 0.1% acidified sodium chlorite and 0.02% peracetic acid, produced reductions in STEC varying from 0.4 to 1.8 $\log_{10}$ CFU/cm^2. Others have reported greater reductions in STEC on trimmings and ground beef following application of lactic acid as a beef safety intervention. Harris et al. [12] reported that STEC were reduced by 1.9 to 2.0 $\log_{10}$ CFU/g or 2.1 to 2.5 $\log_{10}$ CFU/g following application of 2% or 4% lactic acid, respectively. This group recently reported that application of acetic acid (2% or 4%) and acidified sodium chlorite (1000 ppm) produced reductions in STEC on beef trimmings ranging from 0.3 to 0.5 $\log_{10}$ CFU/g ($p < 0.05$) [13]. Nonetheless, researchers described STEC reductions as being of little practical utility for food safety protection.

In addition to exploring the use of traditional antimicrobials for reducing STEC on fresh beef products, researchers have investigated plant-derived antimicrobials (PDAs), including essential oils and their components, for beef safety protection. Application of commercial herb extract-containing products to STEC-inoculated beef trimmings, two rounds of grinding, and up to seven days' refrigerated (4 °C) storage, produced reductions of 0.1 to 0.2 $\log_{10}$ CFU/g in STEC numbers [14]. More recently, researchers reported that the application of 0.05% or 0.1% rutin, or 0.1% or 0.2% resveratrol, did not reduce *E. coli* O157:H7 in ground beef patties during refrigerated storage, but did enhance reductions of the pathogen upon subsequent cooking to an internal temperature of 65 °C [15]. The use of encapsulation strategies, such as surfactant micelles, has been described as providing opportunity for enhanced transport and delivery of entrapped compounds to foodborne microbes in both animal- and plant-based foods [16–18]. The use of micelle-encapsulated eugenol for reducing O157 or non-O157 STEC on fresh beef has not, to the authors' knowledge, been reported in the scientific literature.

Application of such antimicrobial interventions may be useful for beef safety protection in the manufacture of natural beef products. Hence, the objectives of this study were to: (i) quantify the capability of free and micelle-encapsulated eugenol to produce statistically significant reductions in numbers of inoculated STEC on beef trimmings prior to beef grinding when applied at concentrations not likely to produce long-term negative impacts on consumer acceptability; and, (ii) determine the capacity of antimicrobial treatments applied to beef trimmings to inhibit STEC growth and/or reduce STEC numbers on ground beef during refrigerated storage post-treatment.

2. Materials and Methods

2.1. Microorganisms and Revival Procedures

STEC isolates belonging to serotypes O157:H7, O26:H11, and O121:H19, resistant to 100 µg/mL rifampicin (Rif^R), were provided by J.B. Luchansky (USDA Agricultural Research Service, Wyndmoor, PA, USA) and preserved at −80 °C upon receipt in the culture collection of the Food Microbiology Laboratory (Department of Animal Science, Texas A & M University, College Station, TX, USA). Isolates were revived by duplicate identical passages in sterile tryptic soy broth (TSB; Becton, Dickinson and Co., Franklin Lakes, NJ, USA), followed by incubation at 35 ± 1 °C for 24 h. Following revival, isolates were individually streaked onto Petri dishes containing MacConkey Agar (Becton, Dickinson and Company, Sparks, MD, USA) supplemented with 100 µg/mL rifampicin (Sigma-Aldrich Co., St. Louis, MO, USA), and incubated for 24 h at 35 ± 1 °C to verify Rif^R capacity, as well as organisms' ability to utilize lactose and decompose bile salts. Well-isolated colonies were picked with sterile needles and slant cultures of each isolate were prepared on tryptic soy agar (Becton, Dickinson and Company) for later use during experimental trials. Slants were layered with sterile mineral oil and stored at 5 ± 1 °C until being prepared for use via the revival procedure described above.

2.2. Preparation of Surfactant for Maximum Non-Inhibitory Concentration (MNIC) Determination

Sodium dodecyl sulfate (SDS; CAS #151-21-3) was purchased from Sigma-Aldrich Co.; a 30% (*w/v*) stock was prepared by mixing 12.0 g SDS in 40.0 mL sterile distilled water in a sterile container. SDS has been previously reported to exert antimicrobial activity against members of the STEC at concentrations as low as 0.5% SDS [19]. Thus, to determine whether SDS exerted antimicrobial effects against STEC at experimental concentrations on its own, each STEC isolate was individually inoculated into a 96-well microplate and treated with 2-fold serially diluted SDS. STEC isolates were individually serially diluted prior to loading into sample microplate wells to obtain a target 5.0 $\log_{10}$ CFU/mL inoculum in double-strength TSB (2× TSB; 60 g TSB powder/liter water); 100.0 µL of each isolate was added into surfactant solution-containing wells. Surfactant was added first (200.0 µL), and then 100.0 µL was extracted and loaded into the adjacent well containing 100.0 µL sterile distilled water, according to the method of Pendleton et al. [20]. This process was completed as needed to produce sufficient wells containing 2-fold serially diluted SDS before wells were loaded with a STEC isolate. Loaded, inoculated plates were sealed with plate sealers (Thermo-Fisher Scientific, Waltham, MA, USA) and optical density at 630 nm (OD630) read on a UV/Visible Spectrophotometer (BioTek® Instruments, Inc., Winooski, VT, USA). In addition to the experimental wells described, microplate wells containing identically prepared and loaded solutions of SDS, 2× TSB, and sterile water, but no STEC, were prepared and read at OD630. This was completed in order to provide for baseline adjustment in experimental data to allow for identification of minimum inhibitory concentrations (MICs) of SDS and eugenol, using the method of Brandt et al. [21]. STEC-inoculated wells bearing >0.05 change in OD630 following incubation were labeled as non-inhibitory with respect to SDS concentration applied. Wells with the highest content of SDS not inhibitory to STEC, the maximum non-inhibitory concentration (MNIC), were chosen to prepare micelles for subsequent MIC experiments for STEC.

2.3. Preparation of Eugenol-Loaded Micelles and Unencapsulated Eugenol for MIC Determination

Working solutions from a 70% eugenol stock prepared in 95% ethyl alcohol (EtOH) were diluted in 95% EtOH to desired eugenol concentrations; eugenol and EtOH were purchased from Sigma-Aldrich Co. The working stock was stored at 5 ± 1 °C in a foil-wrapped container until ready for use. Following calculation of required eugenol and surfactant for micelle generation [16], eugenol in alcohol and surfactant in sterile water were mixed and brought to volume with sterile distilled water as required. Mixtures were stirred at room temperature to form micelles. Based on results from experiments detailed above (Section 2.2), 20 mL micelle volumes were prepared to contain varying concentrations of eugenol. Double-strength micelle solutions (max. concentrations: 2.0% SDS ± 2.0% eugenol) were prepared and filtered through a 0.45 µm cellulose acetate filter. Non-encapsulated eugenol was prepared in EtOH and sterile distilled water to identical concentrations as those prepared for eugenol-loaded SDS micelles.

Determination of STEC isolate-specific MICs for free and micelle-loaded eugenol was completed according to published methods [16]. Microplate wells containing individual STEC isolates were exposed to free or encapsulated eugenol at 2-fold serial dilutions and then incubated for 24 h at 35 ± 1 °C. OD630 readings were taken at 0 and 24 h, and baseline corrections made as previously detailed using identically prepared microplate wells loaded with eugenol, 2× TSB, and sterile distilled water, but not inoculated with STEC. Wells bearing <0.05 change in OD630 (<0.05 ΔOD630) after baseline correction were identified as inhibitory for the inoculated STEC isolate. The lowest concentration of free or encapsulated eugenol-producing inhibition was identified as the MIC for each STEC isolate. To verify the maximal load of EtOH contacting STEC in wells was not inhibitory to STEC on its own, a separate set of wells containing only EtOH at maximal calculated concentration was tested alongside other experimental wells. Finally, positive and negative controls were incorporated, bearing STEC plus growth medium only (positive control) or growth medium and sterile water but no STEC inoculum (negative control).

2.4. Application of Eugenol-Loaded Micelles to STEC-Inoculated Beef Trimmings and STEC Reductions on Ground Beef Prepared from Treated Trimmings

Frozen beef trimmings (90% lean) were obtained from the Rosenthal Meat Science and Technology Center at Texas A & M University (College Station, TX, USA) and transported to the Food Microbiology Laboratory. Trimmings were thawed at 4 °C for 24 h prior to inoculation and use. On the day of experiment initiation, 1000 g of thawed beef trimmings were inoculated with a three-strain mixture of STEC and sealed in a sterile plastic bag. The STEC mixture was produced by blending equivalent volumes of overnight cultures of revived STEC isolates (Section 2.1) according to previously published methods [22]. Inoculated trimmings were hand-massaged for 1 min in order to distribute inoculum over trimming surfaces, after which beef was left undisturbed in a biological safety cabinet at ambient conditions for 30 min to allow inoculum attachment. Following STEC attachment, a 10 g aliquot was aseptically collected to determine inoculation efficiency by preparation of decimal dilutions in 0.1% peptone diluent and plating onto tryptic soy agar supplemented with 100 µg/mL rifampicin (TSAR)-containing Petri dishes, followed by 24 h incubation at 35 ± 1 °C. Remaining meat was separated into 200 g batches and treated by application of three sprays from a handheld spray bottle (2.4 mL total applied volume) held approximately 30.5–35.6 cm from the trimmings with solutions of sterile distilled water at 25 °C (Water), twice the MIC of free eugenol (2× FreeEug) or three times the MIC of eugenol-loaded SDS micelles (Micelles). These concentrations of free and micelle-loaded eugenol were selected during preliminary trials in which antimicrobial treatments were applied to non-inoculated beef trimmings that were then coarse-ground and stored for 5 days at 5 °C, after which samples were removed and evaluated for residual eugenol (clove essence) odors. These treatments (2× FreeEug, Micelles (3× micelle MIC)) were highest not producing strongly displeasing off-odor of beef samples (data not shown). In addition, beef trimmings were treated by 2% lactic acid pre-warmed to 55 °C (2% LA), a 25 °C sterile distilled water spray (Water), or were left untreated (Control). Spray application, versus immersion application, was selected due to the low likelihood of a small sprayed volume resulting in water uptake in treated beef as compared to immersion application of antimicrobial systems. The USDA forbids addition of water to ground beef beyond a negligible amount (~0.5%) [23].

Following antimicrobial treatment, trimmings were coarse-ground through a 3/8 inch plate using a LEM Products electric meat grinder (Model #781; West Chester, OH, USA). In between the grinding of each batch of treated trimmings, all grinder components were disassembled and residual beef tissue removed by brush-scrubbing while soaking in chlorinated (0.6% FAC) tap water. After all beef was removed, the grinder components and scrubbing brush were soaked for an additional 10 min in chlorinated water (0.6% FAC). Components were then removed and sprayed with 70% EtOH to further sanitize prior to rinsing with water and re-assembly of the grinder. Beef was aseptically separated into 10.0 g samples, randomly assigned to an antimicrobial treatment and storage period, and subjected to assigned antimicrobial intervention treatment. STEC survival was determined immediately after antimicrobial treatment, immediately after grinding, and again at 3 and 5 days of aerobic refrigerated (5 ± 1 °C) storage in order to determine whether STEC reductions would be detected quickly or require additional holding to allow for eugenol release. Samples were placed into stomacher pouches, diluted with 90 mL sterile 0.1% peptone diluent, and stomached for 1 min at 230 rpm. Decimal dilutions were subsequently prepared in 0.1% peptone diluent and surviving STEC enumerated on TSAR following 24 h at 35 ± 1 °C.

2.5. Statistical Analysis

MIC experiments were repeated three times in identical fashion ($n = 3$); the lowest inhibitory concentration of free or micelle-loaded eugenol for each STEC isolate across all replicates was identified as the experimental MIC [21]. For beef decontamination experiments, three identical replicates were executed ($n = 3$); $\log_{10}$-transformed plate counts were determined from sample plate counts prior to statistical analysis. Reductions in STEC on beef were determined by analysis of variance (ANOVA) and statistically differing means separated by Tukey's Honestly Significant Differences (HSD) test at $\alpha = 0.05$.

3. Results and Discussion

3.1. Minimum Inhibitory Concentration of Eugenol-Loaded SDS Micelles against STEC

The maximum non-inhibitory level of SDS for all STEC isolates tested was 1.0% (Table 1). Additionally, eugenol-loaded micelles were inhibitory to all STEC isolates at 0.125% (*w/v*) eugenol in 1% SDS (Table 1). Micelle-loaded eugenol MICs for STEC are similar to the MICs of 0.15% for eugenol-loaded micelles against *E. coli* O157:H7 strains previously reported by Gaysinsky et al. [24]. The MIC for unencapsulated eugenol against *E. coli* O157:H7, O26:H11, and O121:H19 was 0.5% (*w/v*) (Table 1). Similar MICs for other plant-derived antimicrobials against *E. coli* O157:H7 and other *Enterobacteriaceae* have been reported elsewhere [25,26]. Previous research has also demonstrated enhanced antimicrobial efficacy of plant essential oil components following micelle entrapment in complex food matrices, reportedly resulting from enhanced dispersion of the hydrophobic oils into the aqueous fraction of the food and transport of essential oil components into the membrane of STEC isolates and other bacterial organisms [16,18,25,27,28]. Refrigerated storage is not expected to have significantly inhibited eugenol release by SDS micelles, given previous reports in which a 4.1 $\log_{10}$-cycle reduction of *Salmonella Enteritidis* was reported during a 5 min exposure to 1% SDS/levulinic acid micelles at 8 °C [19].

Table 1. Shiga toxin-producing *Escherichia coli* (STEC) isolates, sources, and minimum inhibitory concentrations (MICs) of free and micelle-loaded eugenol.

STEC Serotype	Isolate [1]	Source	Free Eugenol MIC (% *w/v*)	Micelle-Eugenol MIC (% *w/v*) [2]
O157:H7	USDA-FSIS-380-94	Salami	0.5	0.125
O26:H11	H30	Clinical	0.5	0.125
O121:H19	CDC 97-3068	Human Stool	0.5	0.125

[1] Isolates were provided by J.B. Luchansky (U.S. Department of Agriculture-Agricultural Research Service, Wyndmoor, PA, USA). [2] Micelles were comprised of sodium dodecyl sulfate (SDS; 1.0% *w/v*) by mixture of eugenol into aqueous dispersion of SDS, followed by stirring at ambient temperature. 1.0% SDS was the maximum non-inhibitory concentration (MNIC) of the surfactant against STEC isolates. USDA-FSIS: U.S. Department of Agriculture-Food Safety and Inspection Service; CDC: Centers for Disease Control and Prevention.

3.2. Reduction of STEC on Beef Trimmings by Free and Micelle-Encapsulated Eugenol

The mean number of STEC inoculated onto beef trimmings was 6.6 ± 0.4 $\log_{10}$ CFU/g. No treatment produced statistically significant STEC reductions on trimmings versus untreated controls ($p = 0.902$); the greatest numerical reduction in STEC (0.3 $\log_{10}$ CFU/g) as compared to the control was observed for 55 °C lactic acid-treated beef trimmings (Table 2). Similar reductions in *E. coli* O157:H7 numbers (0.1 to 0.2 $\log_{10}$ CFU/g) have been reported following the treatment of beef trimmings (80% lean) with sprays of either 2% or 4% acetic/lactic acid blends heated to 55 °C [29]. Researchers suggested that inclusion of adipose tissue in trimmings may have compromised antimicrobial activity of applied interventions for pathogen reduction, in addition to impacts of grinding and post-treatment storage. Cutter [14] likewise reported low reductions in *E. coli* O157:H7 following plant extract application in micro-encapsulation systems and subsequent holding.

Table 2. Survival of Shiga toxin-producing *Escherichia coli* (STEC) on fresh beef trimmings following application of antimicrobial treatments.

Treatment [1]	STEC Survivors ($\log_{10}$ CFU/g) [2]	$p > F$	Pooled Standard Error
Sterile Water (25 °C)	6.5 ± 0.40		
2× FreeEug	6.5 ± 0.36	0.902	0.294
Micelles	6.4 ± 0.36		
2% LA	6.4 ± 0.25		

[1] Treatments were: Control (inoculated, non-treated); Sterile Water (25 °C spray), 2× FreeEug (twice the minimum inhibitory concentration of eugenol applied by spray), Micelles (three times the minimum inhibitory concentration of micellarized eugenol in vitro, applied by spraying), and 2% LA (lactic acid solution, heated to 55 °C prior to spraying). [2] Values given depict mean STEC survivors from triplicate identical replications ($n = 3$) following inoculation, a 30 min attachment period, and spray-application of antimicrobial treatments ± one sample standard deviation from the mean. STEC mean inoculation on beef pre-treatment: 6.6 ± 0.40 $\log_{10}$ CFU/g.

In contrast to these studies, other studies have reported higher STEC reductions on trimmings when immersed in solutions of traditional antimicrobials. Ellebracht et al. [30] submerged beef trimmings in 95 °C water or 2% lactic acid tempered to 55 °C. Reductions in *E. coli* O157:H7 following hot water and heated acid in this study were 0.5 and 1.1 $\log_{10}$ CFU/g, respectively. In a study applying 5% lactic acid via immersion to lean trimmings inoculated with O157 and non-O157 STEC, researchers reported STEC reductions varied from 0.5 to 1.4 $\log_{10}$ CFU/cm^2, depending on whether the acid solution was applied at 25 °C or 55 °C [31]. This group also reported reductions in *E. coli* O157:H7 numbers of 0.5 or 0.7 $\log_{10}$ CFU/cm^2 on inoculated trimmings immersed in 0.1% acidified sodium chlorite or 0.02% peroxyacetic acid, respectively [11]. Finally, research testing 4.4% lactic acid application onto STEC-inoculated beef trimmings compared pathogen reductions when acid was applied by dipping or spraying. STEC reductions obtained by dipping approximated 1.5 $\log_{10}$ CFU/g following 20 h post-treatment refrigerated storage, whereas spray-treatment produced only a 0.5 $\log_{10}$ CFU/g reduction following post-treatment refrigerated storage [32]. Researchers suggested that dipping in lactic acid solution allowed for enhanced contact of acidulant with STEC on trimmings versus spraying as an explanation for observed differences in STEC reductions [32]. Nevertheless, use of immersion treatment of meat trimmings is of limited utility in the U.S., due in part to sensory impacts and limits on the utility of treatments expected to result in excess water pick-up by meat, thereby resulting in treated products not adhering to the federal standard of identity for such products [23].

3.3. Inhibition of STEC on Ground Beef Following Antimicrobial Treatment during Refrigerated Storage

Analysis of STEC reductions on ground beef at 0, 3, and 5 days of refrigerated storage (5 ± 1 °C) following treatment by water, free or micelle-entrapped eugenol, or 55 °C lactic acid spraying indicated no effect of antimicrobial treatment ($p = 0.371$), and no effect of interaction of antimicrobial treatment with storage duration ($p = 0.812$) (Figure A1 in Appendix A). However, ground beef refrigerated storage period did impact STEC survival on treated ground beef, where STEC counts differed between days 0 and 5 ($p = 0.014$) (Figure 1). Lack of detectable differences in STEC numbers as a function of treatment may have resulted from the homogenization of STEC throughout beef tissue during grinding, or insufficient antimicrobial application despite applying two and three times the respective MICs for free and encapsulated eugenol (Figure 1). Grinding, through the mechanical disruption of beef tissue, exposes previously non-accessible tissue and surfaces to microbes. Likewise, meat grinding would be expected to reduce the efficacy of applied interventions by exposing amino acids capable of buffering against pH change, or fat/lean tissue allowing for STEC to be removed from close proximity of free or micelle-encapsulated eugenol.

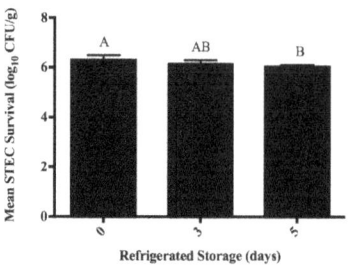

Figure 1. Survival of Shiga toxin-producing *Escherichia coli* (STEC) on ground beef during aerobic refrigerated storage ($p = 0.014$; pooled SE = 0.083). Bars depict means of the main effect of storage period calculated from triplicate identical replicates ($n = 3$); error bars depict one standard deviation from the mean. Columns not sharing letters (A,B) differ at $p < 0.05$. Beef trimmings were ground through a 3/8 inch plate following antimicrobial intervention, separated into 10.0 g samples, and stored for up to five days at 5 ± 1 °C prior to STEC enumeration on Petri dishes containing tryptic soy agar supplemented with 100.0 µg/mL of rifampicin.

Others have also reported numbers of STEC on ground beef to be reduced only to a low extent following application of plant compounds with antimicrobial activity. The application of allyl isothiocyanate (AIT) via impregnated disc to ground beef reduced *E. coli* O157:H7 0.6 to 0.7 $\log_{10}$ CFU/g following five days' storage at 4 °C under vacuum packaging [33]. Reductions in *E. coli* O157:H7 numbers on minced beef following application of plant-derived antimicrobial essential oil components and holding for 3 h at 5 °C approximated 0.1 to 0.5 $\log_{10}$-cycles [34]. Nonetheless, while some researchers have reported that application of plant-derived antimicrobials to ground beef produced no significant pathogen reduction, the application of these interventions enhanced lethality achieved during subsequent processing for inactivation of STEC or *Salmonella* [15,35].

4. Conclusions

The application of eugenol (free, micelle-encapsulated) to members of the O157 and non-O157 STEC in vitro was able to produce growth inhibition at MICs similar to those reported elsewhere. Nonetheless, the application of free or micelle-loaded eugenol to STEC-inoculated beef trimmings, as well as the application of 2% lactic acid (55 ± 1 °C) did not reduce STEC on trimming surfaces (Figure A1). Following grinding and five days of refrigerated storage, statistically significant, albeit biologically non-significant (≥ 1.0 $\log_{10}$-cycle) reductions in STEC were observed as a function of storage period ($p < 0.05$) (Figure 1). Eugenol was hypothesized capable of enhanced antimicrobial activity in the current study by its delivery to beef surfaces in an encapsulated form versus the unencapsulated plant-derived antimicrobial, reported elsewhere to occur in other high-protein animal-derived foods [17]. While this study is the first to the authors' knowledge reporting the application of eugenol-loaded micelles for non-O157 STEC reduction on beef trimmings, analysis of experimental data leads authors to reject the original hypothesis that eugenol micelles would reduce STEC on beef trimmings versus controls when applied via spraying versus other methods. Beef safety researchers should continue investigating and optimizing post-harvest technologies for effective beef safety protection.

Acknowledgments: This material is based upon work that is supported by the National Institute of Food and Agriculture, U.S. Department of Agriculture, under award numbers 2012-68003-30155 and 2010-51110-21079. Author S.R. received graduate assistantship support from Texas A & M University, Department of Nutrition and Food Science, College Station, TX, USA. Authors thanks Lisa M. Lucia, Texas A & M Center for Food Safety, for technical proof-reading of the manuscript during its preparation for submission. Funding to defray the costs of open access publication were not received by investigators from research sponsor.

Author Contributions: T.N.T. and T.M.T. conceived and designed the experiments; S.R. prepared eugenol-loaded micelles; T.N.T. and S.R. completed the inoculation of experimental samples with microbes, and microbiological analysis of STEC survival during experimental trials following antimicrobial treatment; T.N.T., S.R., and T.M.T. analyzed the data; T.N.T., S.R. and T.M.T. wrote the paper.

Conflicts of Interest: The authors declare no conflict of interest. The funding sponsors had no role in the design of the study; in the collection, analyses, or interpretation of data; in the writing of the manuscript, and in the decision to publish the results.

Appendix A

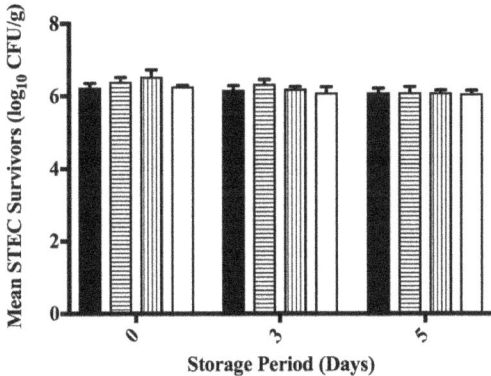

Figure A1. Least squares LS means of Shiga toxin-producing *Escherichia coli* (STEC) as a function of the interaction of antimicrobial treatment x storage period ($p = 0.812$; pooled SE = 0.164). Error bars depict one standard error for treatment mean; means were determined by two-way analysis of variance (ANOVA) and Tukey's Honestly Significant Differences (HSD) means separation test. Beef trimmings were ground through a 3/8-inch plate following antimicrobial intervention, separated into 10.0 g samples, and stored for up to 5 days at 5 ± 1 °C prior to STEC enumeration on Petri dishes containing tryptic soy agar supplemented with 100.0 µg/mL of rifampicin. Antimicrobial treatments were: 25 °C sterile water spray (filled bars), free eugenol applied at twice the MIC in vitro against STEC (horizontally hashed bars), SDS micelle-loaded eugenol applied at three times in vitro MIC (vertically hashed bars), and 2% lactic acid pre-warmed to 55 °C (open bars).

References

1. Brooks, J.T.; Sowers, E.G.; Wells, J.G.; Greene, K.D.; Griffin, P.M.; Hoekstra, R.M.; Strockbine, N.A. Non-O157 Shiga toxin-producing *Escherichia coli* infections in the United States, 1983–2002. *J. Infect. Dis.* **2005**, *192*, 1422–1429. [CrossRef] [PubMed]
2. General Information: *E. coli*. Available online: http://www.cdc.gov/ecoli/general/ (accessed on 17 July 2017).
3. Multistate Outbreak of Shiga Toxin-Producing *Escherichia coli* O157:H7 Infections Linked to Ground Beef (Final Update). Available online: http://www.cdc.gov/ecoli/2014/O157H7-05-14/index.htmL (accessed on 17 July 2017).
4. USDA-FSIS. Shiga toxin-producing *Escherichia coli* in certain raw beef products. *Fed. Regist.* **2011**, *76*, 58157–58165.
5. Hoffmann, S.; Batz, M.B.; Morris, J.G. Annual cost of illness and quality-adjusted life year losses in the United States due to 14 foodborne pathogens. *J. Food Prot.* **2012**, *75*, 1292–1302. [CrossRef] [PubMed]
6. Scharff, R.L. Economic burden from health losses due to foodborne illness in the United States. *J. Food Prot.* **2012**, *75*, 123–131. [CrossRef] [PubMed]
7. Smith, J.L.; Fratamico, P.M.; Gunther, N.W. Shiga toxin-producing *Escherichia coli*. *Adv. Appl. Microbiol.* **2014**, *86*, 145–197. [PubMed]

8. Arthur, T.M.; Bosilevac, J.M.; Nou, X.; Shackelford, S.D.; Wheeler, T.L.; Kent, M.P.; Jaroni, D.; Pauling, B.; Allen, D.M.; Koohmaraie, M. *Escherichia coli* O157 prevalence and enumeration of aerobic bacteria, *Enterobacteriaceae*, and *Escherichia coli* O157 at various steps in commercial beef processing plants. *J. Food Prot.* **2004**, *67*, 658–665. [CrossRef] [PubMed]
9. Arthur, T.M.; Barkocy-Gallagher, G.A.; Rivera-Betancourt, M.; Koohmaraie, M. Prevalence and characterization of non-O157 Shiga toxin-producing *Escherichia coli* on carcasses in commercial beef cattle processing plants. *Appl. Environ. Microbiol.* **2002**, *68*, 4847–4852. [CrossRef] [PubMed]
10. Bosilevac, J.M.; Koohmaraie, M. Prevalence and characterization of non-O157 Shiga toxin-producing *Escherichia coli* isolates from commercial ground beef in the United States. *Appl. Environ. Microbiol.* **2011**, *77*, 2103–2112. [CrossRef] [PubMed]
11. Geornaras, I.; Yang, H.; Moschonas, G.; Nunnelly, M.C.; Belk, K.E.; Nightingale, K.K.; Woerner, D.R.; Smith, G.C.; Sofos, J.N. Efficacy of chemical interventions against *Escherichia coli* O157:H7 and multidrug-resistant and antibiotic-susceptible *Salmonella* on inoculated beef trimmings. *J. Food Prot.* **2012**, *75*, 1960–1967. [CrossRef] [PubMed]
12. Harris, K.; Miller, M.F.; Loneragan, G.H.; Brashears, M.M. Validation of the use of organic acids and acidified sodium chlorite to reduce *Escherichia coli* O157 and *Salmonella* Typhimurium in beef trim and ground beef in a simulated processing environment. *J. Food Prot.* **2006**, *69*, 1802–1807. [CrossRef] [PubMed]
13. Harris, D.; Brashears, M.M.; Garmyn, A.J.; Brooks, J.C.; Miller, M.F. Microbiological and organoleptic characteristics of beef trim and ground beef treated with acetic acid, lactic acid, acidified sodium chlorite, or sterile water in a simulated commercial processing environment to reduce *Escherichia coli* O157:H7 and *Salmonella*. *Meat Sci.* **2012**, *90*, 783–788. [PubMed]
14. Cutter, C.N. Antimicrobial effect of herb extracts against *Escherichia coli* O157:H7, *Listeria monocytogenes*, and *Salmonella* Typhimurium associated with beef. *J. Food Prot.* **2000**, *63*, 601–607. [CrossRef] [PubMed]
15. Surendran Nair, M.; Lau, P.; Belskie, K.; Fancher, S.; Chen, C.-H.; Karumathil, D.P.; Yin, H.-B.; Liu, Y.; Ma, F.; Upadhyaya, I.; et al. Potentiating the heat inactivation of *Escherichia coli* O157:H7 in ground beef patties by natural antimicrobials. *Fron. Microbiol.* **2016**, *7*, 1–8. [CrossRef] [PubMed]
16. Ruengvisesh, S.; Loquercio, A.; Castell-Perez, E.; Taylor, T.M. Inhibition of bacterial pathogens in medium and on spinach leaf surfaces using plant-derived antimicrobials loaded in surfactant micelles. *J. Food Sci.* **2015**, *80*, M2522–M2529. [CrossRef] [PubMed]
17. Gaysinsky, S.; Taylor, T.M.; Davidson, P.M.; Bruce, B.D.; Weiss, J. Antimicrobial efficacy of eugenol microemulsions in milk against *Listeria monocytogenes* and *Escherichia coli* O157:H7. *J. Food Prot.* **2007**, *70*, 2631–2637. [CrossRef] [PubMed]
18. Weiss, J.; McClements, D.J. Mass transport phenomena in oil-in-water emulsions containing surfactant micelles: Solubilization. *Langmuir* **2000**, *16*, 5879–5883. [CrossRef]
19. Zhao, T.; Zhao, P.; Doyle, M.P. Inactivation of *Salmonella* and *Escherichia coli* O157:H7 on lettuce and poultry skin by combinations of levulinic acid and sodium dodecyl sulfate. *J. Food Prot.* **2009**, *72*, 928–936. [CrossRef] [PubMed]
20. Pendleton, S.J.; Story, R.; O'Bryan, C.A.; Crandall, P.G.; Ricke, S.C.; Goodridge, L. A membrane filtration method for determining minimum inhibitory concentrations of essential oils. *Agric. Food Anal. Bacteriol.* **2012**, *2*, 88–93.
21. Brandt, A.L.; Castillo, A.; Harris, K.B.; Keeton, J.T.; Hardin, M.D.; Taylor, T.M. Synergistic inhibition of *Listeria monocytogenes* in vitro through the combination of octanoic acid and acidic calcium sulfate. *J. Food Prot.* **2011**, *74*, 122–125. [CrossRef] [PubMed]
22. Kirsch, K.R.; Taylor, T.M.; Griffin, D.; Castillo, A.; Marx, D.B.; Smith, L. Growth of Shiga toxin-producing *Escerichia coli* (STEC) and impacts of chilling and post-inoculation storage on STEC attachment to beef surfaces. *Food Microbiol.* **2014**, *44*, 236–242. [CrossRef] [PubMed]
23. Title 9, U.S. Code of Federal Regulations, §319.15: Miscellaneous Beef Products. Available online: http://www.ecfr.gov/ (accessed on 23 December 2016).
24. Gaysinsky, S.; Davidson, P.M.; Bruce, B.D.; Weiss, J. Growth inhibition of *Escherichia coli* O157:H7 and *Listeria monocytogenes* by carvacrol and eugenol encapsulated in surfactant micelles. *J. Food Prot.* **2005**, *68*, 2559–2566. [CrossRef] [PubMed]

25. Ma, Q.; Davidson, P.M.; Zhong, Q. Antimicrobial properties of lauric arginate alone or in combination with essential oils in tryptic soy broth and 2% reduced fat milk. *Int. J. Food Microbiol.* **2013**, *166*, 77–84. [CrossRef] [PubMed]
26. Blaszyk, M.; Holley, R.A. Interaction of monolaurin, eugenol and sodium citrate on growth of common meat spoilage and pathogenic organisms. *Int. J. Food Microbiol.* **1998**, *39*, 175–183. [CrossRef]
27. Zhang, H.; Shen, Y.; Bao, Y.; He, Y.; Feng, F.; Zheng, X. Characterization and syergistic antimicrobial activities of food-grade dilution-stable microemulsions against *Bacillus subtilis*. *Food Res. Int.* **2008**, *41*, 495–499. [CrossRef]
28. Hsu, S.T.; Breukink, E.; de Kruijff, B.; Kapstein, R.; Bonvin, A.M.J.J.; van Nuland, N.A.J.J. Mapping the targeted membrane pore formation mechanism by solution NMR: The nisin Z and lipid II interaction in SDS micelles. *Biochemistry* **2002**, *41*, 7670–7676. [CrossRef] [PubMed]
29. Conner, D.E.; Kotrola, J.S.; Mikel, W.B.; Tamblyn, K.C. Effects of acetic-lactic acid treatments applied to beef trim on populations of *Escherichia coli* O157:H7 and *Listeria monocytogenes* in ground beef. *J. Food Prot.* **1997**, *60*, 1560–1563. [CrossRef]
30. Ellebracht, E.A.; Castillo, A.; Lucia, L.M.; Miller, R.K.; Acuff, G.R. Reduction of pathogens using hot water and lactic acid on beef trimmings. *J. Food Sci.* **1999**, *64*, 1094–1099. [CrossRef]
31. Fouladkhah, A.; Geornaras, I.; Yang, H.; Belk, K.E.; Nightingale, K.K.; Woerner, D.R.; Smith, G.C.; Sofos, J.N. Sensitivity of Shiga toxin-producing *Escherichia coli*, multidrug-resistant *Salmonella*, and antibiotic-susceptible *Salmonella* to lactic acid on inoculated beef trimmings. *J. Food Prot.* **2012**, *75*, 1751–1758. [CrossRef] [PubMed]
32. Wolf, M.J.; Miller, M.F.; Parks, A.R.; Loneragan, G.H.; Garmyn, A.J.; Thompson, L.D.; Echeverry, A.; Brashears, M.M. Validation comparing the effectiveness of a lactic acid dip with a lactic acid spray for reducing *Escherichia coli* O157:H7, *Salmonella*, and non-O157 Shiga toxigenic *Escherichia coli* on beef trim and ground beef. *J. Food Prot.* **2012**, *75*, 1968–1973. [CrossRef] [PubMed]
33. Muthukumarasamy, P.; Han, J.H.; Holley, R.A. Bactericidal effects of *Lactobacillus reuteri* and allyl isothiocyanate on *Escherichia coli* O157:H7 in refrigerated ground beef. *J. Food Prot.* **2003**, *66*, 2038–2044. [CrossRef] [PubMed]
34. Barbosa, L.N.; Rall, V.L.M.; Fernandes, A.A.H.; Ushimaru, P.I.; Probst, I.D.S.; Fernandes, A., Jr. Essential oils against foodborne pathogens and spoilage bacteria in minced meat. *Foodborne Pathog. Dis.* **2009**, *6*, 725–728. [CrossRef] [PubMed]
35. Amalaradjou, M.A.R.; Baskaran, S.A.; Ramanathan, R.; Johny, A.K.; Charles, A.S.; Valipe, S.R.; Mattson, T.; Schreiber, D.; Juneja, V.K.; Mancini, R.; et al. Enhancing the thermal destruction of *Escherichia coli* O157:H7 in ground beef patties by trans-cinnamaldehyde. *Food Microbiol.* **2010**, *27*, 841–844. [CrossRef] [PubMed]

© 2017 by the authors. Licensee MDPI, Basel, Switzerland. This article is an open access article distributed under the terms and conditions of the Creative Commons Attribution (CC BY) license (http://creativecommons.org/licenses/by/4.0/).

Article

Mechanisms of Antimicrobial Action of Cinnamon and Oregano Oils, Cinnamaldehyde, Carvacrol, 2,5-Dihydroxybenzaldehyde, and 2-Hydroxy-5-Methoxybenzaldehyde against *Mycobacterium avium* subsp. *paratuberculosis* (Map)

Stella W. Nowotarska [1], Krzysztof Nowotarski [1], Irene R. Grant [1], Christopher T. Elliott [1], Mendel Friedman [2],* and Chen Situ [1],*

[1] Institute for Global Food Security, School of Biological Sciences, Queen's University Belfast, David Keir Building, Stranmillis Road, Belfast BT9 5AG, UK; snowotar@gmail.com (S.W.N.); knowotar@hotmail.com (K.N.); i.grant@qub.ac.uk (I.R.G.); Chris.Elliott@qub.ac.uk (C.T.E.)
[2] Western Regional Research Center, Agricultural Research Service, U.S. Department of Agriculture, Albany, CA 94710, USA
* Correspondence: mendel.friedman@ars.usda.gov (M.F.); c.situ@qub.ac.uk (C.S.); Tel.: +1-510-559-5615 (M.F.); +44-28-9097-6546 (C.S.)

Received: 26 July 2017; Accepted: 21 August 2017; Published: 24 August 2017

Abstract: The antimicrobial modes of action of six naturally occurring compounds, cinnamon oil, cinnamaldehyde, oregano oil, carvacrol, 2,5-dihydroxybenzaldehyde, and 2-hydroxy-5-methoxybenzaldehyde, previously found to inhibit the growth of *Mycobacterium avium* subsp. *paratuberculosis* (Map) reported to infect food animals and humans and to be present in milk, cheese, and meat, were investigated. The incubation of *Map* cultures in the presence of all six compounds caused phosphate ions to leak into the extracellular environment in a time- and concentration-dependent manner. Cinnamon oil and cinnamaldehyde decreased the intracellular adenosine triphosphate (ATP) concentration of *Map* cells, whereas oregano oil and carvacrol caused an initial decrease of intracellular ATP concentration that was restored gradually after incubation at 37 °C for 2 h. Neither 2,5-dihydroxybenzaldehyde nor 2-hydroxy-5-methoxybenzaldehyde had a significant effect on intracellular ATP concentration. None of the compounds tested were found to cause leakage of ATP to the extracellular environment. Monolayer studies involving a Langmuir trough apparatus revealed that all anti-*Map* compounds, especially the essential oil compounds, altered the molecular packing characteristics of phospholipid molecules of model membranes, causing fluidization. The results of the physicochemical model microbial membrane studies suggest that the destruction of the pathogenic bacteria might be associated with the disruption of the bacterial cell membrane.

Keywords: essential oils; oil compounds; benzaldehydes; *Mycobacterium avium* subsp. *paratuberculosis*; Johne's disease; Crohn's disease; type 1 diabetes mechanism; cell membrane; AP release

1. Introduction

Many naturally-occurring compounds, such as plant extracts, secondary metabolites, and phytochemicals, have been extensively evaluated for antimicrobial activity [1–9]. Many of them have been shown to be active against both Gram-positive and Gram-negative bacteria, including *Bacillus cereus* [10,11], *Listeria monocytogenes* [12,13], *Pseudomonas aeruginosa*, *Salmonella typhimurium* and *Staphylococcus aureus* [14,15], *Escherichia coli* [16,17], and *Campylobacter jejuni* [18–20]. Some natural compounds, e.g., cinnamon oil and oregano oil, have exhibited activity against pathogenic bacteria that have developed resistance to conventional antibiotics [21,22].

Map is a bacterial pathogen of animal health and potential public health significance [23]. As the causative agent of Johne's disease (paratuberculosis) in domesticated ruminants, such as cattle, sheep, goats, and rabbits [24–28], as well as hens [29], starlings [30], and wildlife [31], it can cause chronic diarrhea, progressive weight loss, decreased milk production, and infertility in these food animals, as well as significant economic losses to farmers [32–35].

Currently there is no drug approved for the treatment of Johne's disease. Click [36] reported that infection with the probiotic bacterium Dietzia, alone or in combination with dexamethasone, inhibited the growth of the mycobacterium in cattle. Godden, et al. [37] and Verhegghe, et al. [38] describe the use of heat-treated colostrum for reducing *Map* in dairy cows. Vaccines in development also have the potential to protect dairy herds against *Map* [39–42].

Human epidemiological and medical studies suggest that *Map* might also contribute to the etiology of human diseases. These include Crohn's disease of the digestive tract [43,44], type 1 diabetes [45–47], and multiple sclerosis [48]. The cited studies suggest the need to further define the possible conflicting role of *Map* in the cause, mechanism, and prevention of *Map*-induced adverse effects in humans [49].

Once farm animals are identified as being infected with *Map*, they are culled prematurely. However, because of the relatively long latent period of *Map* infections, generally between two and five years, by the time the first clinically-affected animal is identified a significant proportion of the herd could have been infected by the bacterium. *Map* can be readily transmitted through the fecal-oral route between animals and via contaminated water because it can persist in the farm environment for lengthy periods [50–54]. Transmission of *Map* to humans may be via contaminated dairy products, meat, or water [55]. *Map* has been isolated from or detected in dairy products such as cheese, raw and pasteurized milk, and infant milk formula [56–59]. The bacteria can survive extreme conditions such as low pH, high pasteurization temperatures, or low refrigeration temperatures [60].

In a previous study we investigated the effect of a range of naturally-occurring compounds on *Map* cells. Six compounds (cinnamon oil, *trans*-cinnamaldehyde, oregano oil, carvacrol, 2,5-dihydroxybenzaldehyde, and 2-hydroxy-5-methoxybenzaldehyde) inhibited the growth of *Map* [61]. Following appearance of our study, Crandall et al. [62] reported that citrus oils inhibited the growth of *Mycobacterium tuberculosis* species in vitro. These authors suggested that the observed anti-mycobacterium properties of the Valencia orange oil warrant further study designed to elucidate the specific mechanisms of action. In a related study, we explored the use of monolayers of bacterial phospholipids as artificial model membranes to study the interaction these compounds with the artificial cell membranes [63].

To further define the antimicrobial mechanisms, in the present study, the potential anti-mycobacterium mechanisms of these compounds have been investigated with *Map* bacteria. Naturally-occurring compounds, such as potato and tomato glycoalkaloids and plant essential oils and their constituents are generally known to target the cell membrane of microorganisms and animal tissues owing to their hydrophobic nature, which enables them to partition into the hydrophobic part of the phospholipid bilayer and accumulate at the cell membrane [64,65]. However, the molecular interactions between the naturally-occurring compounds and bacterial cells still require further determination [15]. It has been suggested that naturally-occurring antimicrobial compounds might have several modes of action to achieve metabolic inhibition and growth inhibition of microbes, subsequently leading to cell death [66].

Methods for studying antibacterial mechanisms include: measuring the change of cell homeostasis, e.g., using fluorescent probes to measure the change of intracellular pH, the relative change of membrane potential and ATP synthesis [10]; measuring oxygen consumption [16]; proteomic studies to investigate protein expression or repression under stressful, but non-lethal, antimicrobial treatments [67]; observing changes in cell morphology after antimicrobial treatment using transmission [68] and scanning electron microscopy [69]; and measuring cell membrane stability, e.g., whole cell autolysis which could indicate whether the antimicrobials cause the disintegration of cells [70]. In the present study, we determined extracellular phosphate ion concentration, intracellular and extracellular ATP concentrations, and monitored changes in absorbance of supernatants from broth cultures exposed to the six active naturally-occurring compounds. In addition, monolayer model membrane studies using a Langmuir trough apparatus were performed. Monolayer model membrane studies are a biophysical approach to study the interaction of antimicrobials with lipid monolayers that mimic the outer surface of biological membranes. These techniques have recently been employed for mode of action studies [71–73].

Biological membranes have an extremely complex chemical composition including different types of phospholipids [74] which serve as a matrix for other essential components, e.g., proteins, including enzymes and biopolymers for cellular function [75–78]. Due to the complexity of biological membranes, different varieties of model membrane systems, e.g., liposome, planar lipid bilayer, and monolayer have been studied [79]. In this study, a monolayer model membrane was used as a single component system to analyze the influence of antimicrobial substances on lipid behavior in the membrane. We believe this to be the first reported study to determine the cellular response of *Map* to six naturally-occurring compounds previously demonstrated to inhibit growth of this bacterium. Possible modes of action of the plant antimicrobials against *Map* are discussed.

2. Materials and Methods

2.1. Plant Materials

The naturally-occurring compounds 2,5-dihydroxybenzaldehyde, 2-hydroxy-5-methoxybenzaldehyde, carvacrol, and *trans*-cinnamaldehyde were obtained from Sigma-Aldrich (Poole, Dorset, UK); the purity levels of these compounds ranged from 98 to 99% according to the manufacturer's specifications. Cinnamon oil (purity > 95%), containing 85% *trans*-cinnamaldehyde, was obtained from Yerba Buena Co. (Berkeley, CA, USA). Oregano oil (purity > 95%), containing 85% carvacrol, was obtained from Lhasa Karnak Herb Co. (Berkeley, CA, USA). The purity levels of 2,4,6-trihydroxybenzaldehyde, geraniol, and vanillic acid (Sigma-Aldrich, Dorset, UK); ranged from 97% to 98% according to the manufacturer's data. Stock solutions, 50 mg/mL for solid compounds and 50 µL/mL for oil compounds, were prepared by suspension in absolute ethanol. As a high percentage of ethanol is bactericidal, the maximum concentration of ethanol that a strain could tolerate (showing no observable inhibition of growth) was determined in a previous study of the bactericidal assay [61]. The final concentration of ethanol present in all studies using *Map* culture was standardized at 0.4% (v/v).

2.2. Bacterial Strains and Growth Conditions

Mycobacterium avium subsp. *paratuberculosis* NCTC 8578 (a bovine isolate) was originally obtained from the National Collection of Type Cultures, Colindale, London. The strain was maintained in Cryobank vials (Mast Group Ltd., Merseyside, UK) at −70 °C. When a broth culture was required, two cryobeads were inoculated into 10 mL of Middlebrook 7H9 broth (Difco Laboratories, Detroit, MI, USA), supplemented with 0.05% (w/v) Tween 80 (Sigma-Aldrich, Dorset, UK), 10% (v/v) oleic albumin dextrose catalase (OADC) supplement (Difco), and 2 µg/mL of mycobactine J (Synbiotics Europe SAS, Lyon, France), pH 6.6 ± 0.2, and incubated at 37 °C with shaking at 100 rpm for 28 to 35 days until the optical density at 600 nm (OD_{600}) was between 0.7 and 1.0. Fifty milliliters of early stationary phase *Map* culture (OD_{600} = 0.7–1.0, ~5 × 10^7 cfu/mL) was centrifuged at 2500× g for 30 min to pellet the cells. Cell pellets were washed three times in 50 mL of sterile reverse osmosis water (Milli Q water system; Millipore, Molsheim, France) at room temperature. *Map* cells were resuspended differently depending on the analysis to be performed, as indicated below.

2.3. Determination of Extracellular Phosphate Concentration

The phosphate assay was carried out as described by Lambert, et al. [15] with minor modifications. Briefly, the washed *Map* cell pellets were resuspended to the original volume in sterile HPLC water

(Sigma-Aldrich, Dorset, UK). Aliquots (2 mL) of the cell suspension were transferred into sterile Eppendorf tubes to which the test compounds were added. Four of the anti-*Map* compounds (cinnamaldehyde, carvacrol, 2,5-dihydroxybenzaldehyde, and 2-hydroxy-5-methoxynenzaldehyde) and a non-active compound vanillic acid, were tested at three-fold dilutions ranging from eight to 1000 µg/mL. Ethanol (0.4%, v/v) was used as negative control. The samples were incubated at 37 °C for 24 h with aliquots taken at 0, 1, 2, 4, 8, and 24 h time points. Aliquots were transferred into Eppendorf tubes and centrifuged at 16,873× g for 15 min. Supernatants were carefully transferred into fresh Eppendorf tubes. All samples were stored at −20 °C until used. For the phosphate test, aliquots of each sample (50 µL) were pipetted into a flat-bottom 96-well microtitre plate (Sarstedt Ltd., Leicester, UK) and Biomol Green™ phosphate assay reagent (100 µL) (Enzo Life Sciences UK Ltd., Exeter, UK) was dispensed into each well. The plate was sealed and incubated at room temperature for 20 min to allow for color development. The OD_{620} was then measured using a microplate reader (Tecan UK Ltd., Reading, UK). Phosphate standard solution (Enzo Life Sciences UK Ltd., Exeter, UK) was prepared to establish a calibration curve range from 0 to 40 µM to allow the phosphate concentration to be determined. The experiment was repeated twice on different dates.

2.4. Determination of Intra- and Extra-Cellular ATP Concentration

The intracellular and extracellular concentrations of ATP were investigated using the procedures described by Gill and Holley [12] with minor modifications. Briefly, the washed *Map* pellet was resuspended in 7H9 broth base (45 mL) without OADC or mycobactine J and incubated at 37 °C to starve (deplete the intracellular ATP) for six weeks. Aliquots of the cell suspension (3.6 mL) were transferred into small bottles, and supplemented with 0.5% D-glucose. Duplicate bottles were supplemented with natural compound stock (17.76 µL) to achieve the previously-determined minimum inhibitory concentration (MIC) of each compound (MIC: cinnamaldehyde, 24 mg/L; cinnamon oil, 24 mg/L, carvacrol, 74 mg/L, oregano oil, 74 mg/L; 2,5-dihydroxybenzaldehyde, 74 mg/L; and 2-hydroxy-5-methoxybenzaldehyde, 74 mg/L). Two other bottles were supplemented with the non-active compound 2,4,6-trihydroxybenzaldehyde (17.76 µL) stock to achieve a final concentration of 74 mg/L. Another two bottles were supplemented with absolute ethanol (17.76 µL) to a final concentration 0.4% v/v to serve as negative controls. At 0, 1, 2, 4, 8, and 24 h, samples were taken and subjected to the following procedure. A sample (500 µL) from each bottle was transferred to an Eppendorf tube; the cells were pelleted by centrifugation at 2500× g for 15 min, and the supernatant (250 µL) was carefully transferred to an Eppendorf tube containing 200 mM Tris (250 µL) + 4 mM EDTA + 0.05% dodecyl trimethyl ammonium bromide (DTAB) for stabilization and determination of extracellular ATP concentration. The remaining half of the supernatant was carefully discarded. The cell pellet was then resuspended in an 'extractant' (500 µL; 100 mM Tris + 2 mM EDTA + 0.025% DTAB). To facilitate ATP extraction, the cell suspensions mixtures were heated in a boiling bath for 20 min. After heat treatment, samples were placed in an ice bath to facilitate rapid cooling. Triplicate aliquots (50 µL) of each sample were pipetted into a white 96-well plate (Greiner Bio-One Ltd., Gloucestershire, UK). ATP standard (Sigma-Aldrich, Dorset, UK) at a concentration of 1, 2, 4, 8, 16, 32, and 64 nM prepared in the extractant was used to generate a calibration curve. The ATP assay mix reagent (50 µL) (Sigma-Aldrich, Dorset, UK) was dispensed into each sample and standard well. The bioluminescence was then read immediately using a microplate reader (Mithras LB 940, Berthold Technologies UK Ltd., Herts, UK). This experiment was repeated twice.

2.5. Absorbance Scans of Culture Supernatant after Antimicrobial Treatment

The washed *Map* cell pellets were resuspended in the original volume of sterile reverse osmosis water. Aliquots (4 mL) were transferred to small sterile bottles and supplemented with test compounds. Three of the anti-*Map* compounds (carvacrol, 2,5-dihydroxybenzaldehyde and 2-hydroxy-5-methoxynenzaldehyde) and the non-active vanillic acid were tested at 74 µg/mL, and cinnamaldehyde was tested at 24 mg/L. Since all of the natural compounds were suspended in absolute ethanol as a stock solution prior to addition to the *Map* cultures, ethanol (0.4% (*v*/*v*) was used as a negative control. The bottles were incubated at 37 °C for 48 h. At 0, 1, 2, 4, 8, 24, and 48 h, sample aliquots were pipetted into Eppendorf tubes and centrifuged at 16,873× *g* for 15 min. Supernatants were carefully transferred into fresh Eppendorf tubes. For the scan experiment, samples (200 µL) were pipetted into separate wells of a flat-bottom 96-well UV plate (Costar, Corning Ltd., Sunderland, UK). The samples were scanned from 230 nm to 370 nm with a wavelength step size of 5 nm, using a microplate reader (Tecan UK Ltd., Reading, UK). Since most of the natural compounds absorb UV light and might show more than one peak when scanned for a series of wavelengths, a corresponding blank (composed of water and natural compound only, without culture) was prepared for each natural compound and processed under the same conditions as the *Map*-containing sample to allow a comparison of supernatant samples. This experiment was repeated twice.

2.6. Monolayer Studies

A Langmuir trough (Precision Plus) (µTrough XL; Kibron, Helsinki, Finland) equipped with a computer-controlled microbalance (Kibron) and MicroSpot (Kibron) was used to measure surface pressure-area (π-A), using the control software (FilmWare 3.61; Kibron). The total surface area of the trough was 227.15 cm^2, and the volume of the subphase was approximately 0.1 L. Phospholipids 1,2-di-(9Z-octadecenoyl)-*sn*-glycero-3-phosphoethanolamine (DOPE) and 1,2-di-(9Z-octadecenoyl)-*sn*-glycero-3-phospho-(1'-*rac*-glycerol) sodium salt (DOPG) were purchased from Avanti Polar Lipids (Alabaster, Alabama, USA). Stock solutions of the phospholipids (5 mg/mL) were prepared in chloroform (Sigma-Aldrich, Dorset, UK) and stored at −20 °C. The naturally-occurring antimicrobial compounds were prepared as stock solutions in reverse osmosis water for powder compounds (100 mg/mL) and chloroform for oil compounds (500 mg/mL). Reverse osmosis water was freshly obtained and used in all experiments. The stocks of powder compounds were freshly prepared before each experiment and used on the same day. The stocks of oil compounds were stored at −20 °C until required. The compounds were tested at concentrations closed to the MIC determined in previous antibacterial assays [61] was 74 mg/L for powder compounds. For the essential oil compounds, the above stock solution (1 µL) was deposited onto the surface of the subphase. The concentration could not be determined as the oil compounds were surface active and no shaking or stirring was employed to facilitate mixing. The phospholipids prepared in chloroform were deposited onto the water surface (pure water with or without natural compounds in the subphase) interface using a 5-µL Hamilton micro-syringe (Supelco, Bellefonte, PA, USA). The selection of subphases was based on the results of the previous antimicrobial assays by Wong, et al. [61]. After spreading the phospholipids, the monolayer was allowed to equilibrate for 10 min (to ensure evaporation of the solvent). Film compression was initiated by moving the two barriers symmetrically, with a speed of 21.157 Å^2/chain/min to allow for the reorientation and relaxation of the lipids during compression. Surface pressure (π) was measured with an accuracy of ±0.1 mN/m using a metal wire probe (Kibron) linked to a high precision microbalance connected to a computer. All isotherms were recorded at 23 °C. The subphase temperature was controlled thermostatically to within 0.1 °C by a circulating water system (Grant Instruments (Cambridge) Ltd., Cambridgeshire, UK).

2.7. Analysis of Isotherms

The interaction between lipid molecules deposited on subphase containing different antimicrobials and their molecular organization were analyzed by calculating the compression modulus C_S^{-1}, which is a reciprocal of isothermal compressibility (C_S) as previously described [80]. The C_S value of the investigated films at the given surface pressure (π) was obtained from π-A data as follows: $C_S = (-1/A_\pi)(dA/d\pi)_T$, where A_π is the area per molecule at the indicated surface pressure π. The C_S values were calculated using Origin® 8 program (OriginLab Corporation, Northampton, MA, USA). Accordingly, the higher the value of the compressibility modulus C_S^{-1}; the lower the interfacial fluidity will be [81].

2.8. Data Analysis

Graphs were plotted using the mean of the replicates of each experiment. Ordinary ANOVA was performed on data, when appropriate, by using GraphPad InStat (GraphPad Software, Inc., La Jolla, CA, USA).

3. Results

3.1. Extracellular Phosphate Assay

The effect of cinnamaldehyde on phosphate leakage of *Map* cells is shown in Figure 1. The results showed an increase in extracellular phosphate level in the presence of cinnamaldehyde that was concentration- and time- dependent, suggesting increased membrane permeability. Figure 2 shows the effects of four anti-*Map* compounds and two negative controls, non-active compound vanillic acid and ethanol, on phosphate leakage of the *Map* culture. Similar to cinnamaldehyde, the results indicated that membrane permeability increased in the presence of all naturally-occurring compounds, including the non-active compound, and the observed increase was time-dependent.

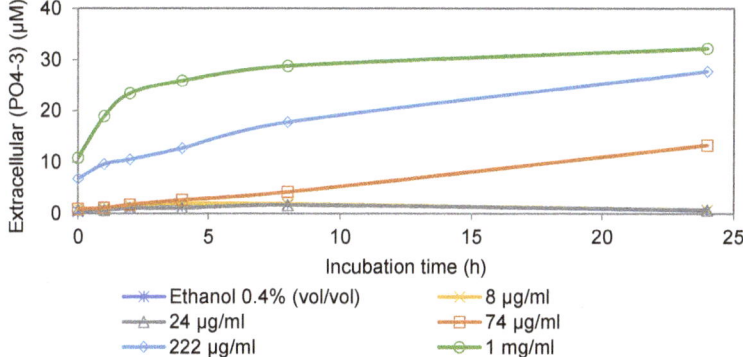

Figure 1. Extracellular levels of phosphate ion in aliquots of *Map* cultures incubated with various concentrations of cinnamaldehyde (MIC 24 mg/L) and non-inhibitory concentration of ethanol (0.4%, v/v) as the negative control.

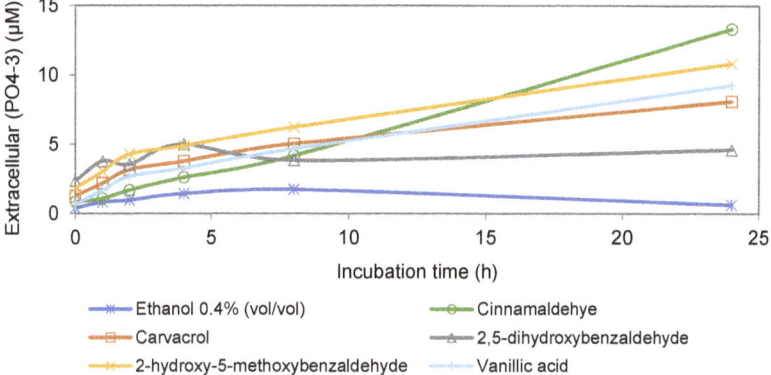

Figure 2. Extracellular concentration of phosphate ion in cultures of *Map* incubated with different active compounds, non-inhibitory compound (vanillic acid) at 74 mg/L, and non-inhibitory concentration of ethanol (0.4%, v/v).

3.2. Intracellular and Extracellular ATP Assays

Cinnamon oil and its active ingredient cinnamaldehyde significantly decreased intracellular ATP ($p < 0.05$). Oregano oil and its active constituent carvacrol resulted in an initial rapid decrease of intracellular ATP concentration, before it rose again (data not shown). The final intracellular ATP concentrations of *Map* cells exposed to these two compounds were still low ($p < 0.05$) compared to the two negative controls. No significant change in intracellular ATP was observed with the other tested compounds.

Low levels of ATP were found in the extracellular environment in all the samples tested including anti-*Map* compounds and negative controls (data not shown). The extracellular ATP concentration was very low (0.5 nM) and remained unchanged throughout the incubation period.

3.3. Absorbance Scans of Culture Supernatant after Antimicrobial Treatment

The absorbance scan (from 230 to 370 nm) of cinnamaldehyde (24 µg/mL) in sterile reverse osmosis water incubated at 37 °C is shown in Figure 3a. A peak was observed and the highest absorbance was measured at 290 nm (A_{290}). The A_{290} reading represents the abundance of cinnamaldehyde in the sample, which decreased from about 2.75 to 2.25 during the two-day incubation period. When a similar scan was performed on the supernatant of the culture incubated with 24 mg/L cinnamaldehyde (the MIC that inhibits the growth of *Map* in broth medium), the A_{290} reading also decreased over the two-day incubation period (Figure 3b). A new peak, which had the highest absorbance at about 250 nm, appeared after one day of incubation.

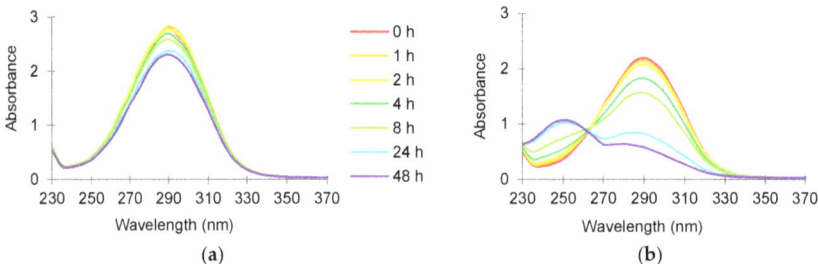

Figure 3. Absorbance scan (230 to 370 nm) of 24 mg/L cinnamaldehyde prepared in sterile reverse osmosis water and incubated in (**a**) absence of and (**b**) presence of *Map* NCTC 8578 at 37 °C for 48 h.

An absorbance scan (230 to 370 nm) of carvacrol (74 mg/L) in sterile reverse osmosis water or the supernatant of *Map* cultures incubated at 37 °C is illustrated in Figure 4a,b. Maximum absorbance was observed at about 270 nm (A_{270}) (Figure 4a). When a similar scan was performed on the supernatant of the *Map* culture incubated with 74 mg/L carvacrol (the MIC that inhibits the growth of *Map* in broth medium) (Figure 4b), the A_{270} reading decreased as the time of incubation increased.

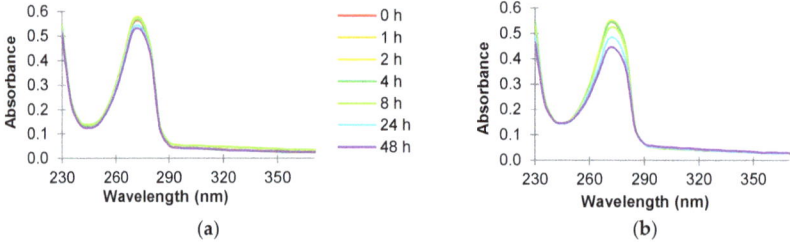

Figure 4. Absorbance scan (230 to 370 nm) of 74 mg/L carvacrol prepared in sterile reverse osmosis water and incubated in (**a**) absence of and (**b**) presence of *Map* NCTC 8578 at 37 °C for 48 h.

3.4. Monolayer Studies

The compression isotherms and compression modulus for the DOPE monolayer deposited on subphases containing natural antimicrobial compounds are shown in Figure 5a,b. In subphase containing pure water only, the lift-off value was approximately 105 Å^2 per molecule and increased gradually into the liquid-condensed (LC) phase up to around 62 Å^2 per molecule, at which point the monolayer collapsed (collapse pressure was about 38 mN/m) (Figure 5a). Analysis of the compression modulus for the DOPE monolayer in the presence of different naturally occurring antimicrobial compounds is shown in Figure 5b.

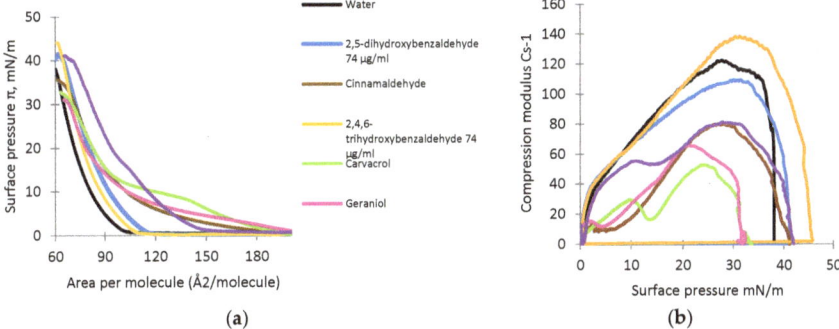

Figure 5. The surface pressure-area (π-A) (**a**) and compression modulus (C_S^{-1}) values versus surface pressure (π); and (**b**) isotherms recorded for monolayers formed by DOPE on the subphases containing pure water with and without naturally-occurring antimicrobial compounds.

The compression isotherms and compression modulus for the DOPG monolayer deposited on subphases containing selected naturally-occurring antimicrobial compounds are shown in Figure 6a,b. In the subphase containing pure water only, the lift-off value was approximately 120 Å^2 per molecule and increased gradually into the liquid-condensed (LC) phase up to around 68 Å^2 per molecule, at which point the monolayer collapsed (collapse pressure was about 42 mN/m) (Figure 6a).

Analysis of the compression modulus for the DOPG monolayer in the presence of different antimicrobial compounds is shown in Figure 6b.

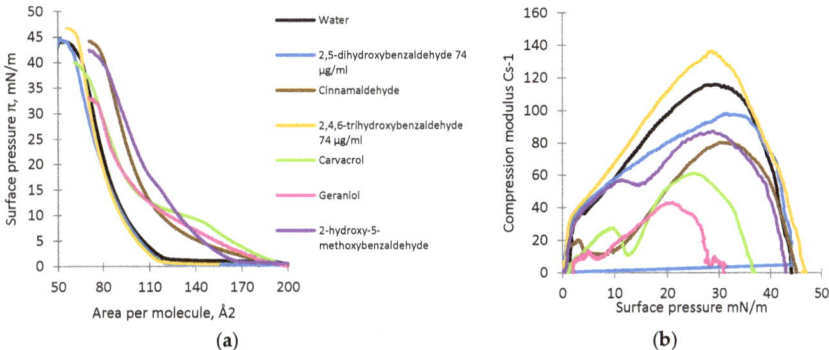

Figure 6. The surface pressure-area (π-A) (**a**) and compression modulus (C_S^{-1}) values versus surface pressure (π); and (**b**) isotherms recorded for the monolayers formed by DOPG on the subphases containing pure water with and without naturally occurring antimicrobial compounds.

4. Discussion

Mechanisms of Antimicrobial Effects against Map

The measurement of intracellular constituents in the extracellular environment, e.g., soluble proteins [69], nucleic acids [82], ATP [83], and phosphate and potassium ions [15] are good indicators of membrane leakage and can reflect the severity of membrane damage. These cellular constituents are important for cellular functions. Presumably, leakage of these constituents might cause further disturbances in cellular metabolism and viability.

As shown in Figures 1 and 2, the degrees of phosphate leakage varied between different compounds in the present study. Cinnamaldehyde caused the highest level of phosphate leakage (Figure 2) in a dose- and time-dependent manner (Figure 1). By contrast, 2,5-dihydroxybenzaldehyde induced the lowest level of leakage. Lambert, et al. [15] reported that oregano essential oil caused leakage of phosphate ion in both the Gram-positive bacterium *S. aureus* and the Gram-negative bacterium *P. aeruginosa*. However, because supplementary controls were not included, it is unclear whether the leakage observed from the two organisms was caused only by the oregano essential oil.

The effects of six anti-*Map* compounds at their MIC values on the intracellular and extracellular ATP concentration of *Map* cells that had been starved for six weeks were also investigated. Significant effects ($p < 0.05$) of cinnamon oil and cinnamaldehyde were observed. The transient effect (an initial rapid decrease) of oregano oil and its active ingredient carvacrol (data not shown), suggests that oregano oil and carvacrol might exert their antimicrobial effect by means of initially stressing *Map*. The data show that *Map* was able to partially overcome such a challenge and to decrease the effect to some degree. Thus ATP synthesis might have resumed or ATP hydrolysis might have slowed down as a result of a self-defense mechanism. In the present study, we found that carvacrol did not deplete the intracellular ATP pool of *Map*. This finding contrasts with observation that carvacrol rapidly depleted the ATP pool in the Gram-positive foodborne pathogen *Bacillus cereus* [10].

A possible explanation for the different effects might be due to the differences in the cell membrane compositions. The *Map* membrane is characterized by a thicker, waxy, and hydrophobic cell wall, which is very rich in mycolic acid, making it more resistant to chemical damage and environmental stress. Low levels of extracellular ATP found in our study may be due to a weak ATP efflux as a result of *Map* being stressed when exposed to the antimicrobial compounds. This also implies that the compounds did not increase the membrane permeability for ATP.

The absorbance scan of cinnamaldehyde (24 µg/mL) in water or *Map* culture showed a decrease of the peak at 290 nm over the two-day incubation period (Figure 3a,b). When comparing the culture supernatant at time 0 min with the corresponding blank, the A_{290} reading is approximately 0.5 absorbance units lower in the supernatant. The explanation for this finding might be due to the adsorption of cinnamaldehyde to the cell surface or uptake of cinnamaldehyde into the cells. Furthermore, a new peak, which had the highest absorbance at about 250 nm, appeared after one day. The new peak could either be a product transformed by *Map* by cinnamaldehyde during the incubation, or an intracellular constituent that had leaked from the cells. Since the peak showed the highest absorbance within the UV region (250 nm), it is possibly an indication of nucleic acid or leakage of other constituents from the cells. The appearance of such a new peak was unique to cinnamaldehyde; culture supernatants from cells exposed to all of the other compounds did not show additional peaks. Attempts were made to identify this peak, using QToF LC/MS and NMR spectroscopy, but without success.

An absorbance scan (230 to 370 nm) of carvacrol in sterile reverse osmosis water (Figure 4a) or supernatant cultures (Figure 4b) shows that the highest absorbance was observed at 270 nm (A_{270}). The A_{270} value decreased from about 0.58 to 0.53 during the two-day incubation period (Figure 4a), similar to the absorbance scan of cinnamaldehyde in water. However, the decrease in A_{270} was much smaller than that with cinnamaldehyde. When a similar scan was performed on the supernatant of the *Map* culture incubated with carvacrol (74 mg/L; the MIC that inhibits the growth in broth medium)

(Figure 4b), the A_{270} reading decreased as the time of incubation increased, i.e., from about 0.55 to 0.44. The decreased quantity of carvacrol suggested the uptake of carvacrol by the *Map* organism. However, in contrast to the cinnamaldehyde experiment, the decrease in absorbance reading in culture supernatant treated with carvacrol was much smaller and no additional peaks were observed.

Lipid monolayers were formed at the air-liquid interface to mimic the outer surface of the bacterial membrane by using DOPE and DOPG. PE and PG phospholipids were selected for this study because they are the predominant zwitterionic and anionic phospholipids found in the membranes of both Gram-positive and Gram-negative bacteria [75,78]. The changes in compressibility modulus in both the DOPE and DOPG monolayers reflect the physical state of the lipid monolayer compressed on the surface of different subphases. The factor that determines compressibility of the isotherm is its slope. This can be calculated as a derivative of area per molecule versus surface pressure, which reflects the rate of change of the area per molecule against surface pressure. The higher the value of the compressibility modulus, the higher the rigidity of the model membrane and, vice versa, a low value of compressibility modulus indicates high fluidity of the model membrane [84].

Isotherms of DOPE deposited on the subphase with naturally-occurring antimicrobial compounds showed the lift-off value increased and varied from approximately 110 to 200 $Å^2$ per molecule (Figure 5a). The increase in the lift-off value indicated these antimicrobial compounds could have been incorporated into the lipid monolayers in the gas state resulting in the observed reduced packing effectiveness of DOPE molecules. In the presence of three oil compounds, cinnamaldehyde, carvacrol, and geraniol, the slopes of the isotherms were the flattest. For the DOPE monolayer compressed on the subphase containing pure water only, the maximal value of C_S^{-1} was observed at approximately 122 mN/m, whereas the value for 2,4,6-trihydroxybenzaldehyde was approximately 138 mN/m, suggesting a rigidifying effect of this compound on the DOPE monolayer (Figure 5b). For the other compounds, the maximal values of the compression modulus varied from 50 to 110 mN/m. Such a decrease in the maximal value of the compression modulus indicated a fluidizing effect possibly in the DOPE monolayer. Carvacrol showed the highest fluidizing effect, whereas 2,5-dihydroxybenzaldehyde exhibited the lowest effect.

Isotherms of DOPG deposited on the subphase with natural antimicrobial compounds showed the lift-off value varied from approximately 117 to 195 $Å^2$ per molecule (Figure 6a). In the presence of two of the oil compounds, carvacrol and geraniol, the slopes of the isotherms were the flattest. 2,4,6-Trihydroxybenzaldehyde and 2,5-dihydroxybenzaldehyde caused a non-significant decrease in the lift-off value ($p > 0.05$). For the DOPG monolayer compressed on a subphase containing pure water only, the maximal value of C_S^{-1} was observed at approximately 118 mN/m, whereas the value for 2,4,6-trihydroxybenzaldehyde was approximately 137 mN/m, indicating a rigidifying effect (Figure 6b). For the other compounds, the maximal values of the compression modulus varied from 42 to 117 mN/m. Geraniol showed the highest fluidizing effect, whereas 2,5-dihydroxybenzaldehyde showed the lowest effect.

It has been reported that antimicrobial compounds interact more easily with the gas or liquid phase of the monolayer than with the liquid-condensed phase [85]. The shape and size of lipid rafts/aggregates seem to be determined by competition between the line tension at the raft boundary and the electrostatic repulsion between molecular polar heads [86]. The present biophysical experiment indicated that antimicrobial compounds interacted differently with the lipid rafts in both lipids, depending on the electrical charge at the polar head as indicated by the higher lift-off values. The difference might be due to the electrostatic interaction between charged head groups and antimicrobials inserted between hydrophobic tails.

In the present study, only 2,4,6-trihydroxybenzaldehyde caused a slight rigidifying effect on both DOPE and DOPG. All other compounds exhibited either a small or large fluidizing effect. The essential oil compounds carvacrol and geraniol showed a greater fluidizing effect in all the monolayers tested than did the solid compound 2,5-dihydroxybenzaldehyde. Sikkema, et al. [87] suggested that the toxicity of a compound is highly related to its ability to disturb the hydrophobic interactions between the lipids and proteins in the cell membrane. The toxicity is, thus, highly related to the decline in membrane integrity. The present results on the relationship between antimicrobial and membrane effects are consistent with this suggestion.

It has been suggested that hydrophobic oil compounds interact with the bacterial cell membrane, changing the membrane structure, stability, and permeability of certain intracellular constituents. Results of this study clearly indicated that natural antimicrobial compounds could modify the lipid monolayer structure, leading to the leakage of phosphate and other essential cell components and a change in the membrane potential and the cell environments, ultimately causing the death of cells. A related study showed that exposure of *Bacillus subtilis* ATCC 6633 cells to *Trachyspermum ammi* essential oil caused an instant loss of cytoplasm membrane integrity causing it to become increasingly permeable to protons and ions that might be responsible for the antibacterial activity [88]. Studies with green tea catechins have showed that hydrogen bonding of phenolic hydroxyl groups of catechins to cell membranes might be correlated with antimicrobial and anti-cancer-cell effects of catechins [89–91].

5. Conclusions

To conclude, the cellular responses of the potentially zoonotic pathogen *Map* in the presence of naturally-occurring compounds were studied. The natural compounds tested caused the leakage of phosphate ions from *Map* cells in relation to the time of exposure to and concentration of the test compounds; however, the extent of phosphate leakage was not consistent with the relative antimicrobial activities of the compounds. Exposure of *Map* cells to cinnamon oil or its constituent cinnamaldehyde caused a decline in intracellular ATP concentration; however, none of the naturally-occurring compounds caused a leakage of ATP to the extracellular environment. Exposure to cinnamaldehyde may have resulted in a leakage of intracellular constituents, possibly protein or nucleic acids, or the transformation to a new product by *Map*. The monolayer model membrane studies showed that natural antimicrobial compounds could modify the lipid monolayer structure by incorporation into the monolayer, formation of aggregates/rafts of antimicrobials and lipids, and reduction in the packing effectiveness of the lipid molecules, resulting in an increase in membrane fluidity. The monolayer studies, therefore, confirmed that the antimicrobial compounds, especially oil compounds, are targeting the cell membrane. The described studies offer insights into the interaction between antimicrobials and membrane lipids and identifying characteristics or actions of the most potent compounds.

Acknowledgments: This work was supported by a Research Studentship from Queen's University Belfast, UK. We thank Carol Levin for facilitating preparation of the manuscript.

Author Contributions: C.S., I.R.G., C.T.E., and M.F. conceived and designed the experiments; S.W.N. and K.N. performed the experiments; and all authors participated in drafting and revising the manuscript.

Conflicts of Interest: The authors declare no conflict of interest.

References

1. Friedman, M.; Henika, P.R.; Levin, C.E. Bactericidal activities of health-promoting, food-derived powders against the foodborne pathogens *Escherichia coli*, *Listeria monocytogenes*, *Salmonella enterica*, and *Staphylococcus aureus*. *J. Food Sci.* **2013**, *78*, M270–M275. [CrossRef] [PubMed]
2. Friedman, M.; Henika, P.R.; Mandrell, R.E. Bactericidal activities of plant essential oils and some of their isolated constituents against *Campylobacter jejuni*, *Escherichia coli*, *Listeria monocytogenes*, and *Salmonella enterica*. *J. Food Prot.* **2002**, *65*, 1545–1560. [CrossRef] [PubMed]
3. Friedman, M. Antimicrobial activities of plant essential oils and their components against antibiotic-susceptible and antibiotic-resistant foodborne pathogens. In *Essential Oils and Nanotechnology for Treatment of Microbial Diseases*; Rai, M., Zachino, S., Derita, M.D., Eds.; CRC Press: Boca Raton, FL, USA, 2017; pp. 14–38.
4. Friedman, M. Antibiotic-resistant bacteria: Prevalence in food and inactivation by food-compatible compounds and plant extracts. *J. Agric. Food Chem.* **2015**, *63*, 3805–3822. [CrossRef] [PubMed]

5. Friedman, M. Chemistry and multi-beneficial bioactivities of carvacrol (4-isopropyl-2-methylphenol), a component of essential oils produced by aromatic plants and spices. *J. Agric. Food Chem.* **2014**, *62*, 7652–7670. [CrossRef] [PubMed]
6. Todd, J.; Friedman, M.; Patel, J.; Jaroni, D.; Ravishankar, S. The antimicrobial effects of cinnamon leaf oil against multi-drug resistant *Salmonella* Newport on organic leafy greens. *Int. J. Food Microbiol.* **2013**, *166*, 193–199. [CrossRef] [PubMed]
7. Moore-Neibel, K.; Gerber, C.; Patel, J.; Friedman, M.; Jaroni, D.; Ravishankar, S. Antimicrobial activity of oregano oil against antibiotic-resistant *Salmonella enterica* on organic leafy greens at varying exposure times and storage temperatures. *Food Microbiol.* **2013**, *34*, 123–129. [CrossRef] [PubMed]
8. Juneja, V.K.; Gonzales-Barron, U.; Butler, F.; Yadav, A.S.; Friedman, M. Predictive thermal inactivation model for the combined effect of temperature, cinnamaldehyde and carvacrol on starvation-stressed multiple *Salmonella* serotypes in ground chicken. *Int. J. Food Microbiol.* **2013**, *165*, 184–199. [CrossRef] [PubMed]
9. Juneja, V.K.; Yadav, A.S.; Hwang, C.-A.; Sheen, S.; Mukhopadhyay, S.; Friedman, M. Kinetics of thermal destruction of *Salmonella* in ground chicken containing *trans*-cinnamaldehyde and carvacrol. *J. Food Prot.* **2012**, *75*, 289–296. [CrossRef] [PubMed]
10. Ultee, A.; Kets, E.P.; Smid, E.J. Mechanisms of action of carvacrol on the food-borne pathogen *Bacillus cereus*. *Appl. Environ. Microbiol.* **1999**, *65*, 4606–4610. [PubMed]
11. Friedman, M.; Henika, P.R.; Levin, C.E.; Mandrell, R.E.; Kozukue, N. Antimicrobial activities of tea catechins and theaflavins and tea extracts against *Bacillus cereus*. *J. Food Prot.* **2006**, *69*, 354–361. [CrossRef] [PubMed]
12. Gill, A.O.; Holley, R.A. Mechanisms of bactericidal action of cinnamaldehyde against *Listeria monocytogenes* and of eugenol against *L. monocytogenes* and *Lactobacillus sakei*. *Appl. Environ. Microbiol.* **2004**, *70*, 5750–5755. [CrossRef] [PubMed]
13. Ravishankar, S.; Jaroni, D.; Zhu, L.; Olsen, C.W.; McHugh, T.H.; Friedman, M. Inactivation of *Listeria monocytogenes* on ham and bologna using pectin-based apple, carrot, and hibiscus edible films containing carvacrol and cinnamaldehyde. *J. Food Sci.* **2012**, *77*, M377–M382. [CrossRef] [PubMed]
14. Je, J.-Y.; Kim, S.-K. Chitosan derivatives killed bacteria by disrupting the outer and inner membrane. *J. Agric. Food Chem.* **2006**, *54*, 6629–6633. [CrossRef] [PubMed]
15. Lambert, R.J.W.; Skandamis, P.N.; Coote, P.J.; Nychas, G.-J.E. A study of the minimum inhibitory concentration and mode of action of oregano essential oil, thymol and carvacrol. *J. Appl. Microbiol.* **2001**, *91*, 453–462. [CrossRef] [PubMed]
16. Fitzgerald, D.J.; Stratford, M.; Gasson, M.J.; Ueckert, J.; Bos, A.; Narbad, A. Mode of antimicrobial of vanillin against *Escherichia coli*, *Lactobacillus plantarum* and *Listeria innocua*. *J. Appl. Microbiol.* **2004**, *97*, 104–113. [CrossRef] [PubMed]
17. Friedman, M.; Zhu, L.; Feinstein, Y.; Ravishankar, S. Carvacrol facilitates heat-induced inactivation of *Escherichia coli* O157:H7 and inhibits formation of heterocyclic amines in grilled ground beef patties. *J. Agric. Food Chem.* **2009**, *57*, 1848–1853. [CrossRef] [PubMed]
18. Friedman, M.; Henika, P.R.; Mandrell, R.E. Antibacterial activities of phenolic benzaldehydes and benzoic acids against *Campylobacter jejuni*, *Escherichia coli*, *Listeria monocytogenes*, and *Salmonella enterica*. *J. Food Prot.* **2003**, *66*, 1811–1821. [CrossRef] [PubMed]
19. Ravishankar, S.; Zhu, L.; Law, B.; Joens, L.; Friedman, M. Plant-derived compounds inactivate antibiotic-resistant *Campylobacter jejuni* strains. *J. Food Prot.* **2008**, *71*, 1145–1149. [CrossRef] [PubMed]
20. Mild, R.M.; Joens, L.A.; Friedman, M.; Olsen, C.W.; McHugh, T.H.; Law, B.; Ravishankar, S. Antimicrobial edible apple films inactivate antibiotic resistant and susceptible *Campylobacter jejuni* strains on chicken breast. *J. Food Sci.* **2011**, *76*, M163–M168. [CrossRef] [PubMed]
21. Friedman, M.; Buick, R.; Elliott, C.T. Antibacterial activities of naturally occurring compounds against antibiotic-resistant *Bacillus cereus* vegetative cells and spores, *Escherichia coli*, and *Staphylococcus aureus*. *J. Food Prot.* **2004**, *67*, 1774–1778. [CrossRef] [PubMed]
22. Ravishankar, S.; Zhu, L.; Olsen, C.W.; McHugh, T.H.; Friedman, M. Edible apple film wraps containing plant antimicrobials inactivate foodborne pathogens on meat and poultry products. *J. Food Sci.* **2009**, *74*, M440–M445. [CrossRef] [PubMed]
23. Naser, S.A.; Ghobrial, G.; Romero, C.; Valentine, J.F. Culture of *Mycobacterium avium* subspecies *paratuberculosis* from the blood of patients with Crohn's disease. *Lancet* **2004**, *364*, 1039–1044. [CrossRef]

24. Lombard, J.E.; Gardner, I.A.; Jafarzadeh, S.R.; Fossler, C.P.; Harris, B.; Capsel, R.T.; Wagner, B.A.; Johnson, W.O. Herd-level prevalence of *Mycobacterium avium* subsp. *paratuberculosis* infection in United States dairy herds in 2007. *Prev. Vet. Med.* **2013**, *108*, 234–238. [CrossRef] [PubMed]
25. Sweeney, R.W.; Collins, M.T.; Koets, A.P.; McGuirk, S.M.; Roussel, A.J. Paratuberculosis (Johne's disease) in cattle and other susceptible species. *J. Vet. Intern. Med.* **2012**, *26*, 1239–1250. [CrossRef] [PubMed]
26. Pithua, P.; Kollias, N.S. Estimated prevalence of caprine paratuberculosis in boer goat herds in Missouri, USA. *Vet. Med. Int.* **2012**, *2012*. [CrossRef] [PubMed]
27. Windsor, P.A. Paratuberculosis in sheep and goats. *Vet. Microbiol.* **2015**, *181*, 161–169. [CrossRef] [PubMed]
28. Arrazuria, R.; Juste, R.A.; Elguezabal, N. Mycobacterial infections in rabbits: From the wild to the laboratory. *Transbound. Emerg. Dis.* **2017**, *64*, 1045–1058. [CrossRef] [PubMed]
29. Shitaye, J.E.; Matlova, L.; Horvathova, A.; Moravkova, M.; Dvorska-Bartosova, L.; Treml, F.; Lamka, J.; Pavlik, I. *Mycobacterium avium* subsp. *avium* distribution studied in a naturally infected hen flock and in the environment by culture, serotyping and IS901 RFLP methods. *Vet. Microbiol.* **2008**, *127*, 155–164. [CrossRef]
30. Gaukler, S.M.; Linz, G.M.; Sherwood, J.S.; Dyer, N.W.; Bleier, W.J.; Wannemuehler, Y.M.; Nolan, L.K.; Logue, C.M. *Escherichia coli*, *Salmonella*, and *Mycobacterium avium* subsp. *paratuberculosis* in Wild European starlings at a Kansas cattle feedlot. *Avian Dis.* **2009**, *53*, 544–551. [CrossRef]
31. Carta, T.; Álvarez, J.; Pérez de la Lastra, J.M.; Gortázar, C. Wildlife and paratuberculosis: A review. *Res. Vet. Sci.* **2013**, *94*, 191–197. [CrossRef] [PubMed]
32. Ott, S.L.; Wells, S.J.; Wagner, B.A. Herd-level economic losses associated with Johne's disease on US dairy operations. *Prev. Vet. Med.* **1999**, *40*, 179–192. [CrossRef]
33. Garcia, A.B.; Shalloo, L. Invited review: The economic impact and control of paratuberculosis in cattle. *J. Dairy Sci.* **2015**, *98*, 5019–5039. [CrossRef] [PubMed]
34. McAloon, C.G.; Whyte, P.; More, S.J.; Green, M.J.; O'Grady, L.; Garcia, A.; Doherty, M.L. The effect of paratuberculosis on milk yield—A systematic review and meta-analysis. *J. Dairy Sci.* **2016**, *99*, 1449–1460. [CrossRef] [PubMed]
35. Kirkeby, C.; Graesboll, K.; Nielsen, S.S.; Toft, N.; Halasa, T. Epidemiological and economic consequences of purchasing livestock infected with *Mycobacterium avium* subsp. *paratuberculosis*. *BMC Vet. Res.* **2017**, *13*, 202. [CrossRef] [PubMed]
36. Click, R.E. Successful treatment of asymptomatic or clinically terminal bovine *Mycobacterium avium* subspecies *paratuberculosis* infection (Johne's disease) with the bacterium Dietzia used as a probiotic alone or in combination with dexamethasone: Adaption to chronic human diarrheal diseases. *Virulence* **2011**, *2*, 131–143. [CrossRef] [PubMed]
37. Godden, S.M.; Wells, S.; Donahue, M.; Stabel, J.; Oakes, J.M.; Sreevatsan, S.; Fetrow, J. Effect of feeding heat-treated colostrum on risk for infection with *Mycobacterium avium* ssp. *paratuberculosis*, milk production, and longevity in Holstein dairy cows. *J. Dairy Sci.* **2015**, *98*, 5630–5641. [CrossRef] [PubMed]
38. Verhegghe, M.; Rasschaert, G.; Herman, L.; Goossens, K.; Vandaele, L.; De Bleecker, K.; Vlaemynck, G.; Heyndrickx, M.; De Block, J. Reduction of *Mycobacterium avium* ssp. *paratuberculosis* in colostrum: Development and validation of 2 methods, one based on curdling and one based on centrifugation. *J. Dairy Sci.* **2017**, *100*, 3497–3512. [CrossRef] [PubMed]
39. Cho, J.; Tauer, L.W.; Schukken, Y.H.; Gómez, M.I.; Smith, R.L.; Lu, Z.; Grohn, Y.T. Economic analysis of *Mycobacterium avium* subspecies *paratuberculosis* vaccines in dairy herds. *J. Dairy Sci.* **2012**, *95*, 1855–1872. [CrossRef] [PubMed]
40. Lu, Z.; Schukken, Y.H.; Smith, R.L.; Mitchell, R.M.; Gröhn, Y.T. Impact of imperfect *Mycobacterium avium* subsp. *paratuberculosis* vaccines in dairy herds: A mathematical modeling approach. *Prev. Vet. Med.* **2013**, *108*, 148–158. [CrossRef] [PubMed]
41. Shippy, D.C.; Lemke, J.J.; Berry, A.; Nelson, K.; Hines, M.E.; Talaat, A.M. Superior protection from live-attenuated vaccines directed against Johne's Disease. *Clin. Vaccine Immunol.* **2017**, *24*, e00478-16. [CrossRef] [PubMed]
42. Chaubey, K.K.; Gupta, R.D.; Gupta, S.; Singh, S.V.; Bhatia, A.K.; Jayaraman, S.; Kumar, N.; Goel, A.; Rathore, A.S.; Sahzad; et al. Trends and advances in the diagnosis and control of paratuberculosis in domestic livestock. *Vet. Q.* **2016**, *36*, 203–227. [CrossRef] [PubMed]
43. McNees, A.L.; Markesich, D.; Zayyani, N.R.; Graham, D.Y. Mycobacterium paratuberculosis as a cause of Crohn's disease. *Expert Rev. Gastroenterol. Hepatol.* **2015**, *9*, 1523–1534. [CrossRef] [PubMed]

44. Waddell, L.A.; Rajic, A.; Stark, K.D.; Mc, E.S. The zoonotic potential of *Mycobacterium avium* ssp. *paratuberculosis*: A systematic review and meta-analyses of the evidence. *Epidemiol. Infect.* **2015**, *143*, 3135–3157. [CrossRef] [PubMed]
45. Naser, S.A.; Thanigachalam, S.; Dow, C.T.; Collins, M.T. Exploring the role of *Mycobacterium avium* subspecies *paratuberculosis* in the pathogenesis of type 1 diabetes mellitus: A pilot study. *Gut Pathog.* **2013**, *5*, 14. [CrossRef] [PubMed]
46. Hesam Shariati, S.; Alaei, A.; Keshavarz, R.; Mosavari, N.; Rabbani, A.; Niegowska, M.; Sechi, L.A.; Feizabadi, M.M. Detection of *Mycobacterium avium* subsp. *paratuberculosis* in Iranian patients with type 1 diabetes mellitus by PCR and ELISA. *J. Infect. Dev. Ctries.* **2016**, *10*, 857–862. [CrossRef] [PubMed]
47. Songini, M.; Mannu, C.; Targhetta, C.; Bruno, G. Type 1 diabetes in Sardinia: Facts and hypotheses in the context of worldwide epidemiological data. *Acta Diabetol.* **2017**, *54*, 9–17. [CrossRef] [PubMed]
48. Cossu, D.; Yokoyama, K.; Hattori, N. Conflicting role of *Mycobacterium* species in multiple sclerosis. *Front. Neurol.* **2017**, *8*, 216. [CrossRef] [PubMed]
49. Singh, A.V.; Chauhan, D.S.; Singh, S.V.; Kumar, V.; Singh, A.; Yadav, A.; Yadav, V.S. Current status of *Mycobacterium avium* subspecies *paratuberculosis* infection in animals & humans in India: What needs to be done? *Indian J. Med. Res.* **2016**, *144*, 661–671. [CrossRef] [PubMed]
50. Corbett, C.S.; De Buck, J.; Orsel, K.; Barkema, H.W. Fecal shedding and tissue infections demonstrate transmission of *Mycobacterium avium* subsp. *paratuberculosis* in group-housed dairy calves. *Vet. Res.* **2017**, *48*, 27. [CrossRef] [PubMed]
51. Sechi, L.A.; Paccagnini, D.; Salza, S.; Pacifico, A.; Ahmed, N.; Zanetti, S. *Mycobacterium avium* subspecies *paratuberculosis* bacteremia in type 1 diabetes mellitus: An infectious trigger? *Clin. Infect. Dis.* **2008**, *46*, 148–149. [CrossRef] [PubMed]
52. Cossu, A.; Rosu, V.; Paccagnini, D.; Cossu, D.; Pacifico, A.; Sechi, L.A. MAP3738c and MptD are specific tags of *Mycobacterium avium* subsp. *paratuberculosis* infection in type I diabetes mellitus. *Clin. Immunol.* **2011**, *141*, 49–57. [CrossRef] [PubMed]
53. Bach, H.; Rosenfeld, G.; Bressler, B. Treatment of Crohn's disease patients with infliximab is detrimental for the survival of *Mycobacterium avium* ssp. *paratuberculosis* within macrophages and shows a remarkable decrease in the immunogenicity of mycobacterial proteins. *J. Crohn's Colitis* **2012**, *6*, 628–629. [CrossRef]
54. Elguezabal, N.; Chamorro, S.; Molina, E.; Garrido, J.M.; Izeta, A.; Rodrigo, L.; Juste, R.A. Lactase persistence, NOD2 status and *Mycobacterium avium* subsp. *paratuberculosis* infection associations to Inflammatory Bowel Disease. *Gut Pathog.* **2012**, *4*. [CrossRef]
55. Gill, C.O.; Saucier, L.; Meadus, W.J. *Mycobacterium avium* subsp. *paratuberculosis* in dairy products, meat, and drinking water. *J. Food Prot.* **2011**, *74*, 480–499. [CrossRef] [PubMed]
56. Eltholth, M.M.; Marsh, V.R.; Van Winden, S.; Guitian, F.J. Contamination of food products with *Mycobacterium avium paratuberculosis*: A systematic review. *J. Appl. Microbiol.* **2009**, *107*, 1061–1071. [CrossRef] [PubMed]
57. Carvalho, I.A.; Pietralonga, P.A.G.; Schwarz, D.G.G.; Faria, A.C.S.; Moreira, M.A.S. Short communication: Recovery of viable *Mycobacterium avium* subspecies *paratuberculosis* from retail pasteurized whole milk in Brazil. *J. Dairy Sci.* **2012**, *95*, 6946–6948. [CrossRef] [PubMed]
58. Giacometti, F.; Serraino, A.; Finazzi, G.; Daminelli, P.; Losio, M.N.; Arrigoni, N.; Piva, S.; Florio, D.; Riu, R.; Zanoni, R.G. Sale of raw milk in Northern Italy: Food safety implications and comparison of different analytical methodologies for detection of foodborne pathogens. *Foodborne Pathog. Dis.* **2012**, *9*, 293–297. [CrossRef] [PubMed]
59. Mundo, S.L.; Gilardoni, L.R.; Hoffman, F.J.; Lopez, O.J. Rapid and sensitive method to identify *Mycobacterium avium* subsp. *paratuberculosis* in cow milk using DNA-methylase Genotyping. *Appl. Environ. Microbiol.* **2012**, *79*, 1612–1618. [CrossRef] [PubMed]
60. Klanicova, B.; Slana, I.; Roubal, P.; Pavlik, I.; Kralik, P. *Mycobacterium avium* subsp. *paratuberculosis* survival during fermentation of soured milk products detected by culture and quantitative real time PCR methods. *Int. J. Food Microbiol.* **2012**, *157*, 150–155. [CrossRef] [PubMed]
61. Wong, S.Y.Y.; Grant, I.R.; Friedman, M.; Elliott, C.T.; Situ, C. Antibacterial activities of naturally occurring compounds against *Mycobacterium avium* subsp. *paratuberculosis*. *Appl. Environ. Microbiol.* **2008**, *74*, 5986–5990. [CrossRef] [PubMed]

62. Crandall, P.G.; Ricke, S.C.; O'Bryan, C.A.; Parrish, N.M. In vitro effects of citrus oils against *Mycobacterium tuberculosis* and non-tuberculous *Mycobacteria* of clinical importance. *J. Environ. Sci. Health B* **2012**, *47*, 736–741. [CrossRef] [PubMed]
63. Nowotarska, S.W.; Nowotarski, K.I.; Friedman, M.; Situ, C. Effect of structure on the interactions between five natural antimicrobial compounds and phospholipids of bacterial cell membrane on model monolayers. *Molecules* **2014**, *19*, 7497–7515. [CrossRef] [PubMed]
64. Blankemeyer, J.T.; White, J.B.; Stringer, B.K.; Friedman, M. Effect of α-tomatine and tomatidine on membrane potential of frog embryos and active transport of ions in frog skin. *Food Chem. Toxicol.* **1997**, *35*, 639–646. [CrossRef]
65. Friedman, M.; Burns, C.F.; Butchko, C.A.; Blankemeyer, J.T. Folic acid protects against potato glycoalkaloid α-chaconine-induced disruption of frog embryo cell membranes and developmental toxicity. *J. Agric. Food Chem.* **1997**, *45*, 3991–3994. [CrossRef]
66. Burt, S. Essential oils: Their antibacterial properties and potential applications in foods—A review. *Int. J. Food Microbiol.* **2004**, *94*, 223–253. [CrossRef] [PubMed]
67. Cho, Y.S.; Schiller, N.L.; Kahng, H.Y.; Oh, K.H. Cellular responses and proteomic analysis of *Escherichia coli* exposed to green tea polyphenols. *Curr. Microbiol.* **2007**, *55*, 501–506. [CrossRef] [PubMed]
68. Raafat, D.; Von Bargen, K.; Haas, A.; Sahl, H.-G. Insights into the mode of action of chitosan as an antibacterial compound. *Appl. Environ. Microbiol.* **2008**, *74*, 3764–3773. [CrossRef] [PubMed]
69. Kwon, J.A.; Yu, C.B.; Park, H.D. Bactericocidal effects and inhibition of cell separation of cinnamic aldehyde on *Bacillus cereus*. *Lett. Appl. Microbiol.* **2003**, *37*, 61–65. [CrossRef] [PubMed]
70. Gustafson, J.E.; Liew, Y.C.; Chew, S.; Markham, J.; Bell, H.C.; Wyllie, S.G.; Warmington, J.R. Effects of tea tree oil on *Escherichia coli*. *Lett. Appl. Microbiol.* **1998**, *26*, 194–198. [CrossRef] [PubMed]
71. Rakotomanga, M.; Saint-Pierre-Chazalet, M.; Loiseau, P.M. Alteration of fatty acid and sterol metabolism in miltefosine-resistant *Leishmania donovani* promastigotes and consequences for drug-membrane interactions. *Antimicrob. Agents Chemother.* **2005**, *49*, 2677–2686. [CrossRef] [PubMed]
72. Gidalevitz, D.; Ishitsuka, Y.; Muresan, A.S.; Konovalov, O.; Waring, A.J.; Lehrer, R.I.; Lee, K.Y. Interaction of antimicrobial peptide protegrin with biomembranes. *Proc. Natl. Acad. Sci. USA* **2003**, *100*, 6302–6307. [CrossRef] [PubMed]
73. Giordani, C.; Molinari, A.; Toccacieli, L.; Calcabrini, A.; Stringaro, A.; Chistolini, P.; Arancia, G.; Diociaiuti, M. Interaction of tea tree oil with model and cellular membranes. *J. Med. Chem.* **2006**, *49*, 4581–4588. [CrossRef] [PubMed]
74. Simons, K.; Vaz, W.L. Model systems, lipid rafts, and cell membranes. *Annu. Rev. Biophys. Biomol. Struct.* **2004**, *33*, 269–295. [CrossRef] [PubMed]
75. Epand, R.M.; Epand, R.F. Domains in bacterial membranes and the action of antimicrobial agents. *Mol. BioSyst.* **2009**, *5*, 580–587. [CrossRef] [PubMed]
76. Janas, T.; Nowotarski, K.; Gruszecki, W.I.; Janas, T. The effect of hexadecaprenol on molecular organisation and transport properties of model membranes. *Acta Biochim. Pol.* **2000**, *47*, 661–673. [PubMed]
77. Lorite, G.S.; Nobre, T.M.; Zaniquelli, M.E.D.; de Paula, E.; Cotta, M.A. Dibucaine effects on structural and elastic properties of lipid bilayers. *Biophys. Chem.* **2009**, *139*, 75–83. [CrossRef] [PubMed]
78. Epand, R.M.; Epand, R.F. Lipid domains in bacterial membranes and the action of antimicrobial agents. *Biochim. Biophys. Acta* **2009**, *1788*, 289–294. [CrossRef] [PubMed]
79. Yoneyama, F.; Imura, Y.; Ohno, K.; Zendo, T.; Nakayama, J.; Matsuzaki, K.; Sonomoto, K. Peptide-lipid huge toroidal pore, a new antimicrobial mechanism mediated by a lactococcal bacteriocin, lacticin Q. *Antimicrob. Agents Chemother.* **2009**, *53*, 3211–3217. [CrossRef] [PubMed]
80. Smaby, J.M.; Kulkarni, V.S.; Momsen, M.; Brown, R.E. The interfacial elastic packing interactions of galactosylceramides, sphingomyelins, and phosphatidylcholines. *Biophys. J.* **1996**, *70*, 868–877. [CrossRef]
81. Hac-Wydro, K.; Wydro, P. The influence of fatty acids on model cholesterol/phospholipid membranes. *Chem. Phys. Lipids* **2007**, *150*, 66–81. [CrossRef] [PubMed]
82. Chen, C.Z.; Cooper, S.L. Interactions between dendrimer biocides and bacterial membranes. *Biomaterials* **2002**, *23*, 3359–3368. [CrossRef]
83. Ultee, A.; Gorris, L.G.M.; Smid, E.J. Bactericidal activity of carvacrol towards the food-borne pathogen *Bacillus cereus*. *J. Appl. Microbiol.* **1998**, *85*, 211–218. [CrossRef] [PubMed]

84. Sabatini, K.; Mattila, J.-P.; Kinnunen, P.K.J. Interfacial behavior of cholesterol, ergosterol, and lanosterol in mixtures with DPPC and DMPC. *Biophys. J.* **2008**, *95*, 2340–2355. [CrossRef] [PubMed]
85. Demel, R.A.; Peelen, T.; Siezen, R.J.; De Kruijff, B.; Kuipers, O.P. Nisin Z, mutant nisin Z and lacticin 481 interactions with anionic lipids correlate with antimicrobial activity: A monolayer study. *Eur. J. Biochem.* **1996**, *235*, 267–274. [CrossRef] [PubMed]
86. Diociaiuti, M.; Ruspantini, I.; Giordani, C.; Bordi, F.; Chistolini, P. Distribution of GD3 in DPPC monolayers: A thermodynamic and atomic force microscopy combined study. *Biophys. J.* **2004**, *86*, 321–328. [CrossRef]
87. Sikkema, J.; De Bont, J.A.M.; Poolman, B. Mechanisms of membrane toxicity of hydrocarbons. *Microbiol. Rev.* **1995**, *59*, 201–222. [PubMed]
88. Paul, S.; Dubey, R.C.; Maheswari, D.K.; Kang, S.C. *Trachyspermum ammi* (L.) fruit essential oil influencing on membrane permeability and surface characteristics in inhibiting food-borne pathogens. *Food Control* **2011**, *22*, 725–731. [CrossRef]
89. Sirk, T.W.; Brown, E.F.; Friedman, M.; Sum, A.K. Molecular binding of catechins to biomembranes: Relationship to biological activity. *J. Agric. Food Chem.* **2009**, *57*, 6720–6728. [CrossRef] [PubMed]
90. Sirk, T.W.; Brown, E.F.; Sum, A.K.; Friedman, M. Molecular dynamics study on the biophysical interactions of seven green tea catechins with lipid bilayers of cell membranes. *J. Agric. Food Chem.* **2008**, *56*, 7750–7758. [CrossRef] [PubMed]
91. Sirk, T.W.; Friedman, M.; Brown, E.F. Molecular binding of black tea theaflavins to biological membranes: Relationship to bioactivities. *J. Agric. Food Chem.* **2011**, *59*, 3780–3787. [CrossRef] [PubMed]

© 2017 by the authors. Licensee MDPI, Basel, Switzerland. This article is an open access article distributed under the terms and conditions of the Creative Commons Attribution (CC BY) license (http://creativecommons.org/licenses/by/4.0/).

Article

Cytotoxicity of the Essential Oil of Fennel (*Foeniculum vulgare*) from Tajikistan

Farukh Sharopov [1,2], Abdujabbor Valiev [1], Prabodh Satyal [3], Isomiddin Gulmurodov [1], Salomudin Yusufi [1], William N. Setzer [3] and Michael Wink [2,*]

1. Department of Pharmaceutical Technology, Avicenna Tajik State Medical University, Rudaki 139, Dushanbe 734003, Tajikistan; shfarukh@mail.ru (F.S.); valizoda83@gmail.com (A.V.); gulmurodov@mail.ru (I.G.); salomudin@mail.ru (S.Y.)
2. Institute of Pharmacy and Molecular Biotechnology, Heidelberg University, Im Neuenheimer Feld 364, Heidelberg 69120, Germany
3. Department of Chemistry, University of Alabama in Huntsville, Huntsville, AL 35899, USA; prabodhsatyal@gmail.com (P.S.); setzerw@uah.edu (W.N.S.)
* Correspondence: wink@uni-heidelberg.de; Tel.: +49-62-2154-4880

Received: 11 August 2017; Accepted: 16 August 2017; Published: 28 August 2017

Abstract: The essential oil of fennel (*Foeniculum vulgare*) is rich in lipophilic secondary metabolites, which can easily cross cell membranes by free diffusion. Several constituents of the oil carry reactive carbonyl groups in their ring structures. Carbonyl groups can react with amino groups of amino acid residues in proteins or in nucleotides of DNA to form Schiff's bases. Fennel essential oil is rich in anise aldehyde, which should interfere with molecular targets in cells. The aim of the present study was to investigate the chemical composition of the essential oil of fennel growing in Tajikistan. Gas chromatographic-mass spectrometric analysis revealed that the main components of *F. vulgare* oil were *trans*-anethole (36.8%); α-ethyl-*p*-methoxy-benzyl alcohol (9.1%); *p*-anisaldehyde (7.7%); carvone (4.9%); 1-phenyl-penta-2,4-diyne (4.8%) and fenchyl butanoate (4.2%). The oil exhibited moderate antioxidant activities. The potential cytotoxic activity was studied against HeLa (human cervical cancer), Caco-2 (human colorectal adenocarcinoma), MCF-7 (human breast adenocarcinoma), CCRF-CEM (human T lymphoblast leukaemia) and CEM/ADR5000 (adriamycin resistant leukaemia) cancer cell lines; IC$_{50}$ values were between 30–210 mg L^{-1} and thus exhibited low cytotoxicity as compared to cytotoxic reference compounds.

Keywords: *Foeniculum vulgare*; essential oil; *trans*-anethole; anise aldehyde; cytotoxicity; cluster analysis

---

1. Introduction

Fennel (Arpabodiyon, local Tajik name), *Foeniculum vulgare* Miller, an important member of the Apiaceae, is widely used for flavouring foods and beverages due to its pleasant spicy aroma [1,2]. In traditional medicine, the plant and its essential oil have been extensively used as carminative, digestive, galactogogue and diuretic and to treat respiratory and gastrointestinal disorders [1]. It is also used as a constituent in cosmetic and pharmaceutical products [3]. The essential oil of *F. vulgare*, in particular anethole, exhibits antispasmodic, carminative, anti-inflammatory, estrogenic and anti-microbial activities [4]. In vitro, fennel oil possesses antioxidant [5,6], antimicrobial [7], insecticidal [8], antithrombotic [9] and hepatoprotective activities [2]. Furthermore, the essential oil of fennel exhibits in vitro anticancer activity [10–12]. The in vitro cytotoxic, genotoxic, and apoptotic activities of estragole were suspected to induce hepatic tumors in susceptible strains of mice [10].

Anethole is toxic in high concentrations [4]. Because of their lipophilic properties, the secondary metabolites of essential oils are able to penetrate cytoplasmic membranes by free diffusion. This process can affect membrane fluidity and permeability, transport, ion equilibrium and membrane potential [13], leading to cell death by apoptosis and necrosis [11].

The essential oil of fennel is rich in secondary metabolites, which carry reactive substituents (among them carbonyl groups) in their ring structures or side chains. Aldehydes are generally long-lived and electrophilic compounds, they can react with molecular targets which carry free amino groups, such as of amino acid residues in proteins or of nucleotides in DNA to form Schiff's bases [14]. Aldehyde-containing essential oils often exhibit cytotoxicity [15,16] by reacting with cellular nucleophiles, including proteins and nucleic acids [13,17].

The chemical composition of the essential oil of *F. vulgare* from different geographical locations has been extensively studied [6,18–20]. According to these studies, the major components of fennel oil are *trans*-anethole, estragole, fenchone, and limonene depending on the chemotype [21–23]. The aim of the present study was to investigate the chemical composition of the essential oil of fennel growing in Tajikistan (Central Asia) and to explore cytotoxic activity against different human cancer cell lines. The biological activity and chemical composition of *F. vulgare* oil from Tajikistan have not been previously reported.

2. Materials and Methods

2.1. Plant Material

The aerial parts of *F. vulgare* plants were collected from the Varzob region, Tajikistan on 29 July 2016. A voucher specimen of the plant material was deposited at the Department of Pharmaceutical Technology, Avicenna Tajik State Medical University under accession number TD2016-24. The material was completely dried and hydrodistilled using a Clevenger-type apparatus for 3 h to give an essential oil yield of 0.5%.

2.2. Gas-Liquid Chromatography-Mass Spectrometry (GLC-MS)

The essential oil from *F. vulgare* oil was analyzed by GLC-MS using an instrument (GCMS-QP2010 Ultra, Shimadzu, Tokyo, Japan) operated in the EI mode (electron energy = 70 eV), scan range = 3.0 scans s^{-1}. The GC column was ZB-5 fused silica capillary with a (5% phenyl)-polymethyl siloxane stationary phase a film thickness of 0.25 mm. The carrier gas was helium with a column head pressure 551 kPa and flow rate of 1.37 mL min^{-1}. Injector temperature was 250 °C and the ion source temperature was 200 °C, increased in temperature rate 2 °C min^{-1} to 260 °C. The GC oven temperature program was programmed from 50 °C initial temperature, increased at a rate of 2 °C min^{-1} to 260 °C. A 5% w/v solution of the sample in CH_2Cl_2 was prepared and 0.1 µL was injected in splitting mode (30:1).

Identification of the oil components was based on their retention indices determined by reference to a homologous series of n-alkanes (Kovats RI), and by comparison of their mass spectral fragmentation patterns with those reported in the literature [24] and stored on the MS library (NIST 11 (National Institute of Standards and Technology, Gaithersburg, MD, USA), WILEY 10 (John Wiley & Sons, Inc., Hoboken, NJ, USA), FFNSC version 1.2 (Shimadzu Corp., Tokyo, Japan)). The percentages of each component are reported as raw percentages based on total ion current without standardization (set 100%).

2.3. Antioxidant Activity

The antioxidant activity of the essential oils was evaluated by 2,2-diphenyl-1-picrylhydrazyl (DPPH), 2,2'-azinobis-(3-ethylbenzthiazoline-6-sulfonic acid) (ABTS) and ferric reducing antioxidant power (FRAP) assays. DPPH, ABTS and FRAP assays were performed as described earlier by us [25,26].

2.4. Cytotoxicity

The potential cytotoxicity of the fennel essential oil against of the five human tumor cell lines (HeLa, Caco-2, MCF-7, CCRF-CEM and CEM/ADR5000) were determined by the MTT assay. The cells were seeded at a density of 2×10^4 cells/well (HeLa, Caco-2, MCF-7) and 3×10^4 cells/well (CCRF-CEM and CEM/ADR5000). The essential oil was serially diluted in media in the presence of DMSO at concentrations between 10 mg/L and 5 g/L; 100 µL of each concentration was applied to the wells of a 96-well plates. Cells were incubated with the essential oil for 24 h (HeLa, Caco-2, MCF-7) and 48 h (CCRF-CEM and CEM/ADR5000) before the medium was removed and replaced with fresh medium containing 0.5 mg/mL 3-(4,5-dimethylthiazol-2-yl)-2,5-diphenyltetrazolium bromide (MTT). The formazan crystals produced were dissolved in DMSO 4 h later; the absorbance was measured at 570 nm with a Biochrom Asys UVM 340 Microplate Reader (Cambridge, UK).

2.5. Hemolytic Activity

The hemolytic activity was investigated by incubation of serially diluted fennel essential oil in phosphate-buffered saline with red blood cells (human O+). The hemolytic activity assay was performed as described earlier [27].

2.6. Hierarchical Cluster Analysis

A total of 68 chemical compositions of *F. vulgare* essential oils, including the sample from this study in addition to 66 compositions obtained from the published literature [5–7,9,23,28–45] were used to carry out the cluster analysis using the XLSTAT software, version 2015.4.01. The essential oil compositions were treated as operational taxonomic units (OTUs) and the percentages of 34 of the most abundant essential oil components (*trans*-anethole, limonene, estragole, fenchone, α-pinene, α-phellandrene, *p*-anisaldehyde, β-phellandrene, β-pinene, *exo*-fenchyl acetate, *p*-cymene, myrcene, (E)-β-ocimene, camphor, 10-nonacosanone, piperitenone oxide, sabinene, neophytadiene, *cis*-anethole, *trans*-dihydrocarvone, γ-terpinene, carvone, phytol, 1,8-cineole, *iso*-isopulegol, *trans*-β-terpineol, *endo*-fenchyl acetate, camphene, carvacrol, apiole, *o*-cymene, δ-3-carene, linalool, and thymol) were used to establish the chemical relationships of the *F. vulgare* essential oil samples using the agglomerative hierarchical cluster (AHC) method. Pearson correlation was selected as a measure of similarity, and the unweighted pair-group method with arithmetic average (UPGMA) was used for definition of the clusters.

2.7. Microscopic Observation

The images of the treated or untreated CCRF cells were obtained and photographed using a by fluorescence microscopy (BZ-9000, Keyence, Osaka, Japan) in order to investigate morphological changes.

2.8. Data Analysis

The experiments were repeated three times. IC_{50} values were calculated using a four parameter logistic curve (Sigma Plot 11.0 (SYSTAT Software, San Jose, CA, USA)). The data are represented as means ± standard deviations. The results of statistical test were determined by using Sigma Plot 11.0 software and also by using the statistical function *t*-test in Microsoft Excel. A *p* value below 0.05 was considered to represent statistical significance.

3. Results and Discussion

3.1. Chemical Composition

The essential oil of *F. vulgare* was analyzed by gas-liquid chromatography—mass spectrometry (GLC-MS). Thirty components were identified representing 97.7% of total oil composition (Table 1). Oxygenated terpenoids were the dominant compounds of the essential oil of *F. vulgare*.

The major components were *trans*-anethole (**1**) (36.8%), *p*-anisaldehyde (**2**) (7.7%), α-ethyl-*p*-methoxybenzyl alcohol (**3**) (9.1%), carvone (4.9%), 1-phenylpenta-2,4-diyne (4.7%) and fenchyl butanoate (4.2%). The main three compounds (*trans*-anethole, *p*-anisaldehyde, α-ethyl-*p*-methoxybenzyl alcohol) are both ethers, having methoxy functional groups (Scheme 1).

Table 1. Chemical composition of the essential oil of *Foeniculum vulgare* according to a GLC-MS analysis.

Compounds	% *	RT **	RI ***
trans-Anethole	36.8	36.022	1286
α-Ethyl-*p*-methoxybenzyl alcohol	9.10	54.059	1569
p-Anisaldehyde	7.73	33.825	1254
Carvone	4.87	33.119	1243
1-Phenylpenta-2,4-diyne	4.75	35.875	1283
Fenchyl butanoate	4.23	46.653	1448
Neomenthol	3.62	28.027	1170
(2*E*)-Dodecenal	3.44	47.807	1467
β-Ethyl-*p*-methoxybenzyl alcohol	3.27	54.498	1577
trans-Thujone	2.95	24.404	1118
Fenchone	2.75	22.408	1089
Carvacrol	2.15	36.802	1297
Linalyl acetate	1.88	33.503	1249
Unidentified	1.39	42.318	1380
(*E*)-Chrysanthenyl acetate	1.38	34.015	1256
Thymol	1.03	36.255	1289
Fenchyl isobutanoate	1.03	47.726	1465
(*E*)-β-Terpineol	1.00	28.642	1179
Linalool	0.75	23.139	1100
cis-Thujone	0.74	23.624	1107
(*E*)-Dihydrocarvone	0.64	30.422	1204
Unidentified	0.64	48.021	1470
Geranial	0.56	34.747	1267
Myrtenyl acetate	0.54	36.160	1288
exo-Fenchyl acetate	0.48	32.269	1231
Penta-1,3-diynylbenzene	0.46	40.505	1353
Dill ether	0.44	29.148	1186
Methylchavicol (=estragole)	0.42	29.973	1198
Unidentified	0.30	53.885	1567
Caryophyllene oxide	0.25	54.759	1581
Camphor	0.23	26.445	1147
iso-Menthone	0.10	27.050	1156
1-Hexadecene	0.08	48.270	1474
Terpene hydrocarbons:	5.21		
Oxygenated terpenoids:	85.78		
Others:	6.70		
Total identified:	97.67		

* Total peak area was set to 100%; ** Retention time; *** Kovats retention index in ZB-5 column.

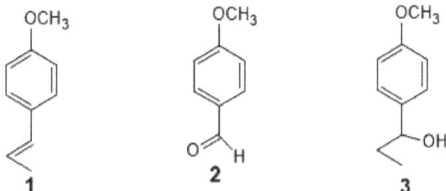

Scheme 1. Structures of main components of the essential oil *Foeniculum vulgare*.

In accordance with previously published data, **1** is the main component [1,46], its content varying from 5.0 to 85%. However, estragole [47,48], fenchyl acetate [7] and limonene [6] have also been reported as main components of the fennel oil from other origins. Fennel essential oil is known as a source for anethole [49].

F. vulgare is subdivided into three main chemotypes according to their relative compositions: (1) estragole chemotype; (2) estragole/anethole chemotype and (3) anethole chemotype [34]. The essential oil of *F. vulgare* from Tajikistan thus belongs to the anethole chemotype, which is widely distributed [47].

3.2. Cluster Analysis

In order to place the chemical composition of Tajik *F. vulgare* into context with previous investigations, a hierarchical cluster analysis was carried out using the essential oil composition from this study in conjunction with compositions from 66 samples previously reported in the literature [5–7,9,23,28–45]. The cluster analysis (Figure 1) reveals the major chemotype of *F. vulgare* to be an anethole-rich chemotype (CT1), which includes the sample from Tajikistan. There is also an estragole-rich chemotype (CT2), represented by seven samples, and several chemotypes represented by only one or two samples each: an estragole/α-phellandrene chemotype (CT3), an anethole/estragole/α-pinene chemotype (CT4), an α-phellandrene chemotype (CT5), and a limonene/β-pinene/myrcene chemotype (CT6). The anethole-rich cluster can be subdivided into three chemotypes: an anethole chemotype (CT1a, including the sample from Tajikistan), an anethole/limonene chemotype (CT1b), and an anethole/camphor chemotype (CT1c) represented by a single sample from Romania (see Figure 1).

3.3. Antioxidant Activity

The investigation of antioxidant activity of essential oils as lipophilic secondary metabolites became an interesting aspect of food and pharmaceutical research. Synthetic food additives are increasingly replaced with plant-based natural ingredients, due to their safety, effectiveness and consumer acceptance [50]. In general, fennel as an edible and medicinal plant represents an interest through the neutralization of reactive oxygen species in order to prevent the damage of protein, lipid, and DNA which are supposed to be the main reason for cell aging, oxidative stress-originated diseases (cardiovascular and neurodegenerative diseases), and cancer.

The essential oil of fennel exhibits low antioxidant activity as compared to the positive control, caffeic acid. The results of the DPPH, ABTS and FRAP analyses are represented Table 2.

Table 2. Antioxidant activity of the essential oil *Foeniculum vulgare* as determined by the ABTS, DPPH, and FRAP assays *.

Sample	DPPH IC_{50} (g L^{-1})	ABTS IC_{50} (g L^{-1})	FRAP µM Fe(II)/mg of Samples
Foeniculum vulgare	15.6 ± 1.1 **	10.9 ± 0.4 **	194 ± 18 **
trans-Anethole	23.4 ± 0.1 **	35.6 ± 0.1 **	104 ± 5.2 **
Caffeic acid	0.0017 ± 0.0002 ***	0.0011 ± 0.0002 ***	2380 ± 46 ***

* The data are represented as means ± standard deviations; ** significant at $p < 0.0025$; *** significant at $p < 0.0001$.

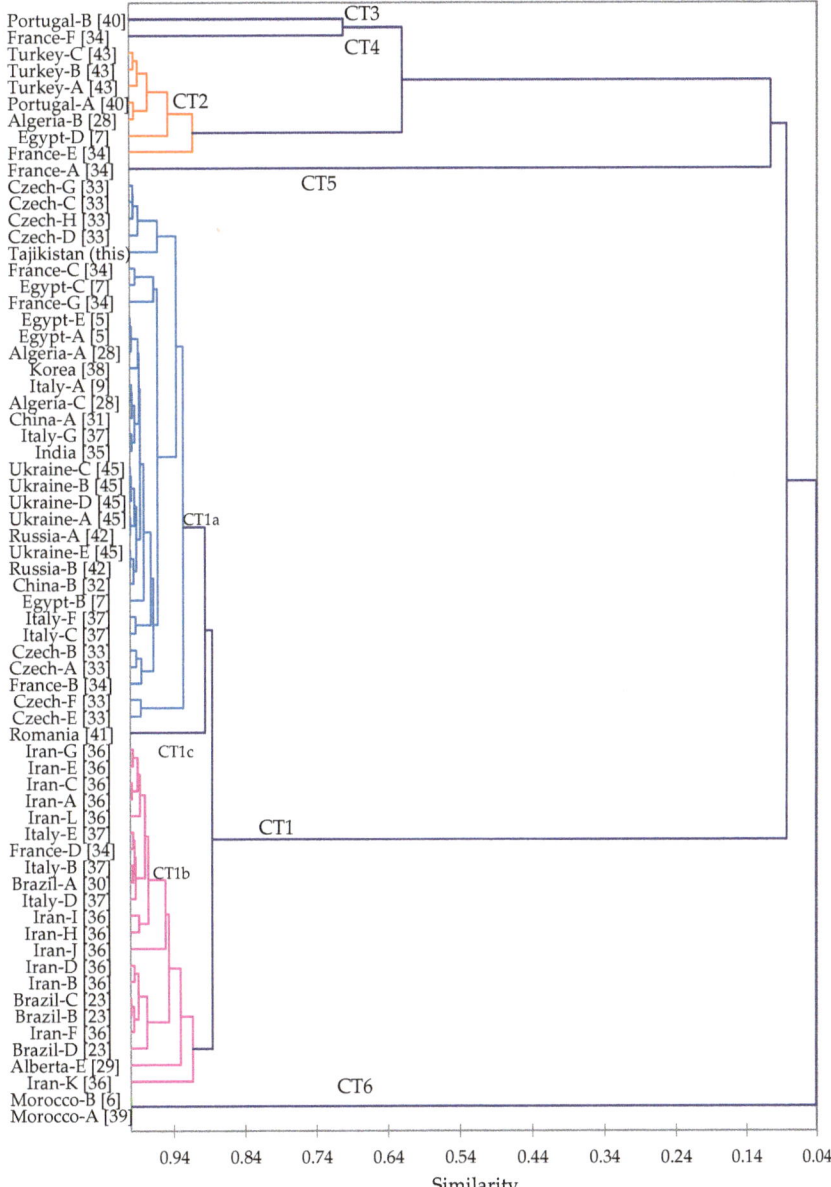

Figure 1. Dendrogram obtained from the agglomerative hierarchical cluster analysis of 68 *Foeniculum vulgare* essential oil compositions. (CT1) anethole-rich chemotype, (CT1a) anethole chemotype, (CT1b) anethole/limonene chemotype, (CT1c) anethole/camphor chemotype, (CT2) estragole chemotype, (CT3) estragole/α-phellandrene chemotype, (CT4) anethole/estragole/α-pinene chemotype, (CT5) α-phellandrene chemotype, and (CT6) limonene/β-pinene/myrcene chemotype.

The concentration of 50% inhibition (IC_{50}) was the parameter used to compare the DPPH and ABTS radical scavenging activity. A lower IC_{50} (for DPPH and ABTS) and higher FRAP values indicate higher antioxidant activity. IC_{50} values for the antioxidant activity were 15.6 mg mL^{-1} (DPPH) and 10.9 mg mL^{-1} (ABTS). The IC_{50} values of the known antioxidant substance—caffeic acid—were 0.0017 mg mL^{-1} for DPPH and 0.0011 mg mL^{-1} for ABTS, respectively. Ferric reducing antioxidant power (FRAP) were equivalent to 193.5 µM Fe(II)/mg for oil and 2380 µM Fe(II)/mg for caffeic acid. In agreement with our results, it was reported that the an IC_{50} value of DPPH radical scavenging activity of *Foeniculum vulgare* essential oil was 15.3 mg mL^{-1} [7]. According to the authors [7], fennel essential oil reacts with free radicals as a primary antioxidant and, therefore, it may limit free-radical damage occurring in the human body. In our previous paper, we reported the antioxidant activity of pure essential oil components, including the main component of the essential oil of fennel (*trans*-anethole). It shows weak antioxidant activity. We assume that the phenolic substances (carvacrol (2.1%) and thymol (1.0%)) are responsible for the observed antioxidant activity. These data are in agreement with previously reported data [25]. However, it is known that the bioactivity of plant extracts is due to the entire composition of the extract [51,52].

3.4. Cytotoxicity

The cytotoxicity of the oil was tested against HeLa, Caco-2, MCF-7, CCRF-CEM and CEM/ADR5000 cancer cell lines (Table 3). IC_{50} values were 207 mg L^{-1} for HeLa, 75 mg L^{-1} for Caco-2, 59 mg L^{-1} for MCF-7, 32 mg L^{-1} for CCRF-CEM, and 165 mg L^{-1} for CEM/ADR5000 cell lines. As compared to the positive control doxorubicin, the essential oil exhibits low cytotoxicity. Doxorubicin, an anthracycline antitumor antibiotic is a hydrophilic drug, and shows broad spectrum anticancer activity [53]. The cytotoxicity of *F. vulgare* oil is most likely due to the lipophilic properties of essential oil and alkylating properties of the major components *trans*-anethole and *p*-anisaldehyde. Caco-2 and CEM/ADR5000 overexpress the ABC transporter p-gp which can actively pump out any lipophilic compound that has entered the cell by free diffusion [54]). Thus, both cell lines are rather insensitive towards lipophilic cytotoxic agents. In contrast, the parent cell line CCRF-CEM should be sensitive. We also suspect that some components of the essential oil are may be substrates for p-gp, as IC_{50} values were higher in CEM/ADR5000 cells.

Table 3. Cytotoxicity of the essential oil of *Foeniculum vulgare*.

Sample	HeLa	Caco-2	MCF-7	CCRF-CEM	CEM/ADR 5000	RBC
	IC_{50}, mg L^{-1} *					
Foeniculum vulgare	207 ± 13 **	75 ± 4 **	59 ± 5 **	32 ± 1 **	165 ± 15 ***	1100 ± 50 **
Doxorubicin	4.5 ± 0.6 **	1.1 ± 0.1 **	1.3 ± 0.3 **	0.25 ± 0.2 **	1.4 ± 0.4 **	-

* The data are represented as means ± standard deviations; ** significant at $p < 0.0006$; *** significant at $p < 0.001$.

To better understand the mechanism of action of *F. vulgare* essential oil, we have investigated its hemolytic effect. The result of hemolytic activity indicates that the oil is able to lyse the cell membrane albeit with a rather high IC_{50} value of 1100 mg L^{-1} (Table 3). Moreover, in order to investigate the effect of essential oil on the cell morphology, the images of untreated and treated CCRF cells with essential oil were captured by fluorescence microscope. The images are illustrated in Figure 2.

Obtained images indicate that the essential oil can change the morphology of cells. Results of both hemolysis and microscopic investigation indicate that essential oil also affects the integrity of cell membranes. This is in agreement with many of the reported data [55].

In addition, *trans*-anethole, the main component of the essential oil, was examined for its cytotoxicity in RC-37 cells. Its IC_{50} value was 100 mg L^{-1} [56]. The incubation of hepatocytes with anethole caused a cell death accompanied by losses of cellular ATP and adenine nucleotide pools [57]. Anethole shows apoptotic activity, as it can damage DNA [58]. Thus anethole could be responsible for the overall cytotoxicity of the essential oil in our study.

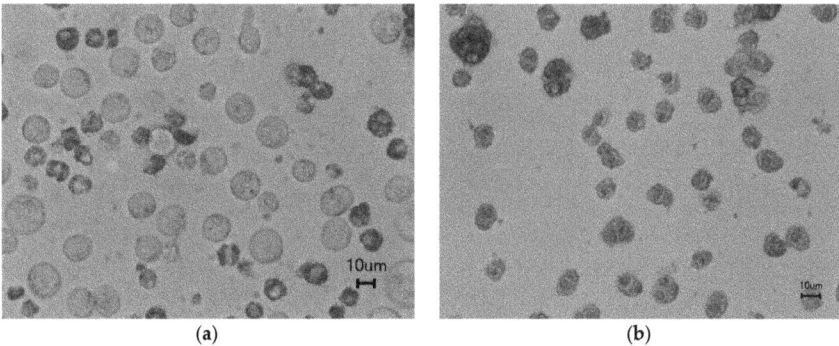

Figure 2. The images of untreated (**a**) and treated (**b**) CCRF cells with essential oil of *Foeniculum vulgare*.

4. Conclusions

The essential oil of fennel contains several bioactive secondary metabolites, such as aldehydes. The oil apparently affects the stability of biomembranes and interacts with molecular targets, such as proteins and DNA, which causes a low cytotoxicity.

Author Contributions: F.S. and M.W. conceived and designed the experiments; F.S., A.V., P.S., I.G., S.I., and W.N.S. performed the experiments; F.S., P.S., W.N.S., and M.W. analyzed the data; P.S., W.N.S., and M.W. contributed reagents/materials/analysis tools; All authors contributed to writing and editing the manuscript.

Conflicts of Interest: The authors declare no conflict of interest.

References

1. Mimica-Dukic, N.; Kujundyic, S.; Sokovic, M.; Couladis, M. Essential oil composition and antifungal activity of *Foeniculum vulgare* Mill. Obtained by different distillation conditions. *Phytother. Res.* **2003**, *17*, 368–371. [CrossRef] [PubMed]
2. Rather, M.A.; Dar, B.A.; Sofi, S.N.; Bhat, B.A.; Qurishi, M.A. *Foeniculum vulgare*: A comprehensive review of its traditional use, phytochemistry, pharmacology, and safety. *Arab. J. Chem.* **2012**, *9*, S1574–S1583. [CrossRef]
3. Diao, W.R.; Hu, Q.P.; Zhang, H.; Xu, J.G. Chemical composition, antibacterial activity and mechanism of action of essential oil from seeds of fennel (*Foeniculum vulgare* Mill.). *Food Control* **2014**, *35*, 109–116. [CrossRef]
4. Van Wyk, B.E.; Wink, M. *Medicinal Plants of the World*; Briza: Pretoria, Africa, 2004.
5. Roby, M.H.; Sarhan, M.A.; Selim, K.A.; Khalel, K.I. Antioxidant and antimicrobial activities of essential oil and extracts of fennel (*Foeniculum vulgare* L.) and chamomile (*Matricaria chamomilla* L.). *Ind. Crops Prod.* **2013**, *44*, 437–445. [CrossRef]
6. Ouariachi, E.E.; Lahhit, N.; Bouyanzer, A.; Hammouti, B.; Paolini, J.; Majidi, L.; Desjobert, J.M.; Costa, J. Chemical composition and antioxidant activity of essential oils and solvent extracts of *Foeniculum vulgare* Mill. from Morocco. *J. Chem. Pharm. Res.* **2014**, *6*, 743–748.
7. Shahat, A.A.; Ibrahim, A.Y.; Hendawy, S.F.; Omer, E.A.; Hammouda, F.M.; Abdel-Rahman, F.H.; Saleh, M.A. Chemical composition, antimicrobial and antioxidant activities of essential oils from organically cultivated fennel cultivars. *Molecules* **2011**, 1366–1377. [CrossRef] [PubMed]
8. Ghanem, I.; Audeh, A.; Alnaser, A.; Tayoub, G. Chemical constituents and insecticidal activity of the essential oil from fruits of *Foeniculum vulgare* Miller on larvae of khapra beetle (*Trogoderma granarium* Everts). *Herba Polonica* **2013**, *59*, 86–96. [CrossRef]
9. Tognolini, M.; Ballabeni, V.; Bertoni, S.; Bruni, R.; Impicciatore, M.; Barocelli, E. Protective effect of *Foeniculum vulgare* essential oil and anethole in an experimental model of thrombosis. *Pharmacol. Res.* **2007**, *56*, 254–260. [CrossRef] [PubMed]

10. Villarini, M.; Pagiotti, R.; Dominici, L.; Fatigoni, C.; Vannini, S.; Levorato, S.; Moretti, M. Investigation of the cytotoxic, genotoxic, and apoptosis-inducing effects of estragole isolated from fennel (*Foeniculum vulgare*). *J. Nat. Prod.* **2014**, *77*, 773–778. [CrossRef] [PubMed]
11. Bhardwaj, P.; Alok, U.; Khanna, A. In vitro cytotoxicity of essensial oils: A review. *Int. J. Res. Pharm. Chem.* **2013**, *3*, 675–681.
12. Heydarzade, A.; Moravvej, G. Contact toxicity and persistence of essential oils from *Foeniculum vulgare*, *Teucrium polium* and *Satureja hortensis* against *Callosobruchus maculatus* (Fabricius) (Coleoptera: Bruchidae) adults. *Turk. J. Entomol.* **2012**, *36*, 507–518.
13. Wink, M. Evolutionary advantage and molecular modes of action of multi-component mixtures used in phytomedicine. *Curr. Drug Metab.* **2008**, *9*, 996–1009. [CrossRef] [PubMed]
14. Bassi, A.M.; Penco, S.; Canuto, R.A.; Muzioa, G.; Ferro, M. Comparative evaluation of cytotoxicity and metabolism of four aldehydes in two hepatoma cell lines. *Drug Chem. Toxicol.* **1997**, *20*, 173–187. [CrossRef] [PubMed]
15. Sonboli, A.; Esmaeili, M.A.; Gholipour, A.; Kanani, M.R. Composition, cytotoxicity and antioxidant activity of the essential oil of *Dracocephalum surmandinum* from Iran. *Nat. Prod. Commun.* **2010**, *5*, 341–344.
16. Sharopov, F.S.; Wink, M.; Khalifaev, D.R.; Zhang, H.; Dosoky, N.S.; Setzer, W.N. Chemical composition and antiproliferative activity of the essential oil of *Galagania fragrantissima* Lipsky (Apiaceae). *Am. J. Essent. Oils Nat. Prod.* **2013**, *1*, 11–13.
17. Esterbauer, H.; Schaur, R.J.; Zollner, H. Chemistry and biochemistry of 4-hydroxynonenal, malonaldehyde and related aldehydes. *Free Radic. Biol. Med.* **1991**, *11*, 81–128. [CrossRef]
18. Zellagui, A.; Gherraf, N.; Elkhateeb, A.; Hegazy, M.F.; Mohamed, T.A.; Touil, A.; Shahat, A.; Rhouati, S. Chemical constitutents from Algerian *Foeniculum vulgare* aerial parts and evaluation of antimicrobial activity. *J. Chil. Chem. Soc.* **2011**, *56*, 759–763. [CrossRef]
19. Chowdhury, J.U.; Mobarak, H.; Bhuiyan, N.I.; Nandi, N.C. Constituents of essential oils from leaves and seeds of *Foeniculum vulgare* Mill. cultivated in Bangladesh. *Bangladesh J. Bot.* **2009**, *38*, 181–183. [CrossRef]
20. Dadaliogylu, I.; Evrendilek, G.A. Chemical compositions and antibacterial effects of essential oils of Turkish oregano (*Origanum minutiflorum*), bay laurel (*Laurus nobilis*), Spanish lavender (*Lavandula stoechas* L.), and fennel (*Foeniculum vulgare*) on common foodborne pathogens. *J. Agric. Food Chem.* **2004**, *52*, 8255–8260. [CrossRef] [PubMed]
21. Aprotosoaie, A.C.; Spac, A.; Hancianu, M.; Miron, A.; Tanasescu, V.F.; Dorneanu, V.; Stanescu, U. The chemical profile of essensial oils obtained from fennel fruits (*Foeniculum vulgare* Mill.). *Farmacia* **2010**, *58*, 46–53.
22. Radulovic, N.S.; Blagojevic, P.D. A note on the volatile secondary metabolites of *Foeniculum vulgare* Mill. (Apiaceae). *Facta Univ.* **2010**, *8*, 25–37. [CrossRef]
23. Stefanini, M.B.; Ming, L.C.; Marques, M.O.; Facanali, R.; Meireles, M.A.; Moura, L.S.; Marchese, J.A.; Sousa, L.A. Essential oil constituents of different organs of fennel (*Foeniculum vulgare* var. *vulgare*). *Braz. J. Med. Plants* **2006**, *8*, 193–198.
24. Adams, R.P. *Identification of Essential Oil Components by Gas Chromatography/Mass Spectrometry*, 4th ed.; Allured Publishing Co. Carol Stream: Carol Stream, IL, USA, 2007.
25. Sharopov, F.S.; Wink, M.; Setzer, W.N. Radical scavenging and antioxidant activities of essential oil components—An experimental and computational investigation. *Nat. Prod. Commun.* **2015**, *10*, 153–156. [PubMed]
26. Sharopov, F.S. Phytochemistry and Bioactivities of Selected Plant Species with Volatile Secondary Metabolites. Ph.D. Thesis, Ruperto-Carola University of Heidelberg, Heidelberg, Germany, 2015.
27. Sharopov, F.; Valiev, A.; Satyal, P.; Setzer, W.N.; Wink, M. Chemical composition and anti-proliferative activity of the essential oil of *Coriandrum sativum* L. *Am. J. Essent. Oils Nat. Prod.* **2017**, *5*, 11–15.
28. Zoubiri, S.; Baaliouamer, A. Chemical composition and insecticidal properties of some aromatic herbs essential oils from Algeria. *Food Chem.* **2011**, *129*, 179–182. [CrossRef]
29. Embong, M.B.; Hadziyev, D.; Molnar, S. Essential oils from spices grown in Alberta. Fennel oil (*Foeniculum vulgare* var. *dulce*). *Can. J. Plant Sci.* **1977**, *57*, 829–837. [CrossRef]
30. De Oliveira, P.F.; Alves, J.M.; Damasceno, J.L.; Oliveira, R.M.; Dias, H.J.; Crotti, A.M.; Tavares, D.C. Cytotoxicity screening of essential oils in cancer cell lines. *Rev. Bras. Farmacogn.* **2015**, *25*, 183–188. [CrossRef]

31. Zhao, N.N.; Zhou, L.; Liu, Z.L.; Du, S.S.; Deng, Z.W. Evaluation of the toxicity of the essential oils of some common Chinese spices against *Liposcelis bostrychophila*. *Food Control* **2012**, *26*, 486–490. [CrossRef]
32. Zeng, H.; Chen, X.; Liang, J. In vitro antifungal activity and mechanism of essential oil from fennel (*Foeniculum vulgare* l.) on dermatophyte species. *J. Med. Microbiol.* **2015**, *64*, 93–103. [CrossRef]
33. Pavela, R.; Zabka, M.; Bednar, J.; Tríska, J.; Vrchotova, N. New knowledge for yield, composition and insecticidal activity of essential oils obtained from the aerial parts or seeds of fennel (*Foeniculum vulgare* Mill.). *Ind. Crops Prod.* **2016**, *83*, 275–282. [CrossRef]
34. Muckensturm, B.; Foechterlen, D.; Reduron, J.P.; Dantont, T.P.; Hildenbrand, M. Phytochemical and chemotaxonomic studies of *Foeniculum vulgare*. *Biochem. Syst. Ecol.* **1997**, *25*, 353–358. [CrossRef]
35. Hashmi, N.; Khan, M.M.; Moinuddin; Idrees, M.; Khan, Z.H.; Ali, A.; Varshney, L. Depolymerized carrageenan ameliorates growth, physiological attributes, essential oil yield and active constituents of *Foeniculum vulgare* Mill. *Carbohydr. Polym.* **2012**, *90*, 407–412. [CrossRef] [PubMed]
36. Rahimmalek, M.; Maghsoudi, H.; Sabzalian, M.R.; Ghasemi Pirbalouti, A. Variability of essential oil content and composition of different Iranian fennel (*Foeniculum vulgare* Mill.) accessions in relation to some morphological and climatic factors. *J. Agric. Sci. Technol.* **2014**, *16*, 1365–1374.
37. Senatore, F.; Oliviero, F.; Scandolera, E.; Taglialatela-Scafati, O.; Roscigno, G.; Zaccardelli, M.; Falco, E.D. Chemical composition, antimicrobial and antioxidant activities of anethole-rich oil from leaves of selected varieties of fennel [*Foeniculum vulgare* Mill. ssp. *vulgare* var. *azoricum* (Mill.) Thell]. *Fitoterapia* **2013**, *90*, 214–219. [PubMed]
38. Han, A.Y.; Lee, H.S.; Seol, G.H. *Foeniculum vulgare* Mill. Increases cytosolic Ca^{2+} concentration and inhibits store-operated Ca^{2+} entry in vascular endothelial cells. *Biomed. Pharmacother.* **2016**, *84*, 800–805. [CrossRef] [PubMed]
39. Lahhit, N.; Bouyanzer, A.; Desjobert, J.M.; Hammouti, B.; Salghi, R.; Costa, J.; Jama, C.; Bentiss, F.; Majidi, L. Fennel (*Foeniculum vulgare*) essential oil as green corrosion inhibitor of carbon steel in hydrochloric acid solution. *Port. Electrochim. Acta* **2011**, *29*, 127–138. [CrossRef]
40. Sousa, R.M.; Rosa, J.S.; Oliveira, L.; Cunha, A.; Fernandes-Ferreira, M. Activities of Apiaceae essential oils and volatile compounds on hatchability, development, reproduction and nutrition of *Pseudaletia unipuncta* (Lepidoptera: Noctuidae). *Ind. Crops Prod.* **2015**, *63*, 226–237. [CrossRef]
41. Cioanca, O.; Hancianu, M.; Mircea, C.; Trifan, A.; Hritcu, L. Essential oils from Apiaceae as valuable resources in neurologicaldisorders: *Foeniculi vulgare aetheroleum*. *Ind. Crops Prod.* **2016**, *88*, 51–57. [CrossRef]
42. Gorbunova, E.V. Obosnovanie Osnovnich Elementov Technologii Kompleksnoy Pererabotki Sirya Fenchelya Obiknovennogo (*Foeniculum vulgare* Mill.). Ph.D. Thesis, Michurinsk State Agricultural University, Michurinsk, Russia, 2015.
43. Oezcan, M.M.; Chalchat, J.C.; Arslan, D.; Ateş, A.; Uenver, A. Comparative essential oil composition and antifungal effect of bitter fennel (*Foeniculum vulgare* ssp. *piperitum*) fruit oils obtained during different vegetation. *J. Med. Food* **2006**, *9*, 552–561.
44. Telci, I.; Demirtas, I.; Sahin, A. Variation in plant properties and essential oil composition of sweet fennel (*Foeniculum vulgare* Mill.) fruits during stages of maturity. *Ind. Crops Prod.* **2009**, *30*, 126–130. [CrossRef]
45. Timasheva, L.A.; Gorbunova, E.V. A promising trend in the processing of fennel (*Foeniculum vulgare* Mill.) whole plants. *Foods Raw Mater.* **2014**, *2*, 51–57. [CrossRef]
46. Singh, G.; Maurya, S.; Lampasona, M.P.; Catalan, C. Chemical constituents, antifungal and antioxidative potential of *Foeniculum vulgare* volatile oil and its acetone extract. *Food Control* **2006**, *17*, 745–752. [CrossRef]
47. Barazani, O.; Cohen, Y.; Fait, A.; Diminshtein, S.; Dudai, N.; Ravid, U.; Putievsky, E.; Friedman, J. Chemotypic differentiation in indigenous populations of *Foeniculum vulgare* var. *vulgare* in israel. *Biochem. Syst. Ecol.* **2002**, *30*, 721–731. [CrossRef]
48. Gross, M.; Friedman, J.; Dudai, N.; Larkov, O.; Cohen, Y.; Bar, E.; Ravid, U.; Putievsky, E.; Lewinsohn, E. Biosynthesis of estragole and t-anethole in bitter fennel (*Foeniculum vulgare* Mill. var. *vulgare*) chemotypes. Changes in sam: Phenylpropene o-methyltransferase activities during development. *Plant Sci.* **2002**, *163*, 1047–1053.
49. Franz, C.; Novak, J. Sources of essential oils. In *Handbook of Essential Oils: Science, Technology, and Applications*; Baser, K.H.C., Buchbauer, G., Eds.; CRC Press: Boca Raton, FL, USA; London, UK; New York, NY, USA, 2010; p. 994.

50. Amorati, R.; Foti, M.C.; Valgimigli, L. Antioxidant activity of essential oils. *J. Agric. Food Chem.* **2013**, *61*, 10835–10847. [CrossRef] [PubMed]
51. Ettorre, A.; Frosali, S.; Andreassi, M.; Stefano, A.D. Lycopene phytocomplex, but not pure lycopene, is able to trigger apoptosis and improve the efficacy of photodynamic therapy in HL60 human leukemia cells. *Exp. Biol. Med.* **2010**, *235*, 1114–1125. [CrossRef] [PubMed]
52. Giovannini, D.; Gismondi, A.; Basso, A.; Canuti, L.; Braglia, R.; Canini, A.; Mariani, F.; Cappelli, G. *Lavandula angustifolia* Mill. essential oil exerts antibacterial and anti-inflammatory effect in macrophage mediated immune response to *Staphylococcus aureus*. *Immunol. Investig.* **2016**, *45*, 11–28.
53. Kulbacka, J.; Daczewska, M.; Dubińska-Magiera, M.; Choromańska, A.; Rembiałkowska, N.; Surowiak, P.; Kulbacki, M.; Kotulska, M.; Saczko, J. Doxorubicin delivery enhanced by electroporation to gastrointestinal adenocarcinoma cells with P-gp overexpression. *Bioelectrochemistry* **2014**, *100*, 96–104. [CrossRef] [PubMed]
54. Eid, S.Y.; El-Readi, Z.M.; Wink, M. Carotenoids reverse multidrug resistance in cancer cells by interfering with abc-transporters. *Phytomedicine* **2012**, *19*, 977–987. [CrossRef]
55. Russo, R.; Corasaniti, M.T.; Bagetta, G.; Morrone, L.A. Exploitation of cytotoxicity of some essential oils for translation in cancer therapy. *Evid. Based Complement. Altern. Med.* **2015**, *2015*. [CrossRef] [PubMed]
56. Astani, A.; Reichling, J.; Schnitzler, P. Screening for antiviral activities of isolated compounds from essential oils. *Evid. Based Complement. Altern. Med.* **2011**, *2011*. [CrossRef] [PubMed]
57. Nakagawa, Y.T.S. Cytotoxic and xenoestrogenic effects via biotransformation of *trans*-anethole on isolated rat hepatocytes and cultured mcf-7 human breast cancer cells. *Biochem. Pharmacol.* **2003**, *66*, 63–73. [CrossRef]
58. Muthukumari, D.; Padma, P.R.; Sumathi, S. In vitro analysis of anethole as an anticancerous agent for triple negative breast cancer. *Int. J. Pharm. Sci. Rev. Res.* **2013**, *23*, 314–318.

© 2017 by the authors. Licensee MDPI, Basel, Switzerland. This article is an open access article distributed under the terms and conditions of the Creative Commons Attribution (CC BY) license (http://creativecommons.org/licenses/by/4.0/).

Article

Thyme and Savory Essential Oil Vapor Treatments Control Brown Rot and Improve the Storage Quality of Peaches and Nectarines, but Could Favor Gray Mold

Karin Santoro [1,2,†], Marco Maghenzani [1,†], Valentina Chiabrando [1], Pietro Bosio [2], Maria Lodovica Gullino [1,2], Davide Spadaro [1,2,*] and Giovanna Giacalone [1]

1. Department of Agricultural, Forestry and Food Sciences (DISAFA), University of Turin, Largo Paolo Braccini 2 (ex-Via L. da Vinci 44), 10095 Grugliasco, Italy; karin.santoro@unito.it (K.S.); marco.maghenzani@unito.it (M.M.); valentina.chiabrando@unito.it (V.C.); marialodovica.gullino@unito.it (M.L.G.); giovanna.giacalone@unito.it (G.G.)
2. AGROINNOVA—Centre of Competence for the Innovation in the Agro-environmental Sector, University of Turin, Largo Paolo Braccini 2 (ex-Via L. da Vinci 44), 10095 Grugliasco, Italy; pietro.bosio@unito.it
* Correspondence: davide.spadaro@unito.it; Tel.: +39-011-6708-942
† These two authors contributed equally to this work.

Received: 6 November 2017; Accepted: 28 December 2017; Published: 5 January 2018

Abstract: The effect of biofumigation, through slow-release diffusors, of thyme and savory essential oils (EO), was evaluated on the control of postharvest diseases and quality of peaches and nectarines. EO fumigation was effective in controlling postharvest rots. Naturally contaminated peaches and nectarines were exposed to EO vapors for 28 days at 0 °C in sealed storage cabinets and then exposed at 20 °C for five days during shelf-life in normal atmosphere, simulating retail conditions. Under low disease pressure, most treatments significantly reduced fruit rot incidence during shelf-life, while, under high disease pressure, only vapors of thyme essential oil at the highest concentration tested (10% v/v in the diffusor) significantly reduced the rots. The application of thyme or savory EO favored a reduction of brown rot incidence, caused by *Monilinia fructicola*, but increased gray mold, caused by *Botrytis cinerea*. In vitro tests confirmed that *M. fructicola* was more sensitive to EO vapors than *B. cinerea*. Essential oil volatile components were characterized in storage cabinets during postharvest. The antifungal components of the essential oils increased during storage, but they were a low fraction of the volatile organic compounds in storage chambers. EO vapors did not influence the overall quality of the fruit, but showed a positive effect in reducing weight loss and in maintaining ascorbic acid and carotenoid content. The application of thyme and savory essential oil vapors represents a promising tool for reducing postharvest losses and preserving the quality of peaches and nectarines.

Keywords: biofumigation; *Monilinia* spp.; *Botrytis* spp.; essential oils; stone fruit; postharvest disease

1. Introduction

Peaches and nectarines (*Prunus persica* (L.) Batsch) are fruit rich in vitamins, fibers and other phytochemical compounds, such as carotenes and polyphenols, which are important for a healthy diet [1,2]. Stone fruit are consumed worldwide and represent one of the most important fruit. In recent years, peach and nectarine production increased progressively [3] and the main global producer is China with over 12 million tons, followed by Spain and Italy, which produce 3 million tons annually [4]. Peaches and nectarines are the 3rd most important fruit crop in the European Union after apples and pears [5].

During storage, the quality characteristics and some commercial parameters of these fruit can decrease, at a rate depending on the storage conditions, due to postharvest diseases and senescence processes [6].

The most common postharvest pathogens on stone fruit are *Monilinia* spp. (*M. fructigena* Honey, *M. fructicola* (G. Winter) Honey, and *M. laxa* (Aderh. and Ruhland) Honey), agents of brown rot, *Botrytis cinerea* Pers. agent of gray mold, *Penicillium expansum* Link, agent of blue mold, *Alternaria* spp., agent of black mold, and *Rhizopus stolonifer*, Ehrenb., agent of Rhizopus rot [7,8]. On peaches, postharvest losses can cause even higher damage than preharvest diseases [9]. Crop protection in Europe should be performed in the orchard because only one fungicide (fludioxonil) can be used on stone fruit after harvesting, but the supermarket chains typically request either no further postharvest treatments or a limited number of active ingredients, as residues, on the fruit. The last fungicide has to be applied 1 or 2 weeks before harvesting, to guarantee a high level of fruit protection against pathogens during storage, and to remain below the maximum residue limits imposed by European legislation [10]. Moreover, consumer attention is attracted by environmentally friendly production practices, preferring foods treated with natural products instead of conventional pesticides [11]. At present, *Monilinia* spp. control depends on an integrated strategy based on orchard fungicide spray programs and maintenance of proper storage conditions in the packinghouse and during distribution [12].

Hence, intense research efforts focus on developing innovative, unconventional, sustainable strategies to preserve fruit quality and decrease food losses. The most promising control approaches are the use of microorganisms and natural products with intrinsic antimicrobial properties [13,14]. Essential oils (EOs) represent a powerful tool to reduce the environmental impact of fruit production [15]. The efficacy of plant EOs has been extensively evaluated in vitro [16], but a few studies have been performed in vivo [17]. However, these treatments may modify the organoleptic characteristics of fruit, changing taste or flavor during cold storage.

The antifungal activity of EOs is determined by their chemical composition. In particular, aldehydes, phenols and ketones considerably inhibit pathogen growth. Thymol, carvacrol and *p*-anisaldehyde have a proven fungicidal activity and EOs rich in these components showed the highest inhibitory activity against many postharvest pathogens, such as *Penicillium digitatum* [18], *Colletotrichum gloeosporioides* [19] and *R. stolonifer* [20]. EOs of thyme (*Thymus vulgaris*) and savory (*Satureja montana*) are mainly composed of thymol and carvacrol [21], which are highly effective in controlling fungal pathogens. Generally, the efficacy of EOs is investigated through direct contact with fruit, by application through spraying or dipping [22]. However, these application methods can have undesired effects, including phytotoxicity and organoleptic modification of treated fruit. Only a few studies have reported the efficacy of EO treatments through biofumigation, focusing on phytopathological aspects [23]. Scientific research recently started to pay particular attention to the assessment of the antifungal activity of EO vapors [24,25]. Fumigation with thyme and savory EOs resulted in effective control of several postharvest pathogens, showing antifungal activity against *Colletotrichum* [26], *Aspergillus*, *Penicillium*, *Mucor* and *Trichoderma* spp. [27] The use of EOs through fumigation avoids the direct contact with the product, reducing the possibility of influencing the sensorial profile.

The aim of this study was to investigate the effect of the vapor phase of thyme and savory EOs, applied by fumigation through slow-release diffusors, on both quality parameters and postharvest diseases of peaches and nectarines, during cold storage and shelf life. Savory and thyme solid diffusors were prepared at two different concentrations and they were used to treat naturally infected peaches and nectarines. In order to clarify how essential oils diffuse and persist in cold rooms, the atmospheric composition of the storage cabinets was analyzed during cold storage. At the same time, the antimicrobial activity of essential oil vapors was evaluated in vitro on conidial germination of *M. fructicola* and *B. cinerea*, two of the main postharvest pathogens of peaches and nectarines.

2. Materials and Methods

The EOs of thyme (*Thymus vulgaris*) and savory (*Satureja montana*) used in the assays were prepared by Soave (Turin, Italy). The compositional analyses were performed using a gas chromatograph

Shimadzu GC-2010 Plus (Shimadzu, Kyoto, Japan) equipped with a mass spectrometer GCMS-QP 2010 Ultra (Shimadzu) and a split-splitless injector. The gas chromatograph was fitted with a 30 m × 0.25 mm fused silica capillary Zebron ZB-5MSi column (Phenomenex, Torrance, CA, USA) with 0.25 µm film thickness. Helium carrier gas using a linear velocity of 37 cm/s with a constant flow rate of 1.0 mL/min was used. The pressure was 55 kPa and total flow was 105 mL/min. Ion electron impact spectra at 70 eV were recorded in scan mode (30–700 m/z).

For savory essential oil, the oven program started with an initial temperature of 50 °C for 3 min, heating at 5 °C/min to 70 °C, 70 °C for 5 min, heating at 1 °C/min to 90 °C, heating at 5 °C/min to 150 °C, and finally heating at 40 °C/min to 270 °C, held for 5 min. For thyme essential oil, the same protocol was used without the isothermal phase at 70 °C for 5 min. For both essential oils, the injection temperature was set at 250 °C and the ion source and the interface were both set at 280 °C.

Pure essential oil of savory and thyme were diluted at 1% and 10% in *n*-hexane (VWR, Radnor, PA, USA) for direct injection using split mode (80%). Sampling in the chambers was performed using SPME fiber assembly 100 µm PDMS (Supelco Analytical, Bellefonte, PA, USA) for 5 min in triplicate at 1, 14 and 28 days of incubation whereby the injector was in splitless mode. Relative composition (percentage) of volatile compounds was calculated by comparing peak area to area of total chromatogram (from 7.5 to 40 min). Absolute quantification was calculated for carvacrol and thymolusing a standard calibration curve between 1 and 50 ppm (mg/L). Relative quantification was determined for the other compounds, by using standard calibration curve of thymol for thyme essential oil and standard calibration curve of carvacrol for savory essential oil.

Peaches ('Vista Rich') and nectarines ('Sweet Red') were harvested from two different orchards located in Lagnasco (Cuneo, Italy, 44°37′33″60 N, 07°33′21″24 E) at the firm-ripe stage and transported immediately to the laboratory of DISAFA, University of Torino, during the summer of 2015. All fruit were sorted by size. Defect-free fruit were randomly divided into five lots of 350 fruit each. Each lot was treated in a different way and further divided into 5 replicates of 70 fruit. Each replicate was a box kept in a container at the same temperature, but different atmosphere according to the treatment.

EO diffusors were made by adding EO (10% v/v), sterilized deionized water (88% v/v) and Tween 20 (2% v/v) (Merck, Darmstadt, Germany) to agar-agar (Merck) (15 g/L). Lower EO concentrations were obtained by serial dilutions. 50 mL of medium were poured into Petri dishes and after agar solidification, 5 diffusors were installed in storage cabinets under the fruit boxes. Fruit were stored in refrigerator cabinets (75 × 70 × 65 cm) at 0 °C and 98% relative humidity for 28 days. Fumigation was performed at 1% and 10% EO concentrations. A total of four treatments were tested: thyme EO at 1%, thyme EO at 10%, savory EO at 1% and savory EO at 10%. An untreated control was included. The analyses were performed at 1, 14 and 28 days of cold storage.

After harvesting, healthy sound fruit were selected. Rotten fruit were counted and incidence of diseased fruit was calculated for each treatment every 7 days up to 28 days of storage, and for 5 days of shelf life at 20 °C. Pathogens were isolated by transferring small pieces of symptomatic fruit tissues, previously washed in 1% sodium hypochlorite and rinsed in sterile deionized water, onto potato dextrose agar (PDA, Merck) plates amended with 25 mg/L streptomycin sulfate (Merck). A 7-day-old culture was used for DNA extraction by using the EZNA Plant DNA Kit (Omega Bio-Tek, Norcross, GA, USA). The internal transcribed spacer (ITS) region of rDNA of 50 isolates was amplified using the ITS1/ITS4 primers [28]. The PCR reaction mixture comprised 2 µL 10 × PCR buffer, 1 µL ITS1 primer at 10 mM, 1 µL of ITS4 primer at 10 mM, 1 µL of nucleotides mixture at 5 mM, 12 µL of MilliQ autoclaved water, 0.8 µL of $MgCl_2$ at 25 mM, 0.2 µL of Taq polymerase and 2 µL of template DNA. PCR cycles included a denaturing step at 95 °C for 2 min and 35 cycles as follows: 94 °C for 30 s, 55 °C for 30 s, 72 °C for 1 min and a final elongation step at 72 °C for 7 min. ITS amplicons were sequenced by BMR Genomics (Padua, Italy), and DNA sequences were compared with those present in the NCBI database and deposited with accession numbers.

The effect of essential oils on conidial germination was investigated on two main peach and nectarine pathogens, *B. cinerea* and *M. fructicola*. Two virulent strains isolated from peaches were stored on agar slant at 4 °C until use. B. cinerea conidial suspension was obtained from 15 days of culture grown on PDA+ streptomycin 25 mg/L at 25 °C. M. fructicola was cultured on tomato agar plate (250 mL of tomato puree, 750 mL of deionized water and 20 g of agar) amended with 25 mg of streptomycin for 5 days. 5 mL of sterile deionized water were added to the plate and the mycelium was gently scraped with L-shaped spreader to detach the conidia. Conidial suspension was filtered through four layers of sterile cheesecloth and 100 µL were spread on PDA+ streptomycin plates. PDA plates were sealed with the essential oil diffusor. EOs were added to the diffusors at 350 µL/L and 35 µL/L, a concentration proportional to the quantity present in the cabinet considering the concentration of EO diffusor, the number of diffusors per cabinet and the volume of the cabinet and the plates. Conidial germination was assessed after 20 h for B. cinerea and 36 h for M. fructicola counting 100 conidia per plate. Three replicates were used for each treatment and the assay was repeated twice. Conidia were considered germinated when the germ tube exceeded the conidial length.

Weight loss was determined by weighing 30 fruit per treatment at the beginning of the trial (zero time) and during storage (7, 14, 21 and 28 days of storage, and at 5 days for shelf life). Values are reported as shown in Equation (1).

$$\% \; weight \; loss = \frac{initial \; weight - final \; weight}{initial \; weight} \times 100 \quad (1)$$

The color parameters were measured weekly during cold storage, with a Minolta chromameter (CR400, Konica Minolta Sensing, Inc., Osaka, Japan), calibrated with a standard white plate, using the CIE L*C*h (lightness, chroma/saturation and hue angle) scale. The surface of 30 fruit (ground and over color) was evaluated per treatment.

The carotenoid content was determined every 14 days, using the method reported by Talcott and Howard [29]. The carotenoids were extracted using 10 mL of extraction solvent (ethanol/acetone w/w with 0.2% butylhydroxytoluene) and 2 g of fresh sample from 10 fruit, homogenized at 24,000 rpm for 1 min using an Ultra-Turrax T-25 Tissue homogenizer (IKA®-Labortechnik, Saufen, Germany). The samples were then centrifuged at 2900 rpm for 20 min at 2 °C (Avanti J-25 centrifuge, Beckman Instruments, Palo Alto, CA, USA). The recovered supernatants were combined with 30 mL of extraction solvent, 25 mL of hexane and 12.5 mL of nanopure water. The tubes were left in the dark at 4 °C for 1 h, then the samples were transferred to quartz cuvettes. Absorbance was measured using a UV-visible spectrophotometer (DU 530, Beckman Coulter, Brea, CA, USA) at 450 nm, with β-carotene as an external standard. The results are expressed as µg β-carotene equivalents per kg weight of fruit and are an average of three replicates per treatment and per time point (at 0, 14 and 28 days of storage).

Ascorbic acid (AA) was determined according to Sánchez-Moreno et al. [30] and González-Molina et al. [31], and evaluated at 0, 14 and 28 days (three replicates per treatment and per time point). The ascorbic acid was extracted using 10 mL of extraction solvent (methanol:water 5:95 v/v) and 10 g of fruit flesh from 10 fruit per treatment by homogenization with a T-25 Ultra-Turrax for 3 min. Then, pH was adjusted to 2.2–2.4, and the extract was adsorbed onto a C18 Sep-Pak cartridge (Waters Associates, Milford, MA, USA). The resultant solution was added to 1,2-phenylenediamine dihydrochloride (Fluka Chemika, Neu-Ulm, Switzerland) and left to stand for 37 min before HPLC analysis. The AA and dehydroascorbic acid contents were expressed as mg/kg fresh weight. Three replicate analyses were performed on the flesh. The chromatographic system (Agilent Technologies, Inc., Santa Clara, CA, USA) was equipped a Kinetex-C18 column (4.6 × 150 mm, 5 µm, Phenomenex, Torrance, CA, USA), a pump and a diode array detector. The system was controlled through HPLC online software (Agilent Technologies, Inc.) at 40 °C. The mobile phase (isocratic) comprised 50 mM monobasic potassium phosphate and 5 mM cetrimide (Sigma-Aldrich Corporation, Saint Louis, MO, USA) in methanol:water (5:95 v/v). The flow rate was 0.9 mL/min. The detector was set at 261 nm for AA and 348 for dehydroascorbic acid (DHAA). External calibration curves for AA and DHAA, respectively, were used for quantification. The total run time was 15 min. The detection limit is 0.5 mg/kg of fresh weight.

Analysis of variance (ANOVA) was performed on the data using Statistica v. 6.0 (Statsoft Inc., Tulsa, OK, USA). Least significant differences (LSD) at a significance level of 0.05 were used to compare treatment means with Tukey's test. Mean values for each time point were considered significantly different at $p \leq 0.05$.

3. Results and Discussion

The vapor phase activity makes EOs potential biofumigants of fruit in storage chambers. Slow release diffusors, based on EO gel emulsions, were used to release EO vapor phase during the storage of peaches and nectarines. Pathogens were not inoculated, so only natural pathogen inoculum could develop both on nectarines and peaches.

EO fumigation was effective in controlling postharvest rots of peaches and nectarines, but the efficacy was different in the two experimental conditions. During cold storage, no rots developed either on nectarines 'Sweet Red' or on 'Vista Rich' peaches. Rot incidence on nectarines 'Sweet Red' and peaches 'Vista Rich' greatly differed during shelf life (5 days at 20 °C). After shelf life, on nectarines the rot incidence in untreated fruit was 23.3%, while most peaches (99.3%) were rotten in untreated control (Figure 1).

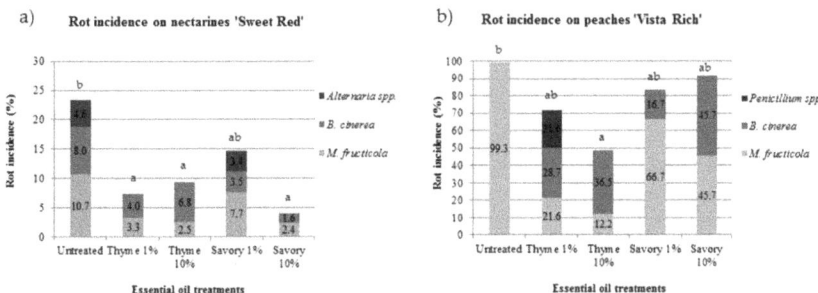

Figure 1. Rot incidence in nectarines 'Sweet Red' (**a**) and peaches 'Vista Rich' (**b**) treated with essential oil biofumigation and pathogen incidence (%) at the end of shelf life (5 days at 20 °C after 28 days of cold storage). Values of the same storage trial, followed by the same letter, are not statistically different by Tukey's Test ($p < 0.05$).

Disease incidence was influenced by the weather conditions during fruit growing. A high incidence of brown rot on peaches, which were harvested one month before nectarines, was favored by fresh and humid weather conditions, while nectarines were harvested in August, after a period characterized by high temperatures and scarce precipitations, which limited the development of brown rot [32].

Untreated control showed the highest percentage of rotten fruit in both trials. The pathogens isolated from rotten fruit were identified using morphological and molecular tools. On nectarines, the postharvest pathogens isolated from untreated fruit were *Monilinia fructicola*, *Botrytis cinerea*, and *Alternaria* spp. (Table 1), with an incidence of 10.7%, 8.0% and 4.6%, respectively.

Table 1. GenBank accession numbers of ITS sequences of some pathogenic isolates from nectarines 'Sweet Red'.

Isolated Strains	GenBank Accession Number
CaF1—*Botrytis cinerea*	KX304007
S1cF3—*Botrytis cinerea*	KX304008
CcF5—*Monilinia fructicola*	KX304009
S1aF1—*Monilinia fructicola*	KX304010
Cb22—*Alternaria* sp.	KX304011
Cc12—*Alternaria* sp.	KX304012

The efficacy of the EO treatments was influenced by the disease incidence: under low disease pressure, three out of four treatments significantly reduced the fruit rot incidence, while under high disease pressure, only vapors of thyme at 10% significantly reduced the rots compared to the control.

On nectarines, savory EO at 10% was the most effective treatment, with only 4.0% of the fruit damaged by postharvest pathogens. All the treatments were effective in controlling postharvest diseases, except for savory EO at 1%, which was not statistically different from the control at the end of the shelf life (Figure 1a). Thyme EO was very effective in controlling *M. fructicola*. The increase in EO concentration resulted in a decrease of brown rot. *B. cinerea* was isolated with an incidence of 4.0% and 6.8% for 1% and 10% thyme EO treatment, respectively.

On nectarines, *M. fructicola* was the major pathogen in untreated fruit (47.2% of rotten fruit), while the relative incidence decreased to 45.0% and 26.8% in fruit treated with thyme EO at 1% and 10%, respectively. *B. cinerea* affected 34.3%, 55.0% and 73.2% of rotten fruit in the control, in thyme at 1% and at 10%, respectively. After the first report of *M. fructicola* in Italy in 2009 [33], the pathogen has mainly substituted the endemic species *M. laxa* in Italian orchards.

Moreover, *Alternaria* spp. was not isolated in fruit fumigated with thyme EO. Savory EO vapors were less effective in controlling this pathogen because only 10% concentration inhibited *Alternaria* spp. growth, while 3.4% of fruit fumigated with 1% savory EO showed *Alternaria* rot. Reduced activity against *Alternaria* spp. was reported for savory essential oil, moreover the essential oil at 400 ppm favored *Alternaria* rot [34]. *Alternaria* spp. is a secondary pathogen of nectarines and the presence on the samples is mainly due to long storage.

On peaches, under high disease pressure, untreated fruit were completely damaged by brown rot. On fruit fumigated with EOs, *M. fructicola*, *B. cinerea* and *Penicillium* spp. were isolated (Figure 1b). The efficacy of thyme EO against *M. fructicola* depended on its concentration. *M. fructicola* affected only 30% and 25% of the rotten fruit fumigated with 1% and 10% thyme EO, respectively.

B. cinerea, the causal agent of gray mold, is uncommon on peaches, but its presence can be higher when the incidence of brown rot is low [35]. The application of thyme or savory EO, both on nectarines and on peaches favored a reduction of brown rot incidence, but a concomitant increase of gray mold.

In accordance with the literature, *M. fructicola* was very sensitive to thyme essential oil [36]. The fungicidal properties of thyme EO are mainly due to thymol, recognized as the most active phenolic compound against postharvest molds [37].

The chemical composition of the EO used in the trial was determined by direct injection. Principal volatile compounds present in pure thyme essential oil were thymol (26.0%), followed by p-cymene, α-terpineol and linalool (Table 2).

As diffusors, based on EO gel emulsions, were used to release EO vapor phase during the fruit storage, we wanted to determine the concentration of EO compounds in the atmosphere of the chambers during fruit cold storage. The analyses performed in chambers with thyme EO diffusors at 1% and 10% showed a very high amount of p-cymene, the main volatile organic compound at 1, 14 and 28 days. Thymol, instead, was on average 2.0% during the three samplings in thyme EO at 10%, while in thyme EO at 1% thymol was 0.40%, 3.66% and 3.67% at day 1, 14 and 28, respectively. Thymol in storage chambers was released slowly and at lower concentration, compared to the pure essential oil composition. This experiment demonstrated that thymol was slowly released by diffusors during the 28 days of fruit storage in cold chambers, and persisted by increasing in absolute concentration during storage.

Regarding savory essential oil, direct injection showed that the principal volatile compound was linalool (22.2%), followed by carvacrol (13.3%), thymol (10.7%) and eucalyptol (Table 3).

Table 2. Thyme essential oil composition and volatilized compounds in storage cabinet at 1, 14 and 28 days.

EO * Components	DI ** (%)	Thyme 10%						Thyme 1%					
		T1		T14		T28		T1		T14		T28	
		ppm	(%)	ppm	(%)	ppm	(%)	ppm	(%)	ppm	(%)	ppm	(%)
α-Pinene	3.59	17.35	2.59	35.32	4.19	48.44	4.64	3.76	4.07	8.31	2.10	12.74	2.60
Camphene	0.98	7.27	1.05	15.76	1.84	21.53	2.04	1.25	1.06	2.40	0.54	4.71	0.91
β-Pinene	0.30	3.29	0.45	6.53	0.74	8.58	0.79	0.36	0.00	1.49	0.30	2.24	0.39
Myrcene	0.89	12.17	1.80	18.66	2.19	29.39	2.80	2.18	2.18	4.25	1.03	7.05	1.40
p-Cimene	23.52	321.89	49.07	372.43	44.56	397.13	38.30	53.21	63.38	78.13	20.59	99.92	20.89
Linalool	8.00	96.47	14.67	135.54	16.19	166.85	16.07	3.17	3.36	94.47	24.91	100.66	21.04
Fenchol	0.45	5.55	0.79	9.23	1.06	13.69	1.29	0.36	0.00	5.39	1.33	6.00	1.18
Terpinen-1-ol	2.30	14.71	2.19	22.45	2.65	31.92	3.05	0.87	0.61	19.67	5.11	24.85	5.14
Camphor	0.37	3.01	0.40	4.07	0.44	6.96	0.64	1.88	1.82	3.31	0.78	4.07	0.78
β-Terpineol	1.03	6.58	0.95	11.02	1.28	15.79	1.49	0.60	0.28	9.20	2.34	11.39	2.31
Isoborneol	0.71	9.05	1.33	13.79	1.61	19.85	1.88	0.36	0.00	9.77	2.49	11.43	2.32
Borneol	1.90	12.65	1.88	22.71	2.68	29.65	2.83	0.36	0.00	29.14	7.62	22.55	4.65
Terpinen-4-ol	0.67	5.36	0.76	7.32	0.83	10.79	1.01	0.36	0.00	6.00	1.49	7.01	1.39
α-Terpineol	13.40	30.12	4.54	53.57	6.37	74.71	7.18	1.51	1.37	50.54	13.28	64.49	13.45
γ-Terpineol	2.60	6.73	0.97	10.74	1.24	14.32	1.35	0.36	0.00	11.19	2.86	13.30	2.71
Thymol	26.02	4.28	0.60	23.56	2.78	28.07	2.67	0.69	0.40	14.17	3.66	17.87	3.67

* EO: essential oil; ** DI: disease index.

Table 3. Savory essential oil composition and volatilized compounds in storage cabinet at 1, 14 and 28 days.

EO * Components	DI ** (%)	Savory 10%						Savory 1%					
		T1		T14		T28		T1		T14		T28	
		ppm	(%)	ppm	(%)	ppm	(%)	ppm	(%)	ppm	(%)	ppm	(%)
α-Pinene	0.76	4.64	0.48	16.27	0.76	12.06	0.64	1.35	0.20	2.03	0.23	3.63	0.40
Myrcene	0.47	5.33	0.56	15.19	0.70	16.70	0.89	1.31	0.19	1.59	0.16	5.15	0.59
p-Cymene	10.63	119.89	13.71	297.20	14.17	248.17	13.62	34.46	7.43	41.12	5.78	55.77	6.96
Eucalyptol	7.71	185.98	21.30	442.63	21.11	394.67	21.67	138.52	30.15	113.11	16.01	160.06	20.09
γ-Terpinen	9.45	128.33	14.68	284.79	13.57	234.37	12.86	38.00	8.20	46.39	6.53	62.31	7.79
trans-Linalool oxide	1.19	11.95	1.32	42.58	2.01	51.48	2.81	2.15	0.38	9.50	1.29	12.76	1.55
cis-Linalool oxide	0.86	9.49	1.04	29.57	1.39	37.81	2.05	1.63	0.26	6.31	0.83	9.31	1.12
Linalool	22.16	183.71	21.03	418.00	19.93	384.31	21.10	138.19	30.08	286.32	40.63	273.29	34.33
Plinol	0.34	4.47	0.46	12.46	0.57	13.33	0.71	2.90	0.54	6.90	0.92	7.25	0.86
Isoborneol	1.09	10.89	1.20	29.90	1.41	31.05	1.68	7.20	1.48	18.72	2.60	18.43	2.26
Borneol	2.24	13.44	1.49	32.25	1.52	36.66	1.99	9.48	1.98	23.08	3.22	27.94	3.46
α-Terpineol	1.36	4.51	0.47	10.31	0.47	12.11	0.64	3.64	0.70	7.27	0.97	9.71	1.17
Carvone	2.09	7.26	0.78	15.48	0.72	17.10	0.92	8.24	1.70	16.99	2.35	16.76	2.05
Borlyl acetate	1.55	9.84	1.08	20.52	0.96	16.98	0.91	11.08	2.32	12.70	1.74	10.59	1.28
Thymol	10.67	1.59	0.17	6.65	0.36	9.43	0.60	1.65	0.34	4.78	0.75	8.77	1.27
Carvacrol	13.29	1.68	0.14	10.38	0.47	11.90	0.63	2.19	0.38	6.41	0.85	11.66	1.41

* EO: essential oil; ** DI: disease index.

In storage room atmosphere, where savory diffusors at 10% were used, linalool and eucalyptol were the main components at the three sampling times. On the contrary, thymol and carvacrol in chambers showed a significant decrease compared to the pure EO, in fact they were present at 0.14% to 0.63% for carvacrol and at 0.17% to 0.60% for thymol at the beginning and at the end of the trial, respectively.

These results showed that antifungal components of thyme and savory essential oils increased during storage, but they were a low fraction of the volatile organic compounds in the storage chambers, compared to their concentration in pure EO. For this reason, diffusors could be considered effective in a slow release of vapor EOs.

The antifungal activity of thyme and savory EO in vapor phase was demonstrated by performing an in vitro test in agar plate, where M. fructicola and B. cinerea could germinate in an atmosphere with the same concentration present in the cabinet (Figure 2).

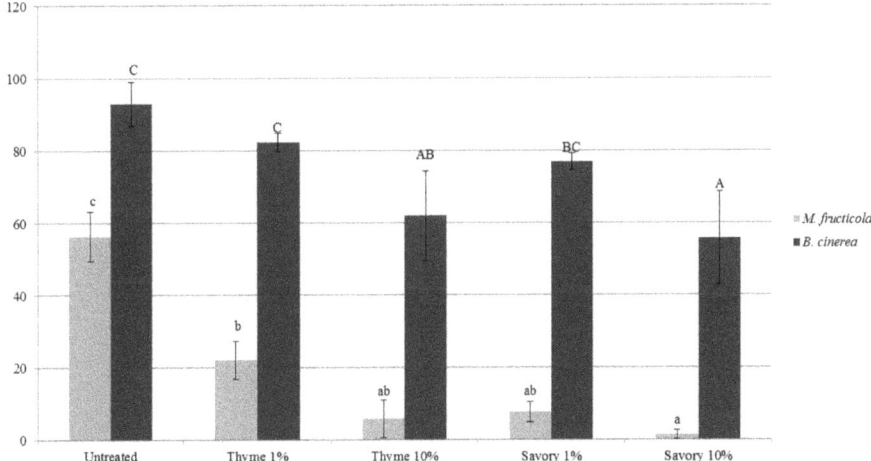

Figure 2. M. fructicola (gray columns) and B. cinerea conidial germination percentage (black columns) after biofumigation without direct contact with essential oil in vitro. Conidial germination was assessed after 20 h for B. cinerea and 36 h for M. fructicola at 20 °C. Values of the same pathogen, followed by the same letter, are not statistically different by Tukey's Test ($p < 0.05$).

The antifungal effects depended on the type and concentration of EO, and on the pathogen species [17]. M. fructicola was almost completely inhibited by savory vapors at 10%. Thyme essential oil vapors led to 40% decrease of conidial germination rate. As expected, vapor treatments were more effective in vitro, when EO concentration increased. All the EO treatments caused a significant decrease of germ tube length with respect to the untreated control (Table 4).

Table 4. Essential oil vapors effect on germ tube length in vitro measured after 36 h at 20 °C for M. fructicola and 20 h at 20 °C for B. cinerea.

	M. fructicola Germ Tube (μm)	B. cinerea Germ Tube (μm)
Untreated control	10.5 [b]	212.7 [c]
Thyme 1%	8.0 [a]	208.5 [bc]
Thyme 10%	6.5 [a]	190.9 [ab]
Savory 1%	8.6 [a]	165.6 [ab]
Savory 10%	5.8 [a]	109.9 [a]

Values of the same column, followed by the same letter within each column, are not statistically different by Tukey's Test ($p < 0.05$).

Previous results showed that thymol vapors inhibited *M. fructicola* mycelial growth and were fatal for conidia viability; the fumigated spores resulted shrunken and with collapsed protoplasts [38]. Thymol is able to crystallize on the outer surface of cell walls and exposed fungal structures were characterized by disrupted cell membranes and disorganized cytoplasmic organelles, reducing to 50% conidial viability at 2 µg/mL and to 17–23% when thymol was applied at 8 µg/mL [39].

B. cinerea is much less sensitive to essential oil antimicrobial activity [40]. In our experiments, the fungus confirmed to be less sensitive to EO vapors, compared to *M. fructicola* and maximum reduction of conidial germination was 40.1% for savory vapors at 10%. Germ tube length of *B. cinerea* growth was inhibited only by 10% thyme treatment, while the other treatments were not statistically different from the untreated control.

In vitro tests confirmed the results obtained in fruit: the antimicrobial activity of vapor EOs does not need a direct contact. Moreover, the higher efficacy against *M. fructicola*, compared to *B. cinerea* in vitro explained the higher reduction of brown rot on fruit, accompanied by a higher incidence of gray mold. This effect was particularly evident on peaches. Untreated fruit were affected exclusively by *M. fructicola*, while other pathogens could develop on fumigated fruits by colonizing the niche left empty by the inhibition of *M. fructicola*. Thanks to the lower sensitivity of *B. cinerea* to EO vapors, the pathogen could start to develop on fumigated fruit causing gray rots.

Besides the efficacy against the postharvest rots, weight loss, color, total soluble solids, titratable acidity, ascorbic acid and carotenoids contents were analyzed during fruit storage.

The use of thyme EO reduced weight loss particularly on peaches (Table 5).

Table 5. Weight loss (% w/w) of nectarines 'Sweet Red' and peaches 'Vista Rich'.

Fruit	Treatments	Weight Loss (% w/w)				
		Days of Storage				
		7	14	21	28	5 Shelf Life
Nectarines	Untreated control	0.55 ab	0.82 a	1.06 a	1.29 a	10.7 a
Nectarines	Thyme 1%	0.80 a	1.00 a	1.20 a	1.35 a	9.01 b
Nectarines	Thyme 10%	0.69 ab	0.85 a	1.04 a	1.20 a	9.22 ab
Nectarines	Savory 1%	0.55 ab	0.79 a	1.00 a	1.15 a	9.46 ab
Nectarines	Savory 10%	0.49 b	0.72 b	0.94 a	1.16 a	9.49 ab
Peaches	Untreated control	1.55 a	1.91 a	2.16 a	2.51 a	-
Peaches	Thyme 1%	1.31 a	1.42 c	1.72 c	1.81 c	-
Peaches	Thyme 10%	0.99 b	1.26 d	1.49 d	1.61 c	-
Peaches	Savory 1%	1.39 a	1.73 b	1.97 b	2.10 b	-
Peaches	Savory 10%	1.54 a	1.77 ab	1.97 b	2.10 b	-

Mean values followed by the same letter within each column are not significantly different by Tukey's Test at $p \leq 0.05$.

Untreated control showed the highest weight loss at the end of the storage in both trials. The efficacy of EO fumigation could be related to the formation of a coating on the fruit surface that modifies gas permeation, reducing respiration rate and water loss. Our results were in agreement with previous experiments on cherries [41], grapes [42], and peaches [43] treated with eugenol, thymol, menthol and cinnamon vapors. The EO vapors were shown to reduce the dehydration process or weight loss in fruit [44]. Other studies showed that the application of essential oils together with edible coatings could reduce the water loss [45]. There are few references reporting the effect of EO treatments on fruit color. Here, ground and overcolor lightness and hue angle were monitored during storage. The lightness values of the nectarines decreased both in ground and overcolor during cold storage (Table 6).

The differences among the treatments were observed at the end of the shelf life, when treated samples showed higher values than the untreated control. Regarding peaches, no differences among the treatments were detected (Table 7).

Table 6. Color parameters (lightness and hue angle) in nectarines with different treatments during storage.

Color Parameters	Ground or Overcolor	Treatments	Storage Times (Days)					
			0	7	14	21	28	5 Shelf Life
Lightness (L^*)	GC	Untreated control	68.70 a	67.86 a	67.78 a	68.6 a	68.28 a	63.71 b
	GC	Thyme 1%	67.75 a	65.38 a	65.64 a	67.57 a	65.97 ab	64.96 ab
	GC	Thyme 10%	67.67 a	65.32 a	65.37 a	67.17 a	65.64 b	64.07 ab
	GC	Savory 1%	68.79 a	65.55 a	66.81 a	67.18 a	67.67 ab	67.75 a
	GC	Savory 10%	68.38 a	66.85 a	65.79 a	67.84 a	68.14 ab	66.78 ab
Hue angle (h)	GC	Untreated control	82.44 a	86.25 a	83.73 a	84.12 a	84.25 a	66.16 a
	GC	Thyme 1%	80.28 a	79.73 b	78.39 a	77.91 b	78.98 ab	66.50 a
	GC	Thyme 10%	78.76 a	75.11 b	79.01 a	77.74 b	78.03 b	69.73 a
	GC	Savory 1%	81.59 a	79.55 b	79.37 a	81.31 ab	81.82 ab	70.29 a
	GC	Savory 10%	83.24 a	81.47 ab	81.43 a	81.35 ab	77.94 b	72.89 a
Lightness (L^*)	OC	Untreated control	40.20 a	48.11 a	41.64 a	38.34 b	39.79 a	44.19 ab
	OC	Thyme 1%	44.73 a	46.96 a	39.00 ab	42.03 a	40.12 a	39.63 b
	OC	Thyme 10%	40.16 a	42.41 b	37.45 b	42.65 a	37.45 a	43.93 ab
	OC	Savory 1%	45.20 a	43.14 b	37.54 b	35.68 b	38.76 a	48.14 a
	OC	Savory 10%	39.34 a	45.96 ab	37.81 ab	37.54 b	36.73 a	43.72 ab
Hue angle (h)	OC	Untreated control	20.28 a	42.58 a	33.75 a	27.32 b	30.88 a	29.58 ab
	OC	Thyme 1%	33.94 a	41.84 ab	32.78 a	34.52 a	31.80 a	20.80 c
	OC	Thyme 10%	25.68 a	36.69 b	31.23 a	29.67 b	28.32 a	28.27 bc
	OC	Savory 1%	33.49 a	38.3 ab	30.79 a	27.46 b	29.16 a	36.20 a
	OC	Savory 10%	25.19 a	40.64 ab	33.05 a	28.48 b	27.07 a	27.47 bc

Nectarines 'Sweet Red': GC: ground color; OC: over color. Mean values followed by the same letter within each column are not significantly different by Tukey's Test at $p \leq 0.05$. Letters in the same column are used to compare the treatment influence.

Table 7. Color parameters (lightness and hue angle) in peaches with different treatments during storage.

Color Parameters	Ground or Overcolor	Treatments	0	Storage Times (Days) 7	14	21	28
Lightness (L*)	GC	Untreated control	49.16 a	49.30 a	49.42 b	54.45 a	53.44 a
	GC	Thyme 1%	49.42 a	50.50 a	51.72 ab	54.24 a	52.97 a
	GC	Thyme 10%	49.43 a	51.55 a	51.52 ab	52.96 a	53.61 a
	GC	Savory 1%	49.62 a	52.08 a	54.46 ab	55.38 a	55.20 a
	GC	Savory 10%	49.20 a	51.07 a	54.46 a	54.04 a	52.85 a
Hue angle (h)	GC	Untreated control	43.12 a	57.21 a	60.76 b	68.78 a	65.62 a
	GC	Thyme 1%	46.06 a	63.87 a	67.13 ab	70.48 a	64.16 a
	GC	Thyme 10%	52.56 a	60.00 a	68.88 ab	66.61 a	66.40 a
	GC	Savory 1%	52.84 a	65.96 a	71.44 a	75.48 a	71.30 a
	GC	Savory 10%	48.81 a	59.94 a	69.11 ab	69.25 a	62.33 a
Lightness (L*)	OC	Untreated control	37.98 a	41.38 c	43.23 a	45.56 a	45.08 a
	OC	Thyme 1%	36.56 a	44.20 ab	44.28 a	43.57 a	45.39 a
	OC	Thyme 10%	34.24 a	44.79 ab	43.09 a	45.12 a	44.14 a
	OC	Savory 1%	34.86 a	45.30 a	42.15 a	43.93 a	45.73 a
	OC	Savory 10%	33.79 a	42.77 bc	43.54 a	43.74 a	46.35 a
Hue angle (h)	OC	Untreated control	15.22 a	35.06 bc	36.60 a	36.52 a	34.26 a
	OC	Thyme 1%	18.45 a	39.76 a	36.98 a	35.14 a	37.52 a
	OC	Thyme 10%	17.25 a	37.91 ab	35.01 a	37.18 a	34.56 a
	OC	Savory 1%	22.42 a	38.01 ab	33.45 a	35.07 a	36.34 a
	OC	Savory 10%	17.88 a	32.04 c	35.02 a	34.98 a	35.70 a

Peaches 'Vista Rich'. GC: ground color; OC: over color. Mean values followed by the same letter within each column are not significantly different by Tukey's Test at $p \leq 0.05$. Lowercase letters (a, b) in the same column are used to compare the treatment influence.

The hue angle is a measure of ripening. In general, the hue angle values of the ground color decrease during postharvest storage, as fruit become yellow. In nectarines, the hue angle remained stable during storage, but some differences among treatments were observed and nectarines treated with EOs were yellower than the control fruit. In peaches, the ground color became yellower during storage as expected, but no differences among treatments were observed. In conclusion, the use of EOs had no negative effect on fruit color. The color variations were connected with the natural ripening process and were slowed down by cold storage.

EO vapors influenced also carotenoid content preserving the amount of these antioxidant compounds in fumigated fruit. Generally, carotenoids decrease during storage. They are photo- and heat-sensitive and tend to oxidize if they are not protected from light and atmosphere [46]. In nectarines, only untreated control and fruit treated with savory EO at 1% showed a significant decrease in total carotenoid content during storage, while carotenoid amounts remained stable in the other fumigated fruit (Figure 3).

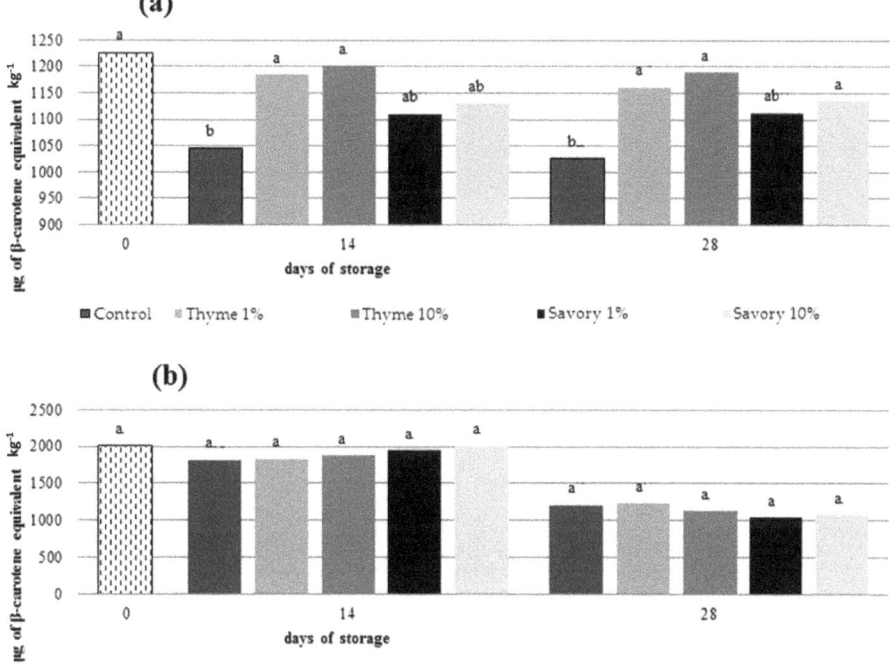

Figure 3. Total content of carotenoids in nectarines 'Sweet Red' (**a**) and peaches 'Vista Rich' (**b**) after 0, 14 and 28 days of cold storage. Mean values at the same time followed by the same letter are not significantly different by Tukey's Test at $p \leq 0.05$.

At the end of the trials, fruit treated with thyme at 1% and 10% had the highest amount of carotenoids (1189 µg/kg and 1162 µg/kg, respectively).

Both on nectarines and peaches, untreated fruit showed the lowest AA content at the end of cold storage resulting statistically different from treated fruit (Figure 4).

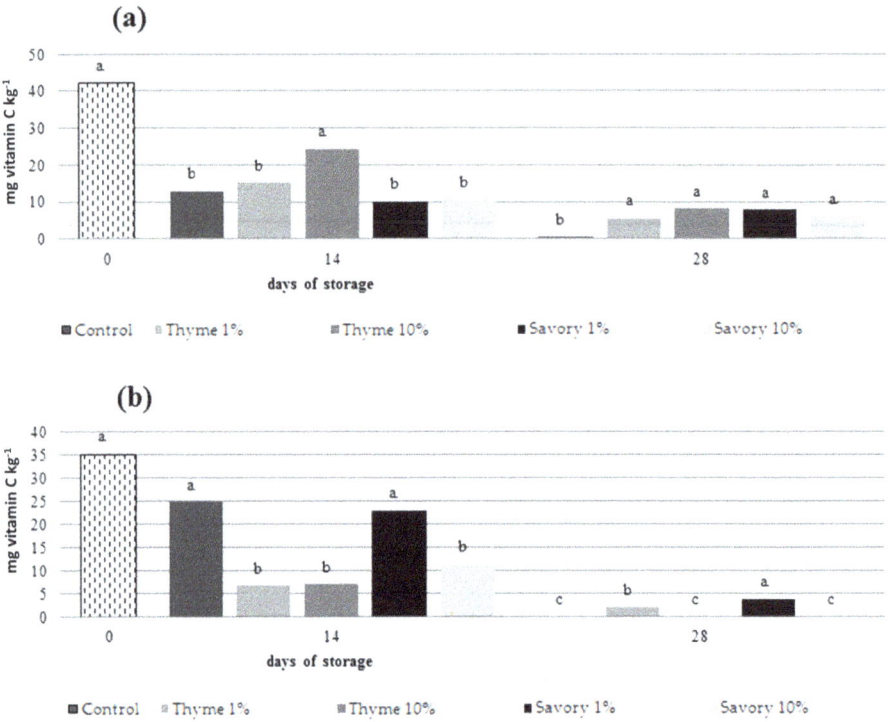

Figure 4. Total content of vitamin C (ascorbic acid and dehydroascorbic acid) in nectarines 'Sweet Red' (**a**) and peaches 'Vista Rich' (**b**) after 0, 14 and 28 days of cold storage. Mean values at the same time followed by the same letter are not significantly different by Tukey's Test at $p \leq 0.05$.

The use of EOs preserved ascorbic acid contents, without showing statistical differences between the treatments. In peaches, fruit fumigated with savory and thyme essential oils at 1% maintained the grater ascorbic acid content at the end of the trial.

The ascorbic acid content decreased significantly during cold storage, as expected, and the EO influenced the process. The decrease in ascorbic acid could be explained by the chemical properties and metabolic functions of AA in the plant cell [47]. AA and dehydroascorbic acid (DHAA) are important antioxidants and are used against the reactive oxygen species, produced naturally by the metabolism of vegetal cells, and accumulated during storage [48].

The use of EOs led to a delay in the loss of total carotenoids content and AA in the pulp. Some EOs (thymol, menthol and eugenol) have shown antioxidant activity and free radical scavenging capability [49]. These effects could explain the EO efficacy in reducing the loss of nutrients. Valero et al. (2006) [50] suggested that the addition of thymol slowed the AA loss in grape. Nevertheless, different effects of EOs on total carotenoids content between nectarines and peaches were evident. The EOs were more effective on the metabolism of nectarines, while in peaches the action of the EOs was less evident.

4. Conclusions

Savory and thyme essential oil vapors demonstrated a high antifungal activity against *M. fructicola* even at low concentrations. *B. cinerea* was less sensitive to EO vapors and could develop when *M. fructicola* was inhibited. EO concentrations require a careful optimization depending on fruit cultivars. Although in in vitro tests the efficacy is directly correlated with EO concentrations, when applied on fruit EO vapors could have phytotoxic effects, which reduce treatment efficacy. EO vapors did not influence the overall quality of the fruit, but showed a positive effect in maintaining nutritional values avoiding ascorbic acid and carotenoids oxidation, preserving the quality of the final product. The application of thyme and savory essential oils represents a promising tool for reducing postharvest losses and preserving quality in peaches and nectarines.

Acknowledgments: Work carried out with a contribution of the LIFE financial instrument of the European Union for the project "Low pesticide IPM in sustainable and safe fruit production" (Contract No. LIFE13 ENV/HR/000580).

Author Contributions: Davide Spadaro, Maria Lodovica Gullino, Valentina Chiabrando and Giovanna Giacalone conceived and designed the experiments; Karin Santoro performed the phytopathological, microbiological and molecular experiments, Marco Maghenzani performed fruit quality analyses, Pietro Bosio performed the gas chromatography analyses, Karin Santoro, Marco Maghenzani and Davide Spadaro wrote the paper.

Conflicts of Interest: The authors declare no conflict of interest. The founding sponsors had no role in the design of the study; in the collection, analyses, or interpretation of data; in the writing of the manuscript, and in the decision to publish the results.

References

1. Di Vaio, C.; Graziani, G.; Marra, L.; Cascone, A.; Ritieni, A. Antioxidant capacities, carotenoids and polyphenols evaluation of fresh and refrigerated peach and nectarine cultivars from Italy. *Eur. Food Res. Technol.* **2008**, *227*, 1225–1231. [CrossRef]
2. Gil, M.I.; Tomas-Barberan, F.A.; Hess-Pierce, B.; Kader, A.A. Antioxidant capacities, phenolic compounds, carotenoids, and vitamin C contents of nectarine, peach, and plum cultivars from California. *J. Agric. Food Chem.* **2002**, *50*, 4976–4982. [CrossRef] [PubMed]
3. Munera, S.; Amigo, J.M.; Blasco, J.; Cubero, S.; Talens, P.; Aleixos, N. Ripeness monitoring of two cultivars of nectarine using VIS-NIR hyperspectral reflectance imaging. *J. Food Eng.* **2017**, *214*, 29–39. [CrossRef]
4. Food and Agricultural Organisation of the United Nations. Available online: http://faostat3.fao.org/faostat-gateway/go/to/home/E (accessed on 29 December 2017).
5. García-Parra, J.; González-Cebrino, F.; Delgado, J.; Lozano, M.; Hernández, T.; Ramírez, R. Effect of thermal and high-pressure processing on the nutritional value and quality attributes of a Nectarine Purée with industrial origin during the refrigerated storage. *J. Food Sci.* **2011**, *76*, 618–625. [CrossRef] [PubMed]
6. Peano, C.; Giacalone, G.; Bounous, G. Changes in fruit quality of peache and nectarine from transport to shelf. *ISHS Acta Hortic.* **2000**, *553*, 739–740.
7. Karabulut, O.A.; Cohen, L.; Wiess, B.; Daus, A.; Lurie, S.; Droby, S. Control of brown rot and blue mold of peach and nectarine by short hot water brushing and yeast antagonists. *Postharvest Biol. Technol.* **2002**, *24*, 103–111. [CrossRef]
8. Zhang, H.; Zheng, X.; Yu, T. Biological control of postharvest diseases of peach with *Cryptococcus laurentii*. *Food Control* **2007**, *18*, 287–291. [CrossRef]
9. Larena, I.; Torres, R.; De Cal, A.; Liñán, M.; Melgarejo, P.; Domenichini, P.; Bellini, A.; Mandrin, J.F.; Lichou, J.; De Eribe, X.O.; et al. Biological control of postharvest brown rot (*Monilinia* spp.) of peaches by field applications of *Epicoccum nigrum*. *Biol. Control* **2005**, *32*, 305–310. [CrossRef]
10. Spadoni, A.; Guidarelli, M.; Sanzani, S.M.; Ippolito, A.; Mari, M. Influence of hot water treatment on brown rot of peach and rapid fruit response to heat stress. *Postharvest Biol. Technol.* **2014**, *94*, 66–73. [CrossRef]
11. Cindi, M.D.; Shittu, T.; Sivakumar, D.; Bautista-Baños, S. Chitosan boehmite-alumina nanocomposite films and thyme oil vapour control brown rot in peaches (*Prunus persica* L.) during postharvest storage. *Crop Prot.* **2015**, *72*, 127–131. [CrossRef]
12. Spadoni, A.; Neri, F.; Mari, M. Physical and chemical control of postharvest diseases. In *Advances in Postharvest Fruit and Vegetable Technology Contemporary Food Engineering*; Wills, R.B.H., Golding, J.B., Eds.; CRC Press: Boca Raton, FL, USA, 2016; pp. 98–102, ISBN 9781482216974.
13. Mari, M.; Bautista-Banos, S.; Sivakumar, D. Decay control in the postharvest system: Role of microbial and plant volatile organic compounds. *Postharvest Biol. Technol.* **2016**, *122*, 70–81. [CrossRef]

14. Spadaro, D.; Sabetta, W.; Acquadro, A.; Portis, E.; Garibaldi, A.; Gullino, M.L. Use of AFLP for differentiation of *Metschnikowia pulcherrima* strains for postharvest disease biological control. *Microbiol. Res.* **2008**, *163*, 523–530. [CrossRef] [PubMed]
15. Burt, S. Essential oils: Their antibacterial properties and potential applications in foods—A review. *Int. J. Food Microbiol.* **2004**, *94*, 223–253. [CrossRef] [PubMed]
16. Bakkali, F.; Averbeck, S.; Averbeck, D.; Idaomar, M. Biological effects of essential oils—A review. *Food Chem. Toxicol.* **2008**, *46*, 446–475. [CrossRef] [PubMed]
17. Lopez-Reyes, J.G.; Spadaro, D.; Prelle, A.; Garibaldi, A.; Gullino, M.L. Efficacy of plant essential oils on postharvest control of rots caused by fungi on different stone fruits in vivo. *J. Food Prot.* **2013**, *76*, 631–639. [CrossRef] [PubMed]
18. Daferera, D.J.; Ziogas, B.N.; Polissiou, M.G. GC-MS analysis of essential oils from some Greek aromatic plants and their fungitoxicity on *Penicillium digitatum*. *J. Agric. Food Chem.* **2000**, *48*, 2576–2581. [CrossRef] [PubMed]
19. Barrera-Nacha, L.L.; Bautista-Banos, S.; Flores-Moctezuma, H.E.; Estudillo, A.R. Efficacy of essential oils on the conidial germination, growth of *Colletrichum gleosporioides* (Penz.) Penz. and Sacc and control of postharvest disease in papaya (*Carica papaya* L.). *Plant Pathol.* **2008**, *7*, 1–5.
20. Spadaro, D.; Gullino, M.L. Use of essential oils to control postharvest rots on pome and stone fruit. In *Post-Harvest Pathology*; Prusky, D., Gullino, M.L., Eds.; Springer International Publishing: Cham, Switzerland, 2014; pp. 101–110, ISBN 978-3-319-07701-7.
21. Lopez-Reyes, J.G.; Spadaro, D.; Gullino, M.L.; Garibaldi, A. Efficacy of plant essential oils on postharvest control of rot caused by fungi on four cultivars of apples in vivo. *Flavour Fragr. J.* **2010**, *25*, 171–177. [CrossRef]
22. Elshafie, H.S.; Camele, I. Investigating the effects of plant essential oils on postharvest fruit decay. In *Fungal Pathogenicity*; InTech: London, UK, 2016; pp. 83–98, ISBN 978-953-51-2393-4.
23. Mehra, L.K.; MacLean, D.D.; Shewfelt, R.L.; Smith, K.C.; Scherm, H. Effect of postharvest biofumigation on fungal decay, sensory quality, and antioxidant levels of blueberry fruit. *Postharvest Biol. Technol.* **2013**, *85*, 109–115. [CrossRef]
24. Plaza, P.; Torres, R.; Usall, J.; Lamarca, N.; Vinas, I. Evaluation of the potential of commercial post-harvest application of essential oils to control citrus decay. *J. Hortic. Sci. Biotechnol.* **2004**, *79*, 935–940. [CrossRef]
25. Sciences, B.; Ziedan, E.H.E.; Farrag, E.S.H. Fumigation of peach fruits with essential oils to control postharvest decay. *Res. J. Agric. Biol. Sci.* **2008**, *4*, 512–519.
26. Sarkhosh, A.; Vargas, A.I.; Schaffer, B.; Palmateer, A.J.; Lopez, P.; Soleymani, A.; Farzaneh, M. Postharvest management of anthracnose in avocado (*Persea americana* Mill.) fruit with plant-extracted oils. *Food Packag. Shelf Life* **2017**, *12*, 16–22. [CrossRef]
27. Šegvić Klarić, M.; Kosalec, I.; Mastelić, J.; Piecková, E.; Pepeljnak, S. Antifungal activity of thyme (*Thymus vulgaris* L.) essential oil and thymol against moulds from damp dwellings. *Lett. Appl. Microbiol.* **2007**, *44*, 36–42. [CrossRef] [PubMed]
28. Glass, N.L.; Donaldson, G.C. Development of primer sets designed for use with the PCR to amplify conserved genes from filamentous ascomycetes. *Appl. Environ. Microbiol.* **1995**, *61*, 1323–1330. [PubMed]
29. Talcott, S.T.; Howard, L.R. Phenolic autoxidation is responsible for color degradation in processed carrot puree. *J. Agric. Food Chem.* **1999**, *47*, 2109–2115. [CrossRef] [PubMed]
30. Sánchez-Moreno, C.; Plaza, L.; De Ancos, B.; Cano, M. Vitamin C, Provitamin A carotenoids, and other carotenoids in high pressurized orange juice during refrigerated storage. *J. Agric. Food Chem.* **2003**, *51*, 647–653. [CrossRef] [PubMed]
31. Gonzàles-Molina, E.; Moreno, D.A.; Garcìa-Viguera, C. Genotype and harvest time influence the phytochemical quality of fino lemon juice (*Citrus limon* (L.) Burm. F.) for industrial use. *J. Agric. Food Chem.* **2008**, *56*, 1669–1675. [CrossRef] [PubMed]
32. Mari, M.; Martini, C.; Guidarelli, M.; Neri, F. Postharvest biocontrol of *Monilinia laxa*, *Monilinia fructicola* and *Monilinia fructigena* on stone fruit by two *Aureobasidium pullulans* strains. *Biol. Control* **2012**, *60*, 132–140. [CrossRef]
33. Pellegrino, C.; Gullino, M.L.; Garibaldi, A.; Spadaro, D. First report of brown rot of stone fruit caused by *Monilinia fructicola* in Italy. *Plant Dis.* **2009**, *93*, 668. [CrossRef]
34. Babagoli, M.A.; Behdad, E. Effects of three essential oils on the growth of the fungus *Alternaria solani*. *J. Res. Agric. Sci.* **2012**, *8*, 45–57.

35. Fourie, J.F.; Holz, G. Initial infection processes by *Botrytis cinerea* on nectarine and plum fruit and the development of decay. *Phytopathology* **1995**, *85*, 82–87. [CrossRef]
36. Lazar-Baker, E.E.; Hetherington, S.D.; Ku, V.V.; Newman, S.M. Evaluation of commercial essential oil samples on the growth of postharvest pathogen *Monilinia fructicola* (G. Winter) Honey. *Lett. Appl. Microbiol.* **2011**, *52*, 227–232. [CrossRef] [PubMed]
37. Chu, C.; Liu, W.; Zhou, T.; Station, V.; Protection, S.C. Fumigation of sweet cherries with thymol and acetic acid to reduce postharvest brown rot and blue mold rot. *Fruits* **2001**, *56*, 123–130. [CrossRef]
38. Liu, W.T.; Chu, C.L.; Zhou, T. Thymol and acetic acid vapors reduce postharvest brown rot of apricots and plums. *HortScience* **2002**, *37*, 151–156.
39. Svircev, A.M.; Smith, R.J.; Zhou, T.; Hernadez, M.; Liu, W.; Chu, C.L. Effects of thymol fumigation on survival and ultrastracture of *Monilinia fructicola*. *Postharvest Biol. Technol.* **2007**, *45*, 228–233. [CrossRef]
40. Arrebola, E.; Sivakumar, D.; Bacigalupo, R.; Korsten, L. Combined application of antagonist *Bacillus amyloliquefaciens* and essential oils for the control of peach postharvest diseases. *Crop Prot.* **2010**, *29*, 369–377. [CrossRef]
41. Serrano, M.; Martínez-Romero, D.; Castillo, S.; Guillén, F.; Valero, D. The use of natural antifungal compounds improves the beneficial effect of MAP in sweet cherry storage. *Innov. Food Sci. Emerg. Technol.* **2005**, *6*, 115–123. [CrossRef]
42. Martinez-Romero, D.; Guillén, F.; Valverde, J.M.; Bailén, G.; Zapata, P.; Serrano, M.; Castillo, S.; Valero, D. Influence of carvacrol on survival of *Botrytis cinerea* inoculated in table grapes. *Int. J. Food Microbiol.* **2007**, *115*, 144–148. [CrossRef] [PubMed]
43. Montero-Prado, P.; Rodriguez-Lafuente, A.; Nerin, C. Active label-based packaging to extend the shelf-life of "Calanda" peach fruit: Changes in fruit quality and enzymatic activity. *Postharvest Biol. Technol.* **2011**, *60*, 211–219. [CrossRef]
44. Sivakumar, D.; Bautista-Baños, S. A review on the use of essential oils for postharvest decay control and maintenance of fruit quality during storage. *Crop Prot.* **2014**, *64*, 27–37. [CrossRef]
45. Kraśniewska, K.; Gniewosz, M.; Kosakowska, O.; Cis, A. Preservation of brussels sprouts by pullulan coating containing oregano essential oil. *J. Food Prot.* **2016**, *79*, 493–500. [CrossRef] [PubMed]
46. Leong, S.Y.; Oey, I. Effects of processing on anthocyanins, carotenoids and vitamin C in summer fruits and vegetables. *Food Chem.* **2012**, *133*, 1577–1587. [CrossRef]
47. Lee, S.K.; Kader, A.A. Preharvest and postharvest factors influencing vitamin C content of horticultural crops. *Postharvest Biol. Technol.* **2000**, *20*, 207–220. [CrossRef]
48. Apel, K.; Hirt, H. Reactive oxygen species: Metabolism, oxidative stress, and signal transduction. *Annu. Rev. Plant Biol.* **2004**, *55*, 373–399. [CrossRef] [PubMed]
49. Wang, C.Y.; Wang, S.Y.; Yin, J.J.; Parry, J.; Yu, L.L. Enhancing antioxidant, antiproliferation, and free radical scavenging activities in strawberries with essential oils. *J. Agric. Food Chem.* **2007**, *55*, 6527–6532. [CrossRef] [PubMed]
50. Valero, D.; Valverde, J.M.; Martínez-Romero, D.; Guillén, F.; Castillo, S.; Serrano, M. The combination of modified atmosphere packaging with eugenol or thymol to maintain quality, safety and functional properties of table grapes. *Postharvest Biol. Technol.* **2006**, *41*, 317–327. [CrossRef]

© 2018 by the authors. Licensee MDPI, Basel, Switzerland. This article is an open access article distributed under the terms and conditions of the Creative Commons Attribution (CC BY) license (http://creativecommons.org/licenses/by/4.0/).

Article

Thyme and Savory Essential Oil Efficacy and Induction of Resistance against *Botrytis cinerea* through Priming of Defense Responses in Apple

Houda Banani [1,2], Leone Olivieri [1,2], Karin Santoro [1,2], Angelo Garibaldi [2], Maria Lodovica Gullino [1,2] and Davide Spadaro [1,2,*]

[1] Department of Agricultural, Forestry and Food Sciences (DISAFA), University of Torino, Largo Braccini 2, 10095 Grugliasco (TO), Italy; houda.banani@unito.it (H.B.); leone.olivieri@gmail.com (L.O.); karin.santoro@unito.it (K.S.); marialodovica.gullino@unito.it (M.L.G.)
[2] Centre of Competence for the Innovation in the Agro-environmental Sector (AGROINNOVA), University of Torino, Largo Braccini 2, 10095 Grugliasco (TO), Italy; angelo.garibaldi@unito.it
[*] Correspondence: davide.spadaro@unito.it; Tel.: +39-011-670-8942

Received: 17 November 2017; Accepted: 18 January 2018; Published: 23 January 2018

Abstract: The efficacy of thyme and savory essential oils were investigated against *Botrytis cinerea* on apple fruit. Apples treated with thyme and savory essential oils showed significantly lower gray mold severity and incidence. Thyme essential oil at 1% concentration showed the highest efficacy, with lower disease incidence and smaller lesion diameter. The expression of specific pathogenesis-related (PR) genes PR-8 and PR-5 was characterized in apple tissues in response to thyme oil application and *B. cinerea* inoculation. After 6 h of pathogen inoculation, thyme essential oil induced a 2.5-fold increase of PR-8 gene expression compared to inoculated fruits. After 24 h of inoculation, PR-8 was highly induced (7-fold) in both thyme oil-treated and untreated apples inoculated with *B. cinerea*. After 48 h of inoculation, PR-8 expression in thyme-treated and inoculated apples was 4- and 6-fold higher than in inoculated and water-treated apples. Neither thyme oil application nor *B. cinerea* inoculation markedly affected PR-5 expression. These results suggest that thyme oil induces resistance against *B. cinerea* through the priming of defense responses in apple fruit, and the PR-8 gene of apple may play a key role in the mechanism by which thyme essential oil effectively inhibits gray mold in apple fruit.

Keywords: apple; *Botrytis cinerea*; essential oils; induced resistance; priming; PR genes

1. Introduction

Apple is one of the most important fruits in international trade; however, it can suffer from severe postharvest losses during long distance transport and storage. *Botrytis cinerea*, which causes gray mold, is one of the main pathogens causing postharvest losses of apples, especially for its conidial germination and mycelium growth at storage temperatures as low as 0 °C [1].

Gray mold control strategies mainly rely on chemical treatments; however, the use of synthetic fungicides is limited by the emergence of resistant strains. Following intensive use, resistance to thiabendazole has been reported in *Botrytis* populations [2]. In addition, public concern over human health and the environmental impact of pesticides have generated interest in developing effective and non-toxic approaches to control postharvest diseases of fruit [3,4].

Plant essential oils are gaining interest due to their apparently safe nature and their potential effectiveness as biopesticides for crop protection. On pome and stone fruit, as on table grapes, many plant essential oils have been effective against brown rot and gray mold rot [5,6]. Thyme and savory oils contain thymol, carvacrol, and p-cymene as volatile compounds, which have shown high antifungal activity [7–9]. The mechanism of activity of these promising fungicidal natural compounds has not been completely elucidated. However, their effectiveness was related to their components with phenolic structures, like carvacrol, eugenol, and thymol, which are highly active against pathogens, and their efficacy is often due to the synergy of different chemical components [9].

Other studies described their role in the induction of host resistance against pathogens. Induced resistance is a promising strategy to enhance a host's defense capacity after treatment with biotic- or abiotic-inducing agents, which provides long-term systemic resistance to a broad spectrum of pathogens and pests [10,11]. Upon treatment with microorganisms or other resistance inducers, many hosts develop an enhanced capacity to activate defense responses, a phenomenon called priming [12]. Thymol could enhance antioxidant levels, enzymatic and non-enzymatic systems, which induce an increase of the fruit resistance to pathogens and a decrease of their physiological degradation [13]. Resistance inducers typically stimulate the expression of a family of genes in the host, defined as pathogenesis-related (PR) genes, which are involved in the defense response to pathogens [14]. In apple, PR-5 and PR-8 were identified and shown to be induced in response to different resistance inducers [15]. PR-5 is a thaumatin-like protein [16], while PR-8 codes for a class III chitinase [15]. However, no information is available regarding the involvement of PR genes induction in the biocontrol activity of plant essential oils against postharvest pathogens.

The objectives of this work were to evaluate the efficacy of important plant essential oils against *B. cinerea* in stored apple fruit, and then to investigate whether the efficacy of the oil application is associated with the priming of defense responses in apples.

2. Materials and Methods

2.1. Food Material and Microorganism

Apples (*Malus x domestica* Borkhausen 'Red Fuji') were harvested from a commercial orchard in Piedmont, Italy. Fruits were surface-sterilized and punctured with a sterile plastic tip. A strain of *Botrytis cinerea* Persoon was isolated from rotten apples and tested for its virulence by inoculation in artificially wounded apples. The strain was maintained on PDA (Potato Dextrose Agar, Merck, Darmstadt, Germany) slants at 4 °C and the spores were harvested after the pathogen was incubated on PDA in Petri dishes at 25 °C for 7 days. The strain was used throughout the experiments at a concentration of 10^5 conidia/mL determined by a Bürker chamber (Knittel).

2.2. Essential Oils

Essential oils from savory (*Satureja montana* L.) and thyme (*Thymus vulgaris* L.) were purchased as commercial preparations with 99% purity from Soave (Turin, Italy). The compositional analyses were performed using a gas chromatograph Shimadzu (Kyoto, Japan) GC-2010 Plus equipped with a mass spectrometer GCMS-QP (Shimadzu, Kyoto, Japan) and a split-splitless injector (Shimadzu, Kyoto, Japan) [17]. A 10% stock emulsion (10% essential oil, 88% sterilized water, and 2% Tween 20, Merck, Darmstadt, Germany) was prepared from each essential oil. Emulsions of 1%, 0.5%, and 0.1% (vol/vol) were prepared for each essential oil application by diluting the stock emulsion with distilled water. All the resultant emulsions were shaken for 30 s before application to ensure a homogeneous essential oil mixture.

2.3. Disease Control Efficacy

The control activity of plant essential oils against *B. cinerea* strain was assessed as follows: 30 µL of each treatment was pipetted into apple wounds. Water served as a control. Twelve hours later, 30 µL of pathogen conidial suspension was inoculated into each wound. Also, a standard chemical (thiabendazole, Tecto 20S, Cerexagri Italia srl, San Carlo di Cesena (FC), Italy; 19.7% active ingredient, a. i.) was employed at 0.3 mg a. i. mL^{-1}. Fruits were incubated at 23 °C. Rot incidence and diameter were measured 6 days after inoculation. Each treatment contained three replicates with 10 fruits per replicate and the experiment was performed three times. Wounded apples were treated with thyme (1%) in each wound. Twelve hours later, wounds were inoculated with *B. cinerea*. Apples treated with thyme or inoculated with *B. cinerea* were included to compare PR gene expression. Sterile distilled water served as a control. Apple tissue samples (exocarp and mesocarp) were obtained from 20 fruits stored at 23 °C at 6, 24, and 48 h post inoculation (hpi).

2.4. RNA Extraction and RT-qPCR

Total RNA was extracted from apple samples using an RNeasy® Extraction Kit (Qiagen, Hilden, Germany), then treated with TURBO DNase (Thermo Fisher, Waltham, MA, USA). Absence of genomic DNA contamination was confirmed by PCR amplification of the elongation factor 1 α (EF1α) gene using a One Step RT-PCR Kit (Qiagen). First-strand cDNA was synthesized using an iScript cDNA Synthesis Kit (Bio-Rad, Hercules, CA, USA).

Reverse transcriptase (RT)-qPCR was performed in triplicate on cDNA obtained from each biological replicate using 2× Power SYBR Green Supermix (Bio-Rad). Amplification and detection were carried out in an iCycler (Bio-Rad), set up with initial denaturation at 95 °C for 10 min followed by 40 cycles comprising a denaturation step at 95 °C for 15 s and an annealing step at 52 °C for PR-8 and at 60 °C for PR-5 for 1 min. Primers PR8-F (5′-GCCACTGCAACCCCGCTAGT-3′), PR8-R (5′-GCGGGCGCGAATCTGACTGA-3′), PR5-F (5′-CAAGCAGCTTCCCTCCTCGGC-3′), and PR5-R (5′-GCCCCAGAAGCGACCAGACC-3′) were used to optimally amplify PR-8 and PR-5 gene sequences. Transcript levels of the elongation factor 1 (EF1α) served as an internal standard, and the primers used were EF1α-F (5′-GACATTGCCCTGTGGAAGTT-3′) and EF1α-R (5′-GGTCTGACCATCCTTGGAAA-3′) [18]. The expression ratio was calculated as $2^{-\Delta\Delta CT}$, where $\Delta\Delta CT$ represents ΔCTsample—ΔCTcontrol [19], and values were normalized to those of control water at each time point.

2.5. Statistical Analysis

Statistical analysis was performed with SPSS version 20.0 (SPSS Inc., Chicago, IL, USA). Data obtained in all experiments were analyzed using analysis of variance (ANOVA). Means of treatment results were separated at the 5% significance level by using Duncan's multiple range tests. Values are presented as the mean ± SD (standard deviation of the mean). Results are the mean of three independent experiments.

3. Results and Discussion

3.1. Efficacy of Essential Oils in the Control of Botrytis cinerea on Apples

Disease incidence and the diameter of lesions of *B. cinerea* rots were measured in 'Red Fuji' apples treated with two plant essential oils (Figure 1). Six days after pathogen inoculation, gray mold rot diameter and disease incidence on apples treated with essential oils of *T. vulgaris* and *S. montana* were significantly diminished as compared to the control. The highest disease reduction was obtained when essential oils were applied at the highest concentration (1%), especially thyme, which showed a disease incidence and rot diameter of about 85% and 21 mm, respectively, compared to 100% and 38 mm of the inoculated control.

Thyme essential oil, and its major components thymol and carvacrol, showed antifungal activity against plant pathogenic fungi [20]. Moreover, the inhibitory effect of thyme essential oil against *B. cinerea* on different apple cultivars was reported by Lopez-Reyes et al. [21], who confirmed that its efficacy is cultivar- and storage time-dependent. The phytotoxicity of the essential oils tested on apples was very low, as determined in previous experiments [21]. A certain level of toxicity to human and animal cell lines in vitro has been reported for some essential oils when used at high concentrations, but it was not reported at the concentrations tested in these experiments [22].

In the present study, the efficacy of thyme essential oil could also be related to the induction of host resistance, since the oil was applied 12 h before *B. cinerea* apple inoculation. However, additional molecular studies were accomplished to prove this hypothesis.

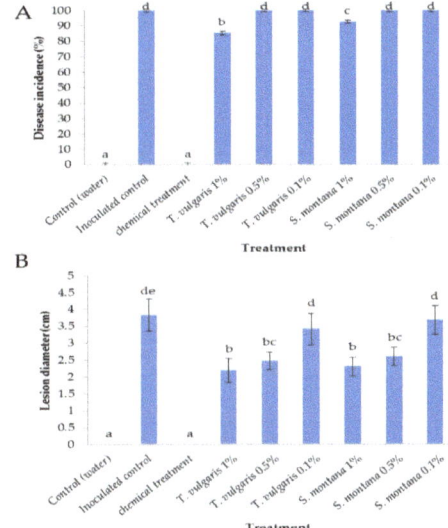

Figure 1. Antifungal activity of essential oils of *Satureja montana* and *Thymus vulgaris* applications at different concentrations (1%, 0.5%, and 0.1%) expressed as disease incidence (**A**) and lesion diameter (**B**) caused by *B. cinerea* on apples. Vertical lines represent the standard error for the average of three biological replicates. Applications followed by different letters are statistically different following Duncan's multiple range test ($p < 0.05$).

3.2. Effect of Thyme Oil Application and B. cinerea Inoculation on Defence Genes Expression in Apple Fruit

In order to analyze the molecular mechanisms involved in thyme-induced resistance in apple, the expression of the two defense-related genes, PR-8 and PR-5, was analyzed in treated apples at different time points (Figures 2 and 3).

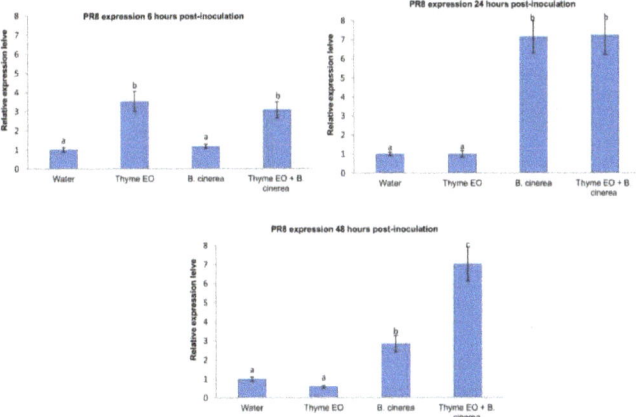

Figure 2. Expression of pathogenesis-related gene PR-8 in apple fruit in response to wounding, thyme essential oil, and *B. cinerea* at different time points (6 h, 24 h, and 48 h). Vertical lines represent the standard error for the average of three biological replicates. Different letters above the columns indicated a significant difference determined by Duncan's multiple comparison test ($p < 0.05$).

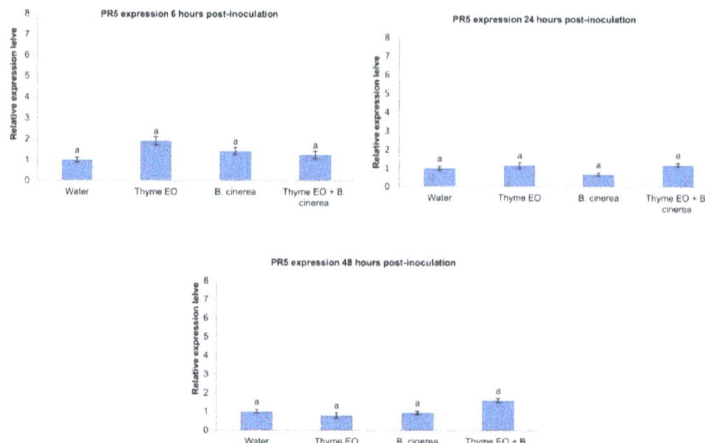

Figure 3. Expression of pathogenesis-related gene PR-5 in apple fruit in response to wounding, thyme essential oil, and *B. cinerea* at different time points (6 h, 24 h, and 48 h). Vertical lines represent the standard error for the average of three biological replicates. Different letters above the columns indicated a significant difference determined by Duncan's multiple comparison test ($p < 0.05$).

After 6 h of pathogen inoculation, thyme essential oil induced a 2.5-fold increase of PR-8 gene expression compared to the negative control (wounded fruits treated with water), while no significant upregulation of PR-8 expression was observed in inoculated fruits.

After 24 h of inoculation, PR-8 expression in thyme-treated apples was similar to the negative control, whereas PR-8 was highly induced (7-fold) in both thyme-treated and untreated apples inoculated with *B. cinerea*. The early induction of PR-8 expression was no longer significant in thyme oil-treated fruit at 36 h after the essential oil treatment.

At this time point, PR-8 was induced similarly in inoculated untreated fruit and in inoculated treated fruit. This could be related to the early response of apple, which tries to counteract the penetration of *B. cinerea* mycelium. In a recently performed experiment on the germination of *B. cinerea* conidia on apple at 20 °C [23], the time points for germination were set at pregermination (1 h), postgermination (2.5 h), appressoria formation (4 h), and early mycelium (15 h). Therefore, we could presume that at 6 h, the pathogen has not yet penetrated the fruit, and thus PR-8 is not induced in inoculated fruit, while at 24 h the pathogen has already penetrated and the first mycelium is growing. The higher induction of PR-8 in inoculated fruit at 24 h compared to 6 h could be explained by the fungal development in the host fruit, since *B. cinerea* conidia formed appressorium-like terminal thickenings within 4 h of incubation, indicating the initiation of penetration [23]. The fruit induced PR-8 as an early response against the pathogen. Previous studies also showed that certain postharvest infections can induce host resistance [24].

Therefore, after penetration into the host tissue during the first 24 h after inoculation, *B. cinerea* could produce elicitors either directly or indirectly that are able to trigger a defense response strong enough to significantly increase the resistance of the fruit to a subsequent pathogen attack [23].

After 48 h of inoculation, PR-8 expression in apples treated with thyme oil and inoculated with the pathogen was 4- and 6-fold greater than that in inoculated and water-treated apples. This is the most significant effect, as 48 h after pathogen infection inoculated fruit no longer show an increase of PR-8 expression, while the response in fruits treated with oil and inoculated with *B. cinerea* is significantly higher.

Thyme essential oil influenced PR-5 expression during the trial, as shown in Figure 3. In particular, PR-5 expression was significantly increased after 6 h in apples treated with thyme essential oil with respect to the other treatments. After 24 h, PR-5 expression was similar in all fruits, while at 48 h the expression level was significantly higher in apples inoculated with *B. cinerea* and treated with thyme essential oil.

The treatment of plants and fruits with different inducers, such as cell walls, plant extracts, essential oils, compounds of biological origin, and synthetic chemical compounds, was shown to trigger resistance to pathogen attack locally and systemically [25]. There are two types of host induced resistance: induced systemic resistance (ISR) and systemic acquired resistance (SAR). SAR requires the signal molecule salicylic acid (SA) and is associated with the accumulation of pathogenesis-related (PR) proteins, which are thought to contribute to resistance [26]. Thyme essential oil demonstrated the ability to trigger defense response in avocado fruit. Thyme oil was applied through fumigation and induced the expression of β-1,3-glucanase and chitinase genes. The mRNA levels of the two enzymes were shown to be higher in fumigated fruit especially in the ripened stage. Fumigation with thyme oil caused the initiation of the induced defense response at the enzymatic and transcript level that made avocados less susceptible to anthracnose development, resulting in a treatment as effective as prochloraz treatment [27]. β-1,3-glucanases are PR-2 proteins able to damage the cell wall of many pathogenic fungi, while chitinase acts on C-bonds in chitin, an important and common component of the fungal cell wall [28]. Similar results were obtained in peaches, though the host response varied depending on the cultivar [29]. On avocado fruit, thyme essential oil also increased ammonia-lyase and peroxidase levels as well as antioxidant enzymes [30,31].

In our study, thyme essential oil significantly induced apple resistance against *B. cinerea* since it favored the accumulation of the pathogenesis-related protein PR-8, which codes for a class III chitinase.

After 6 h of pathogen inoculation, thyme caused a low direct induction of resistance (PR-8 expression level was 2.5-fold higher than that in water-treated fruits) since this signal activated the plant to a state of alertness. After pathogen infection, fruits strongly and efficiently responded, showing a long-lasting period of protection (PR-8 expression level was 6-fold greater than that in water-treated fruits after 24 and 48 h of pathogen inoculation). This effect is also known as the 'priming effect', which is beneficial since it is considered as a host solution to the trade-off dilemma between disease protection and costs involved in direct defense activation, and therefore the costs become affordable only when the host is exposed to pathogen attack [32]. Similarly, *Candida oleophila* was reported to elicit a long-lasting activation of PR-8 at 24 and 48 h, but a high level of PR-8 protein was present even at 8 h. PR-8 expression was higher than that in fruit inoculated with *B. cinerea*, and it increased during the trial. The rapid host response to *C. oleophila* could be due to the general activation of apple fruit defense when exposed to microbes [17]. The difference in PR-8 expression level and speed of defense activation when the fruit was exposed to thyme essential oil could be attributed to the nature of the elicitors, which could induce biotic or abiotic stress.

In contrast, a less clear response was achieved for PR-5 expression. As for PR-8 expression, the PR-5 level was also increased with respect to the untreated, inoculated or inoculated and treated fruit after 6 h. After 48 h, the only increase in PR-5 expression was obtained in inoculated fruit treated with thyme essential oil. Conversely, the presence of the pathogen did not induce any increase in PR-5 levels. Nevertheless, the magnitude of variation was very slight and it would be difficult to attribute any role of this gene to the induction of resistance under the studied conditions. Similar results were reported in literature on apples inoculated with *B. cinerea* or treated with *C. oleophila*. After 8 and 24 h, PR-5 gene expression was stable and similar to that observed in the untreated control. Only after 48 h were PR-5 levels higher in *B. cinerea*-inoculated apples in comparison to other treatments. However, since the expression level was even lower than that at time 0, in that case it was also difficult to attribute any biological significance to the observed pattern of expression [17].

4. Conclusions

Thyme essential oil at 1% could be used as an efficient postharvest treatment against *B. cinerea* in stored apple. Based on gene expression results, it is postulated that one mechanism by which thyme effectively controls gray mold disease in apple fruit is through the induction of the PR-8 gene in apple fruit, besides its known antifungal activity. Deeper studies are required to understand the role of the PR-8 protein as a pathogen defense mechanism, its expression in various apple cultivars against a wide range of pathogens, and how specific pathogens may interfere with PR-8 expression.

Acknowledgments: This work was carried out with a contribution from the LIFE financial instrument of the European Union for the project "Low pesticide IPM in sustainable and safe fruit production" (Contract No. LIFE13 ENV/HR/000580).

Author Contributions: Davide Spadaro and Houda Banani conceived and designed the experiments; Leone Olivieri performed the experiments; Maria Lodovica Gullino and Angelo Garibaldi contributed reagents/materials/analysis tools; Houda Banani, Karin Santoro and Davide Spadaro analyzed data and wrote the paper.

Conflicts of Interest: The authors declare no conflict of interest. The founding sponsors had no role in the design of the study; in the collection, analyses, or interpretation of data; in the writing of the manuscript, and in the decision to publish the results.

References

1. Lahlali, R.; Serrhini, M.N.; Friel, D.; Jijakli, M.H. Predictive modelling of temperature and water activity (solutes) on the in vitro radial growth of Botrytis cinerea Pers. *Int. J. Food Microbiol.* **2007**, *114*, 1–9. [CrossRef] [PubMed]
2. Bus, V.G.; Bongers, A.J.; Risse, L.A. Occurrence of *Penicillium digitatum* and *P. italicum* Resistant to Benomyl, Thiabendazole, and Imazalil on Citrus Fruit from Different Geographic Origins. *Plant Dis.* **1991**, *75*, 1098–1100. [CrossRef]
3. Casals, C.; Teixidó, N.; Viñas, I.; Silvera, E.; Lamarca, N.; Usall, J. Combination of hot water, *Bacillus subtilis* CPA-8 and sodium bicarbonate treatments to control postharvest brown rot on peaches and nectarines. *Eur. J. Plant Pathol.* **2010**, *128*, 51–63. [CrossRef]
4. Spadaro, D.; Ciavorella, A.; Dianpeng, Z.; Garibaldi, A.; Gullino, M.L. Effect of culture media and pH on the biomass production and biocontrol efficacy of a *Metschnikowia pulcherrima* strain to be used as a biofungicide for postharvest disease control. *Can. J. Microbiol.* **2010**, *56*, 128–137. [CrossRef] [PubMed]
5. Lopez-Reyes, J.G.; Spadaro, D.; Prelle, A.; Garibaldi, A.; Gullino, M.L. Efficacy of plant essential oils on postharvest control of rots caused by fungi on different stone fruits in vivo. *J. Food Prot.* **2013**, *76*, 631–639. [CrossRef] [PubMed]
6. Servili, A.; Feliziani, E.; Romanazzi, G. Exposure to volatiles of essential oils alone or under hypobaric treatment to control postharvest gray mold of table grapes. *Postharvest Biol. Technol.* **2017**, *133*, 36–40. [CrossRef]
7. Sellamuthu, P.S.; Mafune, M.; Sivakumar, D.; Soundy, P. Thyme oil vapor and modified atmosphere packaging reduce anthracnose incidence and maintain fruit quality in avocado. *J. Sci. Food Agric.* **2013**, *93*, 3024–3031. [CrossRef] [PubMed]
8. Soković, M.D.; Vukojević, J.; Marin, P.D.; Brkić, D.D.; Vajs, V.; van Griensven, L.J.L.D. Chemical composition of essential oils of Thymus and Mentha species and their antifungal activities. *Molecules* **2009**, *14*, 238–249. [CrossRef] [PubMed]
9. Spadaro, D.; Gullino, M.L. Use of Essential Oils to Control Postharvest Rots on Pome and Stone Fruit. In *Post-Harvest Pathology*; Prusky, D., Gullino, M.L., Eds.; Springer International Publishing: Cham, Switzerland, 2014; pp. 101–110.
10. Harm, A.; Kassemeyer, H.-H.; Seibicke, T.; Regner, F. Evaluation of chemical and natural resistance inducers against Downy Mildew. *Am. J. Enol. Vitic.* **2011**, *62*, 184–192. [CrossRef]
11. Banani, H.; Roatti, B.; Ezzahi, B.; Giovannini, O.; Gessler, G.; Pertot, I.; Perazzolli, M. Characterization of resistance mechanisms activated by *Trichoderma harzianum* T39 and benzothiadiazole to downy mildew in different grapevine cultivars. *Plant Pathol.* **2014**, *63*, 334–343. [CrossRef]
12. Conrath, U.; Beckers, G.J.M.; Flors, V.; García-Agustín, P.; Jakab, G.; Mauch, F.; Newman, M.-A.; Pieterse, C.M.J.; Poinssot, B.; Pozo, M.J.; et al. Priming: Getting ready for battle. *Mol. Pant-Microbe Interact.* **2006**, *19*, 1062–1071. [CrossRef] [PubMed]
13. Bautista-Baños, S.; Sivakumar, D.; Bello-Pérez, A.; Villanueva-Arce, R.; Hernández-López, M. A review of the management alternatives for controlling fungi on papaya fruit during the postharvest supply chain. *Crop Prot.* **2013**, *49*, 8–20.

14. Sels, J.; Mathys, J.; De Coninck, B.M.A.; Cammue, B.P.A.; De Bolle, M.F.C. Plant pathogenesis-related (PR) proteins: A focus on PR peptides. *Plant Physiol. Biochem.* **2008**, *46*, 941–950. [CrossRef] [PubMed]
15. Bonasera, J.M.; Kim, J.F.; Beer, S.V. PR genes of apple: Identification and expression in response to elicitors and inoculation with *Erwinia amylovora*. *BMC Plant Biol.* **2006**, *6*, 23. [CrossRef] [PubMed]
16. Krebitz, M.; Wagner, B.; Ferreira, F.; Peterbauer, C.; Campillo, N.; Witty, M.; Kolarich, D.; Steinkellner, H.; Scheiner, O.; Breiteneder, H. Plant-based heterologous expression of Mal d 2, a thaumatin-like protein and allergen of apple (*Malus domestica*), and its characterization as an antifungal protein. *J. Mol. Biol.* **2003**, *329*, 721–730. [CrossRef]
17. Liu, J.; Wisniewski, M.; Artlip, T.; Sui, Y.; Droby, S.; Norelli, J. The potential role of PR-8 gene of apple fruit in the mode of action of the yeast antagonist, *Candida oleophila*, in postharvest biocontrol of Botrytis cinerea. *Postharvest Biol. Technol.* **2013**, *85*, 203–209. [CrossRef]
18. Santoro, K.; Maghenzani, M.; Chiabrando, V.; Bosio, P.; Gullino, M.L.; Spadaro, D.; Giacalone, G. Thyme and savory essential oil vapor treatments control brown rot and improve the storage quality of peaches and nectarines, but could favor gray mold. *Foods* **2018**, *7*, 7. [CrossRef] [PubMed]
19. Livak, K.J.; Schmittgen, T.D. Analysis of relative gene expression data using real-time quantitative PCR and the 2(-Delta Delta C(T)) Method. *Methods* **2001**, *25*, 402–408. [CrossRef] [PubMed]
20. Adorjan, B.; Buchbauer, G. Biological properties of essential oils: An updated review. *Flavour Fragr. J.* **2010**, *25*, 407–426. [CrossRef]
21. Lopez-Reyes, J.G.; Spadaro, D.; Gullino, M.L.; Garibaldi, A. Efficacy of plant essential oils on postharvest control of rot caused by fungi on four cultivars of apples in vivo. *Flavour Fragr. J.* **2010**, *25*, 171–177. [CrossRef]
22. Leroch, M.; Kleber, A.; Silva, E.; Coenen, T.; Koppenhöfer, D.; Shmaryahu, A.; Valenzuela, P.D.T.; Hahn, M. Transcriptome profiling of Botrytis cinerea conidial germination reveals upregulation of infection-related genes during the prepenetration stage. *Eukaryot. Cell* **2013**, *12*, 614–626. [CrossRef] [PubMed]
23. Mari, M.; Bautista-Baños, S.; Sivakumar, D. Decay control in the postharvest system: Role of microbial and plant volatile organic compounds. *Postharvest Biol. Technol.* **2016**, *122*, 70–81. [CrossRef]
24. Lyon, G.D. Agents That Can Elicit Induced Resistance. In *Induced Resistance for Plant Defense*; John Wiley & Sons, Ltd.: Chichester, UK, 2014; pp. 11–40.
25. Walters, D.R.; Fountaine, J.M. Practical application of induced resistance to plant diseases: An appraisal of effectiveness under field conditions. *J. Agric. Sci.* **2009**, *147*, 523–535. [CrossRef]
26. Durrant, W.E.; Dong, X. Systemic Acquired Resistance. *Annu. Rev. Phytopathol.* **2004**, *42*, 185–209. [CrossRef] [PubMed]
27. Bill, M.; Sivakumar, D.; Beukes, M.; Korsten, L. Expression of pathogenesis-related (PR) genes in avocados fumigated with thyme oil vapours and control of anthracnose. *Food Chem.* **2016**, *194*, 938–943. [CrossRef] [PubMed]
28. Thanseem, I.; Joseph, A.; Thulaseedharan, A. Induction and differential expression of beta-1,3-glucanase mRNAs in tolerant and susceptible *Hevea* clones in response to infection by *Phytophthora meadii*. *Tree Physiol.* **2005**, *25*, 1361–1368. [CrossRef] [PubMed]
29. Cindi, M.D.; Soundy, P.; Romanazzi, G.; Sivakumar, D. Different defense responses and brown rot control in two *Prunus persica* cultivars to essential oil vapours after storage. *Postharvest Biol. Technol.* **2016**, *119*, 9–17. [CrossRef]
30. Sellamuthu, P.S.; Sivakumar, D.; Soundy, P.; Korsten, L. Essential oil vapours suppress the development of anthracnose and enhance defence related and antioxidant enzyme activities in avocado fruit. *Postharvest Biol. Technol.* **2013**, *81*, 66–72. [CrossRef]
31. Bill, M.; Sivakumar, D.; Korsten, L.; Thompson, A.K. The efficacy of combined application of edible coatings and thyme oil in inducing resistance components in avocado (*Persea americana* Mill.) against anthracnose during post-harvest storage. *Crop Prot.* **2014**, *64*, 159–167. [CrossRef]
32. Jung, H.W.; Tschaplinski, T.J.; Wang, L.; Glazebrook, J.; Greenberg, J.T. Priming in systemic plant immunity. *Science* **2009**, *324*, 89–91. [CrossRef] [PubMed]

© 2018 by the authors. Licensee MDPI, Basel, Switzerland. This article is an open access article distributed under the terms and conditions of the Creative Commons Attribution (CC BY) license (http://creativecommons.org/licenses/by/4.0/).

Article

Characterization of Essential Oils Obtained from Abruzzo Autochthonous Plants: Antioxidant and Antimicrobial Activities Assessment for Food Application

Marika Pellegrini, Antonella Ricci *, Annalisa Serio, Clemencia Chaves-López, Giovanni Mazzarrino, Serena D'Amato, Claudio Lo Sterzo and Antonello Paparella

Facoltà di Bioscienze e Tecnologie Agro-Alimentari e Ambientali, Università degli Studi di Teramo, Via R. Balzarini 1, 64100 Teramo, Italy; mpellegrini@unite.it (M.P.); aserio@unite.it (A.S.); cchaveslopez@unite.it (C.C.-L.); g.mazzarrino@virgilio.it (G.M.); sdamato@unite.it (S.D.); closterzo@unite.it (C.L.S.); apaparella@unite.it (A.P.)
* Correspondence: aricci@unite.it; Tel.: +39-0861-266-904

Received: 21 December 2017; Accepted: 30 January 2018; Published: 2 February 2018

Abstract: In the present study, the essential oils (EOs) of some officinal plants from Abruzzo territory (Italy) were evaluated for their antimicrobial and antioxidant activities and their volatile fraction chemical characterization. The EOs were extracted from *Rosmarinus officinalis*, *Origanum vulgare*, *Salvia officinalis*, *Mentha piperita*, *Allium sativum*, *Foeniculum vulgare*, *Satureja montana*, *Thymus vulgaris* and *Coriandrum sativum* seeds. The antimicrobial activity was screened against thirteen Gram-positive and Gram-negative strains to determine the Minimal Inhibitory Concentration (MIC). The total phenolic content (TPC) and the antioxidant capacity (AOC) were assessed by means of Folin-Ciocâlteu method, and Trolox Equivalent Antioxidant Capacity with 2,2′-azinobis-(3-ethylbenzothiazoline-6-sulfonic acid (TEAC/ABTS), Ferric Reducing Antioxidant Power (FRAP) and 2,2-diphenyl-1-picrylhydrazyl (DPPH) assays respectively. Among the nine EOs tested, *T. vulgaris*, *S. montana*, *O. vulgare* and *C. sativum* EOs showed MIC values ranging from 0.625 to 5 µL/mL. The AOC and TPC results for these species were also interesting. The major components for these EOs were thymol for *T. vulgaris* (44%) and *O. vulgare* (40%), linalool (77%) for *C. sativum*, and carvacrol for *S. montana* (54%). The results allowed the study to establish that these EOs are good candidates for potential application as biopreservatives in foods and/or food manufacture environments.

Keywords: essential oils; antimicrobial; antioxidant; GC-MS

1. Introduction

Food spoilage can be defined as the alteration of a product due to microbial, chemical, or physical mechanisms that lead a food to become undesirable or unacceptable for human consumption [1]. In food products manufacture, many effective preservation strategies are applied against food spoilage, involving mainly the employment of synthetic preservatives. However, the increasing negative consumer perception of synthetic additives and the worldwide growing problem of allergies, is causing the food industry to search for more effective preservation strategies [2].

An alternative strategy to synthetic chemical preservatives is represented by the employment of essential oils (EOs). Commonly employed in foods as aromatizing and flavoring agents [2], these plant volatile fractions can be exploited by the food industry for their antimicrobial [3,4] and antioxidant [5] properties. EOs, in fact, possess the ability to permeabilize the membrane of microorganisms, with consequent loss of vital intracellular constituents and interruption of the cellular metabolism and enzyme kinetics [6]. In addition, terpenes and terpenoids, alkaloids and phenolic compounds present in these volatile fractions are recognized antioxidant substances [7–9].

According to European Pharmacopeia, the EOs can be obtained by steam distillation or by hydrodistillation [10] and their yield and composition are influenced by the presence of several factors, such as location, climate, plant species, methodology and experimental procedures [11,12].

In the Italian territory, Abruzzo is one of the central area regions characterized by a multitude of environments and microclimates and with the richest flora of Italy and the Mediterranean basin [13]. In the Abruzzo territory, different plant species are cultivated and exploited for their therapeutic and alimentary properties [14]; among them, *Rosmarinus officinalis, Origanum vulgare, Salvia officinalis, Mentha piperita, Allium sativum, Foeniculum vulgare, Satureja montana, Thymus vulgaris*, and *Coriandrum sativum*, are the aromatic plants commonly employed in the Mediterranean diet [15–17].

In scientific literature, different data that showed the antimicrobial and antioxidant potentials of the EOs recovered from these vegetal species are reported [18–21]. However, limited data are available for the EOs obtained from these Abruzzo plant species. In this perspective, the aims of the study were the extraction and the Gas Chromatography-Mass Spectrometry (GC-MS) characterization of the EOs from Abruzzo officinal plants and assessment of their antimicrobial properties against several food-borne strains, as well as their antioxidant capacities and total phenolic contents.

2. Materials and Methods

2.1. Plant Material

The matrices were obtained from Abruzzo territory farmers. The cultures were obtained with organic agriculture and after the harvesting, the matrices were dried on fields and stored at room temperature in dry and dark conditions for few days. The matrices were then transferred in the laboratory for extractions and analyses. Regarding *A. sativum*, after the harvesting, the bulbs were transferred in the laboratory, cleaned and the resultant cloves were vacuum-packed and refrigerated until extraction and analyses.

2.2. Essential Oils Extraction

Essential oils were extracted from the matrices by means of an E0105 12 lt PLUS Essential Oils Extractor (Albrigi Luigi Srl, Verona, Italy). For all plant materials, after two hours of distillation, no significant volume increase was observed in the collector tube, thus all matrices were subjected to 2 h steam distillation, except for garlic cloves which were subjected to 2 h hydrodistillation. After extraction, the EOs were transferred to an amber glass vial with anhydrous sodium sulfate (Sigma Aldrich, Saint Louis, MO, USA), conditioned with argon and sealed. Each matrix extraction was conducted in triplicate. The collected EOs were stored under refrigeration at 4 °C.

2.3. Chemical Compositions of EOs

The GC-MS analyses of the EOs were carried out by a Clarus 580 GC (PerkinElmer, Waltham, MA, USA) coupled to a Clarus GC/MS SQ (PerkinElmer), in full scan mode (50 to 600 amu). The identifications of the volatile compounds were obtained matching the mass spectra with the NIST Mass Spectral Library 2.0 (NIST, Gaithersburg, MD, USA) and confirmed by calculating the retention index, as proposed by Lee et al. [22], referred to a series of *n*-hydrocarbons (C8–C40 *n*-alkanes, Sigma Aldrich), compared with those present in the NIST Chemistry WebBook (http://webbook.nist.gov/chemistry/). The semi-quantitative results were calculated by means of the Turbomass 6.1.0.1963 software (PerkinElmer).

The GC apparatus was equipped with a fused silica Rxi-5ms column (30 m × 250 µm × 0.25 µm Restek, Milan, Italy). For all the EOs, excepting *A. sativum*, the oven temperature program started from 45 °C (holding 10 min) and ramped at a rate of 2.5 °C/min to 180 °C (holding 5 min); for *A. sativum* EOs, the oven temperature program started from 50 °C (holding 1 min), ramped at a rate of 5 °C/min to 145 °C (holding 15 min), ramped at a rate of 7 °C/min to 175 °C and then ramped at a rate of

4 °C/min to 250 °C (holding 15 min); the carrier gas was helium at flow 1 mL/min; the injector temperature and the transfer line temperature were set at 250 °C. A 1% v/v solution of the EOs sample in hexane was prepared and 1 µL was injected in a splitless mode.

2.4. Antioxidant Capacity and Total Phenolic Content

To assess the antioxidant capacity and total phenolic content, 0.2–2 mg/mL methanolic solutions of each EO were subjected to the different spectrophotometric assays carried out by a Lambda Bio 20 ultraviolet-visible (UV/vis) spectrophotometer (PerkinElmer). The different assays conditions were presented below.

2.4.1. Trolox Equivalent Antioxidant Capacity with 2,2'-azinobis-(3-ethylbenzothiazoline-6-sulfonic acid (TEAC/ABTS) Assay

The TEAC/ABTS assay was determined as described by Masaldan et al. [23]. The TEAC/ABTS results of the samples were estimated in terms of mmol Trolox equivalent (TE)/g EO as the mean of three replicates.

2.4.2. Ferric Reducing Antioxidant Power (FRAP) Assay

The FRAP was determined by using the potassium ferricyanide-ferric chloride method described by Oyaizu [24]. The FRAP of the samples was estimated in terms of mg Trolox equivalent (TE)/g EO as the mean of three replicates.

2.4.3. 2,2-diphenyl-1-picrylhydrazyl (DPPH) Assay

The radical-scavenging activity of the EOs methanolic solutions was measured according to the method described by Brand-Williams et al. [25]. The DPPH results were expressed in terms of µg Trolox equivalent (TE)/g EO as the mean of three replicates.

2.4.4. Total Phenolic Content (TPC)

TPC was determined by the Folin-Ciocâlteu method described by Lateef Gharib & Teixeira da Silva [26]. The TPC results were expressed in terms of mg Gallic acid equivalents (GAE)/g EO as the mean of three replicates.

2.5. Antimicrobial Activity

2.5.1. Microbial Strains and Growth Conditions

Thirteen strains, listed in Table 1, and belonging to the Faculty of Bioscience and Technology for Food, Agriculture and Environment collection, were employed in the assessment of antimicrobial activity. The strains were stored at −80 °C in cryovials, containing anti-freezing agent (glycerol 20% v/v Sigma) and periodically confirmed by means of plate counts. Before each trial, bacterial strains were cultured overnight in Tryptone Soy agar medium (TSA, Oxoid Thermofisher, Rodano, Italy); after 24–48 h, the cells were inoculated into Tryptone Soy broth (TSB, Oxoid Thermofisher) and incubated to obtain a working fresh culture (early stationary phase). Fresh cultures were collected by centrifugation at 1300 rpm (Eppendorf-Centrifuge 5415D, Hamburg, Germany) for 5 min and washed for three times with phosphate buffer saline (50 mM pH 7.0). Inocula were standardized at about 5×10^5 CFU/mL, by means of Lambda Bio 20 spectrophotometer (PerkinElmer). Strains origin and incubation conditions were also presented in Table 1.

Table 1. Strains employed for the trial and culture and standardization conditions.

Strains		Origin	Incubation Temperature (°C)	Incubation Time (h)
Pseudomonas fluorescens	P34	Dairy products	28	24
Brochothrix thermosphacta	B2	Poultry meat	30	48
Brochothrix thermosphacta	B1	Poultry meat	30	48
Salmonella Enteritidis	S2	Meat	37	24
Salmonella Typhimurium	S4	Meat	37	24
Enterococcus faecium	P14	Fish	30	48
Enterococcus faecium	ATCC 19434	Type strain	30	48
Listeria monocytogenes	LM 4	Meat products	37	48
Listeria monocytogenes	ATCC 19144	Type strain	37	48
Listeria monocytogenes	ATCC 7644	Type strain	37	48
Staphylococcus aureus	STA 32	Dairy products	37	48
Staphylococcus aureus	STA 47	Dairy products	37	48
Staphylococcus aureus	STA 39	Dairy products	37	48

2.5.2. Determination of Minimal Inhibitory Concentration

The EOs were investigated for their Minimal Inhibitory Concentration (MIC) values according to the microdilution method, as described by Clinical and Laboratory Standards Institute (CLSI) guidelines [27]. The EOs were dissolved in PBS (Phosphate Buffer Saline) 50 mM pH 7.0 and Tween 80 (1%) to reach the initial concentration of 4.0%; working emulsions were obtained by vortexing for 5 min. The emulsions were sterilized through 0.22 µm politetrafluoroetilene (PTFE) Minisart syringe filter (Sartorius, Göttingen, Germany). The inocula were prepared as described in Section 2.5.1. A positive (100 µL of TSB medium and 100 µL inoculum) and a negative control (200 µL of sterile TSB medium) were considered for each strain. The lowest EOs concentrations that prevented growth after 48 h of incubation, was interpreted as the MIC. The Minimum Bactericidal Concentration (MBC) was determined by inoculating the content of wells were no growth was observed, on TSA plates and by incubating the plates at the temperatures reported in Table 1. The MBC was recorded as the lowest concentration not allowing bacterial growth on plates [28].

2.6. Statistical Analysis

Experimental results were expressed as means ± standard deviations. Data obtained were subjected to ANOVA (analysis of variance), and a Tukey's HSD post-hoc test was applied at $p < 0.05$, using Microsoft Xlstat 2016 statistical software (Addinsoft, Paris, France). Correlations between TPC and AOC (antioxidant capacity) results and antimicrobial activities, were calculated using Microsoft Xlstat 2016 statistical software (Addinsoft) by means of Pearson Correlation.

3. Results & Discussion

3.1. Essential Oil Extractions

The extraction yields were calculated considering the mass (g) of the obtained EOs and the mass (g) of dried material processed. The yield results were expressed as the mean of the three replicates of the extraction ± standard deviation.

R. officinalis, O. vulgare, S. officinalis, M. piperita, A. sativum, F. vulgare, C. sativum, S. montana, T. vulgaris yields % were: 0.487 ± 0.011, 2.900 ± 0.012, 0.249 ± 0.001, 1.034 ± 0.057, 0.371 ± 0.011, 0.340 ± 0.016, 0.265 ± 0.010, 0.491 ± 0.027, 1.506 ± 0.096, respectively. The obtained yields were similar to ranges usually reported in the literature for the same species [26,29–33].

3.2. Chemical Characterization

The chemical compositions of the different EOs were reported in Table 2.

Table 2. Gas Chromatography-Mass Spectrometry (GC-MS) characterization of essential oils (EOs).

ID	RID	RIE	R. officinalis	O. vulgare	S. officinalis	A. sativum	F. vulgare	M. piperita	C. sativum	S. montana	T. vulgaris
Diallyl sulfide	848	847	-	-	-	0.55 ± 0.04 [c]	-	-	-	-	-
Methyl allyl disulfide	910	911	-	-	-	0.29 ± 0.00 [c]	-	-	-	-	-
α-Pinene	939	939	16.64 ± 0.22 [b]	0.47 ± 0.02 [i]	1.20 ± 0.10 [f,g]	-	5.18 ± 0.73 [c]	0.86 ± 0.03 [e]	0.28 ± 0.00 [e]	-	0.37 ± 0.01 [f,g]
Camphene	953	956	3.39 ± 0.04 [f]	-	1.38 ± 0.03 [f]	-	-	-	-	-	-
Thuja-2,4(10)-diene	957	960	0.32 ± 0.01 [i]	-	-	-	-	-	-	-	-
1-Octen-3-ol	978	979	-	0.57 ± 0.02 [h,i]	-	-	-	-	-	-	-
β-Pinene	979	981	2.35 ± 0.03 [g]	-	2.77 ± 0.16 [e]	-	1.03 ± 0.05 [e]	0.52 ± 0.01 [e]	-	1.43 ± 0.02 [e]	1.87 ± 0.09 [f]
β-Myrcene	992	993	0.72 ± 0.01 [k]	-	-	-	0.65 ± 0.06 [e]	-	0.28 ± 0.03 [e]	0.55 ± 0.03 [e]	0.56 ± 0.02 [g,h]
α-Phellandrene	1005	1006	-	-	-	-	10.49 ± 0.02 [b]	-	-	-	-
trans-β-Ocimene	1015	1014	0.38 ± 0.02 [l]	-	-	-	-	-	-	-	-
p-Cymene	1024	1021	1.75 ± 0.01 [i]	8.30 ± 0.02 [c]	0.52 ± 0.03 [g]	-	3.33 ± 0.24 [d]	-	0.31 ± 0.00 [e]	10.78 ± 0.41 [b]	18.57 ± 0.71 [b]
Limonene	1029	1029	-	-	-	-	4.56 ± 0.38 [c,d]	-	0.33 ± 0.00 [e]	0.69 ± 0.04 [e]	-
1,8-Cineole	1032	1034	15.71 ± 0.18 [c]	-	10.02 ± 0.36 [c]	-	-	5.35 ± 0.38 [c,d]	-	0.53 ± 0.01 [e]	-
γ-Terpinene	1060	1061	0.46 ± 0.02 [k,l]	9.38 ± 0.01 [c]	-	-	-	-	1.19 ± 0.07 [d,e]	6.46 ± 0.71 [c]	4.92 ± 0.13 [c,d]
cis-Sabinene hydrate	1066	1064	-	-	-	-	-	-	-	-	3.17 ± 0.03 [e]
Diallyl disulfide	1080	1079	-	-	-	20.16 ± 2.84 [b]	-	-	-	-	-
Terpinolene	1087	1085	-	-	-	-	-	-	-	-	-
Fenchone	1088	1088	-	-	-	-	10.12 ± 0.07 [b]	-	-	-	4.54 ± 0.06 [d]
(S)-(+)-Linalool	1100	1099	2.02 ± 0.01 [h]	1.95 ± 0.10 [e,f]	-	-	-	0.86 ± 0.04 [e]	-	2.09 ± 0.10 [d,e]	0.37 ± 0.01 [g,h]
α-Thujone	1102	1104	-	-	30.46 ± 0.49 [a]	-	-	-	77.07 ± 1.82 [a]	-	-
1-Octen-3-ol, acetate	1110	1113	-	-	-	-	-	-	-	-	1.27 ± 0.01 [f,g]
Menthone	1126	1116	-	-	-	-	-	6.87 ± 0.11 [b,c]	-	-	-
L-Pinocarveol	1135	1132	0.23 ± 0.01 [l]	-	-	-	-	-	2.60 ± 0.10 [c,d]	-	-
Camphor	1139	1137	22.07 ± 0.23 [a]	-	11.53 ± 0.34 [b]	-	-	-	0.48 ± 0.01 [e]	4.51 ± 0.37 [c,d]	0.29 ± 0.02 [h]
Borneol	1162	1160	11.99 ± 0.04 [d]	0.66 ± 0.01 [g,h,i]	3.92 ± 0.02 [d]	-	-	-	-	-	-
Menthofuran	1164	1165	-	-	-	-	-	7.81 ± 0.59 [b]	-	-	-
Menthol	1171	1178	-	-	-	-	-	53.39 ± 0.24 [a]	-	-	-
Isocamphopinone	1175	1174	1.08 ± 0.00 [j]	-	-	-	-	-	-	-	-
Terpinene-4-ol	1179	1176	0.26 ± 0.01 [l]	0.38 ± 0.01 [i]	-	-	-	-	0.55 ± 0.03 [e]	-	-
2-Vinyl-1,3-dithiane	1182	1084	-	-	1.43 ± 0.09 [f]	4.60 ± 0.09 [c]	-	-	-	-	-
Isomenthol	1194	1192	-	-	-	-	-	-	-	-	-
α-Terpineol	1195	1195	1.49 ± 0.08 [i]	1.64 ± 0.04 [f,g,h,i]	0.51 ± 0.01 [g]	-	0.49 ± 0.03 [e]	-	0.59 ± 0.03 [e]	1.61 ± 0.02 [e]	4.48 ± 0.09 [d]
Myrtenol	1196	1194	2.35 ± 0.03 [g]	-	-	-	-	-	-	-	2.82 ± 0.15 [e]
Estragole	1199	1198	-	-	-	-	44.86 ± 0.26 [a]	-	-	-	-
Verbenone	1205	1203	0.44 ± 0.05 [l]	-	-	-	-	2.01 ± 0.03 [e]	-	-	-
Isopulegone	1237	1237	-	-	-	-	-	0.21 ± 0.02 [e]	-	-	-
Piperitone	1253	1250	-	-	-	-	-	-	-	-	-
cis-Geraniol	1254	1256	-	-	-	-	-	-	5.24 ± 0.39 [b]	-	-
Thymol methyl ether	1255	1257	-	-	-	-	-	-	-	-	-
Neomenthyl acetate	1273	1270	-	1.04 ± 0.01 [f,g,h]	-	-	-	0.81 ± 0.06 [e]	-	-	-
trans-anethol	1285	1282	-	-	-	-	6.55 ± 0.06 [c]	-	-	-	-

Table 2. Cont.

ID	RID	RIE	R. officinalis	O. vulgare	S. officinalis	A. sativum	F. vulgare	M. piperita	C. sativum	S. montana	T. vulgaris
Bornyl acetate	1286	1286	5.62 ± 0.01 [e]	-	-	-	-	-	-	-	-
Thymol	1290	1290	-	40.32 ± 1.12 [a]	-	-	-	-	-	2.53 ± 0.14 [d,e]	43.68 ± 0.54 [a]
Menthyl acetate	1295	1294	-	-	-	-	-	4.61 ± 0.01 [d]	-	-	-
Carvacrol	1299	1299	-	16.20 ± 0.05 [b]	-	-	0.63 ± 0.01 [e]	-	1.03 ± 0.03 [d,e]	54.17 ± 2.33 [a]	5.51 ± 0.12 [c]
Diallyl trisulfide	1301	1300	-	-	-	65.39 ± 2.50 [a]	-	-	-	-	-
Isocaryophyllene	1438	1434	3.37 ± 0.20 [f]	2.90 ± 0.07 [e]	10.49 ± 0.00 [c]	-	1.05 ± 0.05 [e]	1.67 ± 0.03 [e]	0.62 ± 0.02 [e]	2.91 ± 0.11 [d,e]	1.61 ± 0.03 [f]
Humulene	1467	1467	0.72 ± 0.02 [k]	0.77 ± 0.03 [g,h,i]	10.01 ± 0.35 [c]	-	0.49 ± 0.01 [e]	-	-	-	-
Germacrene-D	1487	1490	-	0.90 ± 0.01 [f,g,h,i]	-	-	-	0.87 ± 0.02 [e]	-	-	-
β-Bisabolene	1506	1509	-	4.64 ± 0.06 [d]	-	-	-	-	0.83 ± 0.04 [d,e]	1.82 ± 0.03 [e]	0.55 ± 0.01 [g,h]
γ-Cadinene	1513	1514	-	-	-	-	-	-	-	0.54 ± 0.02 [e]	1.64 ± 0.01 [f]
δ-Cadinene	1523	1522	-	0.65 ± 0.01 [g,h,i]	0.45 ± 0.01 [g]	-	-	-	-	0.54 ± 0.02 [e]	-
Diallyl tetrasulfide	1555	1557	-	-	-	1.49 ± 0.07 [c]	-	-	-	-	-
Caryophyllene oxide	1581	1583	-	1.73 ± 0.01 [f,g]	1.92 ± 0.05 [e,f]	-	-	1.21 ± 0.04 [e]	3.16 ± 0.17 [c]	1.41 ± 0.05 [e]	-
Ledene	1585	1589	-	-	10.12 ± 0.44 [c]	-	-	-	-	-	-
Total identified compounds			93.35 ± 0.43	92.52 ± 0.84	97.04 ± 0.46	92.47 ± 0.39	90.44 ± 0.87	93.17 ± 0.39	94.55 ± 1.69	92.56 ± 3.94	96.22 ± 1.47

Results were expressed as mean relative abundances % of three replicates. In the table: ID, component name; RID, retention index retrieved from http://webbook.nist.gov/chemistry/ for the same analysis conditions; RIE, experimental retention index referred to C8-C40 n-alkane mixture standard. Statistical groups were defined by progressive alphabetical letters (case-letter). For the same matrix (same column), results followed by the same case-letter are not significantly different according to Tukey' HSD post hoc test ($p > 0.05$).

Regarding *R. officinalis* EO, the components identified were in accordance with those reported by other authors [34–36] for this officinal plant. The major components ($p < 0.05$) of the mixture were camphor (22%), α-pinene (17%), 1,8-cineole (16%) and borneol (12%). These approximately equal ratios have been already recognized to be characteristic of some *R. officinalis* species from Italy and nearby countries [15,37]; however, 1,8-cineole chemotype is generally reported for rosemary plants cultivated in different other locations of Italy [35,37,38].

For *O. vulgare* EO, the major constituent ($p < 0.05$) was thymol (40%), followed by carvacrol (16%), γ-terpinene (9%) and *p*-cymene (8%). The obtained data were similar with those reported by De Martino et al. [39] for thymol/carvacrol chemotypes cultivated in a southern region of Italy, by Vazirian et al. [40] and Daferera et al. [41] for Iranian and Greek oregano EOs, respectively. The main compound of *O. vulgare* EO is usually carvacrol or thymol, while other authors stated that camphor was the main constituent [15,42,43].

S. officinalis EO showed α-tujone (41%) as main constituent ($p < 0.05$), followed by camphor (12%) and equal ratios ($p > 0.05$) of 1,8-cineole/isocaryophyllene/humulene/ledene (total abundance of 42%). The chemical composition was in accordance with those reported in literature by different authors for some European and Iranian sages [44,45], anyhow in these works lower concentrations of α-tujone were recorded.

For *A. sativum* EO a total of six compounds were identified. The principal component ($p < 0.05$) was diallyl disulfide (65%), followed by diallyl trisulfide (20%), in accordance with the results reported by Dziri et al. [46]. These compounds represent two of the main compounds produced during the thermal or long-term decomposition of allicin, the unstable garlic main constituent released from the alliin upon an injury and by means of the activity of the enzyme alliinase [47].

T. vulgaris EO presented thymol (44%) as major compound ($p < 0.05$), thus in our case the thyme chemotype was thymol. In scientific literature there are contrasting data about the area cultivation-related chemotype, being *T. vulgaris* characterized by an evident chemotype variation that lead to different monoterpene co-occurrence and composition [48].

Regarding *F. vulgare* EO, the major component ($p < 0.05$) was estragole (45%), followed by similar values ($p > 0.05$) of fenchone (10%) and α-phellandrene (10%). For *M. piperita*, menthol (53%) was the EO main compound ($p < 0.05$), followed by menthofuran (8%) and menthone (7%). (S)-(+)-Linalool was the principal constituent ($p < 0.05$) of *C. sativum* EO obtained from plant seeds, for which a 77% of the total volatile mixture was accountable. In *S. montana* EO, carvacrol was the compound with the highest ($p < 0.05$) relative abundance (54%). For these last four EOs, the obtained data were in accordance with those reported in the literature from other authors [49–54].

The GC-MS chemical characterization of the analyzed samples allowed to identify the main components of the extracted EOs (total identified compounds > 90%); in addition, the data comparison with scientific literature underlined the influence of the environmental conditions of plant cultures on the composition of their volatile fraction.

3.3. Total Phenolic Content and Antioxidant Activity

Total phenolic content (TPC) results were showed in Table 3. The highest TPC ($p < 0.05$) was recorded for *T. vulgaris* EO (6.42 mg GAE/g EO), followed by *O. vulgare* (4.69 mg GAE/g EO) and *S. montana* (4.40 mg GAE/g EO). The other EOs showed lower values ($p < 0.05$) with a TPC range of 0.05–0.28 mg GAE/g EO and no significant differences among them ($p > 0.05$).

Table 3. Total phenolic content (TPC) and antioxidant activity results Ferric Reducing Antioxidant Power (FRAP), 2,2-diphenyl-1-picrylhydrazyl (DPPH) and Trolox Equivalent Antioxidant Capacity with 2,2′-azinobis-(3-ethylbenzothiazoline-6-sulfonic acid (TEAC/ABTS) of EOs and Pearson correlation coefficients between the different antioxidant activity assays and total phenolic content.

Assay	TPC	FRAP	DPPH	ABTS
Rosmarinus officinalis	0.111 ± 0.002 [c]	188.270 ± 0.437 [a]	10.288 ± 0.258 [c,d]	0.084 ± 0.001 [e]
Origanum vulgare	4.688 ± 0.304 [b]	168.220 ± 1.837 [b]	23.963 ± 2.435 [b]	1.765 ± 0.005 [b]
Salvia officinalis	0.178 ± 0.008 [c]	12.304 ± 0.022 [f]	8.709 ± 0.885 [c,d]	0.098 ± 0.005 [e]
Mentha piperita	0.338 ± 0.018 [c]	0.543 ± 0.044 [h]	11.289 ± 0.514 [c]	0.154 ± 0.006 [d]
Allium sativum	0.050 ± 0.001 [c]	3.924 ± 0.142 [g]	7.868 ± 0.158 [d]	0.037 ± 0.003 [g]
Foeniculum vulgare	0.283 ± 0.013 [c]	15.202 ± 0.175 [e]	11.466 ± 0.636 [c]	0.043 ± 0.003 [g]
Coriandrum sativum	0.046 ± 0.004 [c]	4.122 ± 0.241 [g]	10.656 ± 1.043 [c,d]	0.067 ± 0.004 [f]
Satureja montana	4.398 ± 0.252 [b]	159.280 ± 1.575 [c]	27.015 ± 0.959 [a]	1.997 ± 0.003 [a]
Thymus vulgaris	6.419 ± 0.219 [a]	126.869 ± 0.175 [d]	21.751 ± 0.862 [b]	1.131 ± 0.012 [c]
Pearson Correlation Coefficients				
Assay	FRAP	ABTS	DPPH	
TPC	0.642	0.691	0.905	

Regarding TPC and AOC (antioxidant activity): results were expressed as mg Gallic acid equivalents (GAE)/g EO for TPC assay; mg Trolox equivalent (TE)/g EO for FRAP assay; µg Trolox equivalent (TE)/g EO for DPPH assay; mmol Trolox equivalent/g EO for ABTS assay. The showed values were the mean of three replicates. For the same assay (same column), results followed by the same case-letter are not significantly different according to Tukey' HSD post hoc test ($p > 0.05$). For Pearson Correlation Coefficients: the positive/negative strength of correlation was considered: low for $±0.1 < r < ±0.3$, moderate for $±0.3 < r < ±0.7$, and strong for $r > ±0.7$; for values of $r < ±0.1$ the variables were considered not correlated.

Antioxidant activity (FRAP, DPPH, TEAC/ABTS) results were also reported in Table 3. The different assays established that *O. vulgare*, *S. montana* and *T. vulgaris* were the EOs with the best antioxidant capacity according to free radical scavenging methods (DPPH and TEAC/ABTS). The FRAP assay underlined also the antioxidant potential of *R. officinalis* EO.

Even if the vegetal matrix had different origins, the methodology of the investigation and expression of results made difficult a direct comparison between TPC and AOC data and the literature. The presented ranges were similar to those presented by several authors for different essential oils [15,20,26,43,55].

A Pearson correlation test between the AOC and TPC data was carried out and the coefficients results obtained were presented in Table 3. As reported, among the different assays, a moderate (TPC with FRAP and ABTS) and strong (TPC with DPPH) positive correlation were revealed. Thus, the detected antioxidant activity could be attributed to total phenols content assessed in the EOs. These positive correlations between AOC and TPC have been already reported for plant species of the Mediterranean area [56].

3.4. Antimicrobial Activity

The antibacterial activity of the tested EOs against selected Gram-positive and Gram-negative bacteria was reported in Table 4. The strains were selected among spoiling (*P. fluorescens*, *B. thermosphacta* and *E. faecium*) and pathogenic (*Salmonella enterica* serotype Enteritidis and *Salmonella enterica* serotype Typhimurium, *L. monocytogenes* and *S. aureus*) bacteria commonly isolated from food products of different origins, to have an overview of the potentiality of the selected essential oils.

Generally, the results observed as MIC were also confirmed as MBC. In some cases, the MIC concentration had to be doubled to obtain a bactericidal activity (i.e., MBC of *T. vulgaris* and *C. sativum* EOs was respectively 5 and 10 µL/mL for both *B. thermosphacta* B1 and B2).

For *F. vulgare* EO, the results established that the obtained EO was unable to inhibit the tested microbial strains at concentrations lower or equal than 20 µL/mL. The results were in accordance with those reported by Çetin et al. [57], who assessed that for fennel EOs obtained from the aerial parts, as in our case, the different MIC values ranged from 31.25 to 500 µg/mL. Lower MIC values could be obtained from EOs extracted from seeds [42,58] and fruits [59] of the plant; in these cases, the EOs main compound is trans-anethol, present only in minor quantities in our EO.

Regarding *R. officinalis*, *S. officinalis*, *M. piperita* and *A. sativum*, the EO tested showed a limited spectrum of activity; good results (5 µL/mL) were obtained against different strains, however higher MIC values obtained for the other strains belonging to the same species seemed to underline a strain-dependent activity. Thus, for these EOs, a variable antimicrobial activity against the Gram-negative and Gram-positive bacteria tested, was generally recognized at concentrations higher than 10 µL/mL. Nevertheless, significant results were observed for *A. sativum* EO against the two *Listeria monocytogenes* type strains. Good results were also obtained for *R. officinalis* EO; in fact, it usually shows a good antioxidant activity [60] and a lower antimicrobial activity with respect to other EOs such as oregano, thyme or tea tree [43], while in our case it showed good inhibitory activity, particularly on *L. monocytogenes* ATCC7644 and *S. aureus* STA47. This activity is probably due to the presence of camphor and 1,8-cineol among the principal constituents, as reported in Table 2.

For *O. vulgare*, the MIC values showed a wide spectrum of activity, ranging from 1.25 to 10 µL/mL for both Gram-positive and Gram-negative bacteria. In this case, the antimicrobial activity could be related to the important presence of thymol and carvacrol in the volatile fraction, as described in Section 3.1 (Table 2); the high contents of thymol, in fact, results in good antimicrobial activities [39,61].

The most effective EOs were those obtained from *S. montana*, *T. vulgaris* and *C. sativum*. For these EOs the MIC values ranged from 0.625 to 5 µL/mL. For these EOs thymol, (S)-(+)-linalool, and carvacrol have been already confirmed to be responsible for their antimicrobial activity, with ranges similar to those obtained in the present study [43,62–64]. In particular, while the antimicrobial activity of *O. vulgare* and *T. vulgaris* EOs against *L. monocytogenes* is well known [65,66], very interesting results were observed for *C sativum* against *Listeria*, but also the other tested pathogens, such as *S. aureus* (especially strain STA32) and *Salmonella* strains. These results are particularly significant, as Gram-negative bacteria are usually less sensitive to EOs than Gram-positive, because of the presence of the lipopolysaccharide layer, that provides a higher resistance to hydrophobic compounds such as essential oils [67]. On the contrary, the Gram-positive *B. thermosphacta* strains B1 and B2 were among the most resistant strains, nevertheless, they were inhibited by low concentrations of *T. vulgaris* and *S. montana* EOs.

Table 4. Minimum Inhibitory Concentration (MIC) (µL/mL) of selected essential oils against the different strains.

Strains		Rosmarinus officinalis	Origanum vulgare	Salvia officinalis	Mentha piperita	Allium sativum	Foeniculum vulgare	Satureja montana	Thymus vulgaris	Coriandrum sativum
P. fluorescens	P34	10	1.25	10	>20	10	>20	1.25	2.5	5
B. thermosphacta	B2	>20	10	>20	>20	>20	>20	2.5	2.5	5
B. thermosphacta	B1	>20	10	>20	>20	>20	>20	5	2.5	5
S. Enteritidis	S2	20	2.5	>20	>20	>20	>20	1.25	1.25	5
S. Typhimurium	S4	>20	2.5	>20	>20	>20	>20	5	2.5	5
E. faecium	P14	>20	5	>20	>20	10	>20	5	5	5
E. faecium	ATCC 19434	10	5	>20	>20	10	>20	5	2.5	2.5
L. monocytogenes	LM 4	>20	5	10	>20	>20	>20	2.5	1.25	0.625
L. monocytogenes	ATCC 19144	10	5	5	20	2.5	>20	2.5	1.25	0.625
L. monocytogenes	ATCC 7644	5	10	10	10	2.5	>20	5	2.5	0.625
S. aureus	STA 32	10	5	>20	>20	10	>20	2.5	1.25	0.625
S. aureus	STA 47	5	5	10	2.5	5	>20	5	1.25	1.25
S. aureus	STA 39	>20	5	>20	>20	10	>20	5	1.25	1.25

4. Conclusions

The results obtained from this study established that the essential oils obtained from Abruzzo region officinal plants, mainly from *T. vulgaris*, *S. montana* and *C. sativum*, showed interesting biological potentiality. The antimicrobial and antioxidant properties assessed are excellent bases for further in vitro assays that could be used to define these essential oils as potential candidates for natural biopreservatives in combination with or in substitution to synthetic chemical ones. Moreover, additional studies should be undertaken in order to understand their potentiality in model systems and in real food samples. Study should particularly aim to establish the most effective EO concentration depending on the food matrix, its organoleptic properties, and the microorganisms it should inhibit. Anyhow, these results represent a valid basis for future evaluations and enriched current understanding about the specificity of Abruzzo region plant species and their essential oils.

Acknowledgments: This research was supported by the grant of Regione Abruzzo, for the project "PSR 2017–2013 Misura 1.2.4" cod. CUA 2446850691, title "Sviluppo di sistemi convenzionali e innovazioni per la produzione di composti bioattivi da materie prime vegetali per l'impiego nel settore alimentare".

Author Contributions: Claudio Lo Sterzo and Antonello Paparella conceived and designed the experiments; Marika Pellegrini, Giovanni Mazzarrino and Serena D'Amato performed the experiments; Marika Pellegrini, Antonella Ricci, Annalisa Serio and Clemencia Chaves-López analyzed the data and wrote the paper.

Conflicts of Interest: Authors declare no conflict of interest.

References

1. Blackburn, C. Introduction. In *Food Spoilage Microorganisms*, 1st ed.; Blackburn, C., Ed.; Woodhead Publishing Ltd.: Cambridge, UK, 2006; pp. xvii–xxiii, ISBN 9781845691417.
2. Hyldgaard, M.; Mygind, T.; Meyer, R.L.; Debabov, D. Essential oils in food preservation: Mode of action, synergies, and interactions with food matrix components. *Front. Microbiol.* **2012**, *3*, 1–24. [CrossRef] [PubMed]
3. Oussalah, M.; Caillet, S.; Saucier, L.; Lacroix, M. Inhibitory effects of selected plant essential oils on the growth of four pathogenic bacteria: *E. coli* O157:H7, *Salmonella* Typhimurium, *Staphylococcus aureus* and *Listeria monocytogenes*. *Food Control* **2007**, *18*, 414–420. [CrossRef]
4. Tserennadmid, R.; Takó, M.; Galgóczy, L.; Papp, T.; Pesti, M.; Vágvölgyi, C.; Almássy, K.; Krisch, J. Anti yeast activities of some essential oils in growth medium, fruit juices and milk. *Int. J. Food Microbiol.* **2011**, *144*, 480–486. [CrossRef] [PubMed]
5. Tsai, M.L.; Lin, C.C.; Lin, W.C.; Yang, C.H. Antimicrobial, Antioxidant, and Anti-Inflammatory Activities of Essential Oils from Five Selected Herbs. *Biosci. Biotechnol. Biochem.* **2014**, *75*, 1977–1983. [CrossRef]
6. Swamy, M.K.; Akhtar, M.S.; Sinniah, U.R. Antimicrobial Properties of Plant Essential Oils against Human Pathogens and Their Mode of Action: An Updated Review. *eCAM* **2016**, *2016*. [CrossRef] [PubMed]
7. Grassmann, J. Terpenoids as Plant Antioxidants. *Vitam. Horm.* **2005**, *72*, 505–535. [PubMed]
8. Martins, N.; Barros, L.; Ferreira, I.C.F.R. In vivo antioxidant activity of phenolic compounds: Facts and gaps. *Trends Food Sci. Technol.* **2016**, *48*, 1–12. [CrossRef]
9. Muthupandi, M.A.; Rajagopal, S.S. Phytochemical Evaluation and in vitro Antioxidant Activity of Various Solvent Extracts of *Leucas aspera* (Willd.) Link Leaves. *Free Radic. Antioxid.* **2017**, *7*, 166–171.
10. Council of Europe. *European Pharmacopoeia*, 3rd ed.; Council of Europe: Strasbourg, France, 1997; ISBN 9287129916.
11. Sefidkon, F. Influence of drying and extraction methods on yield and chemical composition of the essential oil of *Satureja hortensis*. *Food Chem.* **2006**, *99*, 19–23. [CrossRef]
12. Şanli, A.; Karadoğan, T. Geographical Impact on Essential Oil Composition of Endemic *Kundmannia anatolica* Hub.-Mor. (Apiaceae). *Afr. J. Tradit. Complement. Altern. Med.* **2016**, *14*, 131–137.
13. Silveri, A.; Manzi, A. Horticultural biodiversity and gardening in the region of Abruzzo. In *Crop Genetic Resources in European Home Gardens, Proceedings of a Workshop, Ljubljana, Slovenia, 3–4 October 2007*; Bailey, A., Eyzaguirre, P., Maggioni, L., Eds.; Bioversity International: Rome, Italy, 2009; pp. 26–36.
14. Guarrera, P.M. Food medicine and minor nourishment in the folk traditions of Central Italy (Marche, Abruzzo ans Latium). *Fitoterapia* **2003**, *74*, 515–544. [CrossRef]

15. Viuda-Martos, M.; Ruiz Navajas, Y.; Sánchez Zapata, E.; Fernández-lópez, J.; Pérez-álvarez, J.A. Antioxidant activity of essential oils of five spice plants widely used in a Mediterranean diet. *Flavour Frag. J.* **2009**, *25*, 13–19. [CrossRef]
16. Hadjichambis, A.C.H.; Paraskeva-Hadjichambi, D.; Della, A.; Giusti, M.E.; De Pasquale, C.; Lenzarini, C.; Censorii, E.; Gonzales-Tejero, M.R.; Sanchez-Rojas, C.P.; Ramiro-Gutierrez, J.M.; et al. Wild and semi-domesticated food plant consumption in seven circum-Mediterranean areas. *Int. J. Food Sci. Nutr.* **2008**, *59*, 383–414. [CrossRef] [PubMed]
17. Carrubba, A.; Scalenghe, R. The scent of Mare Nostrum: Medicinal and aromatic plants in Mediterranean soils. *J. Sci. Food Agric.* **2012**, *92*, 1150–1170. [CrossRef] [PubMed]
18. Lai, P.K.; Roy, J. Antimicrobial and Chemopreventive Properties of Herbs and Spices. *Curr. Med. Chem.* **2004**, *11*, 1451–1460. [CrossRef] [PubMed]
19. Tajkarimi, M.M.; Ibrahim, S.A.; Cliver, D.O. Antimicrobial herb and spice compounds in food. *Food Control* **2010**, *21*, 1199–1218. [CrossRef]
20. Yashin, A.; Yashin, Y.; Xia, X.; Nemzer, B. Antioxidant Activity of Spices and Their Impact on Human Health: A Review. *Antioxidants* **2017**, *6*, 70. [CrossRef] [PubMed]
21. Sajid Arshad, M.; Ayesha Batool, S. Natural Antimicrobials, their Sources and Food Safety. In *Food Additives*; Karunaratne, D.N., Pamunuwa, G., Eds.; InTech: Rijeka, Croatia, 2017; pp. 87–102.
22. Lee, L.M.; Vassilaros, D.L.; White, C.M. Retention indices for programmed-temperature capillary-column gas chromatography of polycyclic aromatic hydrocarbons. *Anal. Chem.* **1979**, *51*, 768–773. [CrossRef]
23. Masaldan, S.; Iyer, V.V. Antioxidant and antiproliferative activities of methanolic extract of Aloe vera leaves in human cancer cell lines. *J. Pharm. Res.* **2011**, *4*, 2791–2796.
24. Oyaizu, M. Studies on products of browning reaction: Antioxidative activity of products of browning reaction prepared from glucosamine. *Japan. J. Nutr.* **1986**, *44*, 307–315. [CrossRef]
25. Brand-Williams, W.; Cuvelier, M.E.; Berset, C. Use of a free radical method to evaluate antioxidant activity. *LWT Food Sci. Technol.* **1995**, *28*, 25–30. [CrossRef]
26. El-Lateef Gharib, F.A.; Teixeira da Silva, J.A. Composition, Total Phenolic Content and Antioxidant Activity of the Essential Oil of Four Lamiaceae Herbs. *Med. Aromat. Plant Sci. Biotechnol.* **2013**, *7*, 19–27.
27. Clinical and Laboratory Standards Institute. *Performance Standards for Antimicrobial Susceptibility Testing*; Twenty-First Informational Supplement; M100-S21; CLSI: Wayne, MI, USA, 2011.
28. Rossi, C.; Chaves-López, C.; Serio, A.; Annibali, F.; Valbonetti, L.; Paparella, A. Effect of *Origanum vulgare* Essential Oil on Biofilm Formation and Motility Capacity of *Pseudomonas fluorescens* Strains Isolated from Discolored Mozzarella Cheese. *J. Appl. Microbiol.* **2018**. Accepted. [CrossRef] [PubMed]
29. Panizzi, L.; Flamini, G.; Cioni, P.L.; Morelli, I. Composition and Antimicrobial Properties of Essential Oils of 4 Mediterranean Lamiaceae. *J. Ethnopharmacol.* **1993**, *39*, 167–170. [CrossRef]
30. Burdock, G.A.; Carabin, J.G. Safety assessment of coriander (*Coriandrum sativum* L.) essential oil as a food ingredient. *Food Chem. Toxicol.* **2009**, *47*, 22–34. [CrossRef] [PubMed]
31. Russo, M.; Galletti, G.C.; Bocchini, P.; Carnacini, A. Essential Oil Chemical Composition of Wild Populations of Italian Oregano Spice (*Origanum vulgare* ssp. hirtum (Link) Ietswaart): A Preliminary Evaluation of Their Use in Chemotaxonomy by Cluster Analysis. 1. Inflorescences. *J. Food Chem.* **1998**, *8561*, 3741–3746. [CrossRef]
32. Sowbhagya, H.B.; Purnima, K.T.; Florence, S.P.; Rao, A.G.A.; Srinivas, P. Evaluation of enzyme-assisted extraction on quality of garlic volatile oil. *Food Chem.* **2009**, *113*, 1234–1238. [CrossRef]
33. Piccaglia, R.; Marotti, M. Characterization of several aromatic plants grown in northern Italy. *Flavour Fragr. J.* **1993**, *8*, 115–122. [CrossRef]
34. Yesil Celiktas, O.; Hames Kocabas, E.E.; Bedir, E.; Vardar Sukan, F.; Ozek, T.; Baser, K.H.C. Antimicrobial activities of methanol extracts and essential oils of *Rosmarinus officinalis*, depending on location and seasonal variations. *Food Chem.* **2007**, *100*, 553–559. [CrossRef]
35. Angioni, A.; Barra, A.; Cereti, E.; Barile, D.; Coïsson, J.D.; Arlorio, M.; Dessi, S.; Coroneo, V.; Cabras, P. Chemical Composition, Plant Genetic Differences, Antimicrobial and Antifungal Activity Investigation of the Essential Oil of *Rosmarinus officinalis* L. *J. Agric. Food Chem.* **2004**, *52*, 3530–3535. [CrossRef] [PubMed]

36. Takayama, C.; Meira de-Faria, F.; Alves de Almeida, A.C.; Dunder, R.J.; Manzo, L.P.; Rabelo Socca, E.A.; Batista, L.M.; Salvador, M.J.; Monteiro Souza-Brito, A.R.; Luiz-Ferreira, A. Chemical composition of *Rosmarinus officinalis* essential oil and antioxidant action against gastric damage induced by absolute ethanol in the rat. *Asian Pac. J. Trop. Biomed.* **2016**, *6*, 677–681. [CrossRef]
37. Pintore, G.; Usai, M.; Bradesi, P.; Juliano, C.; Boatto, G.; Tomi, F.; Chessa, M.; Cerri, R.; Casanova, J. Chemical composition and antimicrobial activity of *Rosmarinus officinalis* L. oils from Sardinia and Corsica. *Flavour Fragr. J.* **2002**, *17*, 15–19. [CrossRef]
38. Lo Presti, M.; Ragusa, S.; Trozzi, A.; Dugo, P.; Visinoni, F.; Fazio, A.; Dugo, G.; Mondello, L. A comparison between different techniques for the isolation of rosemary essential oil. *J. Sep. Sci.* **2005**, *28*, 273–280. [CrossRef] [PubMed]
39. De Martino, L.; De Feo, V.; Formisano, C.; Mignola, E.; Senatore, F. Chemical composition and antimicrobial activity of the essential oils from three chemotypes of *Origanum vulgare* L. ssp. *hirtum* (Link) Ietswaart growing wild in campania (Southern Italy). *Molecules* **2009**, *14*, 2735–2746. [CrossRef] [PubMed]
40. Vazirian, M.; Mohammadi, M.; Farzaei, M.H.; Amin, G.; Amanzadeh, Y. Chemical composition and antioxidant activity of *Origanum vulgare* subsp. *vulgare* essential oil from Iran. *Res. J. Pharmacogn.* **2015**, *2*, 41–46.
41. Daferera, D.J.; Ziogas, B.N.; Polissiou, M.G. GC-MS analysis of essential oils from some Greek aromatic plants and their fungitoxicity on *Penicillium digitatum*. *J. Agric. Food Chem.* **2000**, *48*, 2576–2581. [CrossRef] [PubMed]
42. Dadalioglu, I.; Evrendilek, G.A. Chemical compositions and antibacterial effects of essential oils of Turkish oregano (*Origanum minutiflorum*), bay laurel (*Laurus nobilis*), Spanish lavender (*Lavandula stoechas* L.), and fennel (*Foeniculum vulgare*) on common foodborne pathogens. *J. Agric. Food Chem.* **2004**, *52*, 8255–8260. [CrossRef] [PubMed]
43. Mazzarrino, G.; Paparella, A.; Chaves-López, C.; Faberi, A.; Sergi, M.; Sigismondi, C.; Compagnone, D.; Serio, A. *Salmonella enterica* and *Listeria monocytogenes* inactivation dynamics after treatment with selected essential oils. *Food Control* **2015**, *50*, 794–803. [CrossRef]
44. Raal, A.; Orav, A.; Arak, E. Composition of the essential oil of *Salvia officinalis* L. from various European countries. *Nat. Prod. Res.* **2007**, *21*, 406–411. [CrossRef] [PubMed]
45. Badiee, P.; Nasirzadeh, A.R.; Motaffaf, M. Comparison of *Salvia officinalis* L. essential oil and antifungal agents against candida species. *J. Pharm. Technol. Drug Res.* **2012**, *1*, 7. [CrossRef]
46. Dziri, S.; Casabianca, H.; Hanchi, B.; Hosni, K. Composition of garlic essential oil (*Allium sativum* L.) as influenced by drying method. *J. Essent. Oil Res.* **2014**, *26*, 91–96. [CrossRef]
47. Yu, T.H.; Wu, C.M.; Liou, Y.C. Volatile Compounds from Garlic. *J. Agric. Food Chem.* **1989**, *37*, 725–730. [CrossRef]
48. Thompson, J.D.; Chalchat, J.C.; Michet, A.; Linhart, Y.B.; Ehlers, B. Qualitative and Quantitative Variation in Monoterpene co-Occurrence and Composition in the Essential Oil of *Thymus vulgaris* Chemotypes. *J. Chem. Ecol.* **2003**, *29*, 859–880. [CrossRef] [PubMed]
49. Piccaglia, R.; Marotti, M. Characterization of some Italian types of wild fennel (*Foeniculum vulgare* Mill.). *J. Agric. Food Chem.* **2001**, *49*, 239–244. [CrossRef] [PubMed]
50. Sun, Z.; Wang, H.; Wang, J.; Zhou, L.; Yang, P. Chemical composition and anti-inflammatory, cytotoxic and antioxidant activities of essential oil from leaves of *Mentha piperita* grown in China. *PLoS ONE* **2014**, *9*, e114767. [CrossRef] [PubMed]
51. Saharkhiz, M.J.; Motamedi, M.; Zomorodian, K.; Pakshir, K.; Miri, R.; Hemyari, K. Chemical Composition, Antifungal and Antibiofilm Activities of the Essential Oil of *Mentha piperita* L. *ISRN Pharm.* **2012**, *2012*, 1–6. [CrossRef] [PubMed]
52. Mandal, S.; Mandal, M. Coriander (*Coriandrum sativum* L.) essential oil: Chemistry and biological activity. *Asian Pac. J. Trop. Biomed.* **2015**, *5*, 421–428. [CrossRef]
53. Miladi, H.; Slama, R.B.; Mili, D.; Zouari, S.; Bakhrouf, A.; Ammar, E. Chemical Composition and Cytotoxic and Antioxidant Activities of *Satureja montana* L. Essential Oil and Its Antibacterial Potential against *Salmonella* Spp. Strains. *J. Chem.* **2013**, *2013*, 1–9. [CrossRef]
54. Lo Cantore, P.; Iacobellis, N.S.; De Marco, A.; Capasso, F.; Senatore, F. Antibacterial activity of *Coriandrum sativum* L. and *Foeniculum vulgare* Miller Var. vulgare (Miller) essential oils. *J. Agric. Food Chem.* **2004**, *52*, 7862–7866. [CrossRef] [PubMed]

55. Wang, H.F.; Hway, K.H.; Yang, C.H.; Huang, K.F. Anti-oxidant activity and major chemical component analyses of twenty-six commercially available essential oils. *J. Food Drug Anal.* **2017**, *25*, 881–889. [CrossRef] [PubMed]
56. Piluzza, G.; Bullitta, S. Correlations between phenolic content and antioxidant properties in twenty-four plant species of traditional ethnoveterinary use in the Mediterranean area. *Pharm. Biol.* **2011**, *49*, 240–247. [CrossRef] [PubMed]
57. Çetin, B.; Özer, H.; Cakir, A.; Polat, T.; Dursun, A.; Mete, E.; Öztürk, E.; Ekinci, M. Antimicrobial Activities of Essential Oil and Hexane Extract of Florence Fennel [*Foeniculum vulgare* var. azoricum (Mill.) Thell.] Against Foodborne Microorganisms. *J. Med. Food* **2010**, *13*, 196–204. [CrossRef] [PubMed]
58. Mahboubi, M.; Kazempour, N.; Mahboubi, M. Antimicrobial activity of Rosemary, Fennel and Galbanum essential oils against clinical isolates of *Staphylococcus aureus*. *Biharean Biol.* **2011**, *5*, 4–7.
59. Tarek, N.; Hassan, H.M.; AbdelGhani, S.M.M.; Radwan, I.A.; Hammouda, O.; El-Gendy, A.O. Comparative chemical and antimicrobial study of nine essential oils obtained from medicinal plants growing in Egypt. *Beni-Suef Univ. J. Basic Appl. Sci.* **2014**, *3*, 149–156. [CrossRef]
60. Gachkar, L.; Yadegari, D.; Bagher, M.; Taghizadeh, M.; Astaneh, S.A.; Rasooli, I. Food Chemistry Chemical and biological characteristics of *Cuminum cyminum* and *Rosmarinus officinalis* essential oils. *Food Chem.* **2007**, *102*, 898–904. [CrossRef]
61. Burt, S. Essential oils: Their antibacterial properties and potential applications in foods—A review. *Int. J. Food Microbiol.* **2004**, *94*, 223–253. [CrossRef] [PubMed]
62. Pirbalouti, A.G.; Rahimmalek, M.; Malekpoor, F.; Karimi, A. Variation in antibacterial activity, thymol and carvacrol contents of wild populations of *Thymus daenensis* subsp. *daenensis* Celak. *Plant Omics* **2011**, *4*, 209–214.
63. Rota, M.C.; Herrera, A.; Martínez, R.M.; Sotomayor, J.A.; Jordán, M.J. Antimicrobial activity and chemical composition of *Thymus vulgaris*, *Thymus zygis* and *Thymus hyemalis* essential oils. *Food Control* **2008**, *19*, 681–687. [CrossRef]
64. Delaquis, P.J.; Stanich, K.; Girard, B.; Mazza, G. Antimicrobial activity of individual and mixed fraction of dill, celandra, coriander and eucalyptus essential oil. *Int. J. Food Microbiol.* **2002**, *74*, 101–109. [CrossRef]
65. Paparella, A.; Taccogna, L.; Aguzzi, I.; Chaves-López, C.; Serio, A.; Marsilio, F.; Suzzi, G. Flow cytometric assessment of the antimicrobial activity of essential oils against *Listeria monocytogenes*. *Food Control* **2008**, *19*, 1174–1182. [CrossRef]
66. Serio, A.; Chiarini, M.; Tettamanti, E.; Paparella, A. Electronic paramagnetic resonance investigation of the activity of *Origanum vulgare* L. essential oil on the *Listeria monocytogenes* membrane. *Lett. Appl. Microbiol.* **2010**, *51*, 149–157. [CrossRef] [PubMed]
67. D'Amato, S.; Serio, A.; Chaves-López, C.; Paparella, A. Hydrosols: Biological activity and potential as antimicrobials for food applications. *Food Control* **2018**, *86*, 126–137. [CrossRef]

© 2018 by the authors. Licensee MDPI, Basel, Switzerland. This article is an open access article distributed under the terms and conditions of the Creative Commons Attribution (CC BY) license (http://creativecommons.org/licenses/by/4.0/).

MDPI
St. Alban-Anlage 66
4052 Basel
Switzerland
Tel. +41 61 683 77 34
Fax +41 61 302 89 18
www.mdpi.com

Foods Editorial Office
E-mail: foods@mdpi.com
www.mdpi.com/journal/foods

www.ingramcontent.com/pod-product-compliance
Lightning Source LLC
Chambersburg PA
CBHW040225040426
42333CB00052B/3368